# THE MISANTHROPE
## and
# OTHER FRENCH CLASSICS:
### Four Plays

•

Edited by

## Eric Bentley

**APPLAUSE**
THEATRE BOOKS

**Library of Congress Cataloging-in-Publication Data**

The Misanthrope : and other French classics.

   (Eric Bentley's dramatic repertoire ; v. 3)
   These 4 plays (with 2 additional plays) previously published in 1961 as v. 4 of the Classic theatre under title: Six French plays.
   Bibliography.
   Contents: The Cid / Pierre Corneille — The misanthrope / Molière — Phaedra / Jean Racine — Figaro's marriage / Beaumarchais.
   1. French drama—Translations into English. 2. French drama—17th century—Translations into English. 3. English drama—Translations from French. I. Bentley, Eric, 1916- II. Series.
PQ1240.E5M5 1986    842',4'08    86-17268
ISBN 0-936839-19-8

**APPLAUSE THEATRE BOOK PUBLISHERS**
211 W. 71st St., New York, NY 10023
Phone: (212) 595-4735   Fax: (212) 721-2856

First Applause Printing, 1986.
Second Applause Printing, 1991.

# CONTENTS

# THE CID

## A TRAGEDY

BY

## PIERRE CORNEILLE

*English Version by James Schevill*
*In collaboration with Robert and Angela Goldsby*

This translation is dedicated to the memory of Rudolph Schevill, whose devotion and scholarly insight into French and Spanish literature influenced many generations of American students in the classroom, and whose books and articles will continue to influence many new generations of students.

ll enquiries concerning the amateur and professional production rights to THE CID ould be addressed to the translator's agent, Helen Merrill, 361 West 17th Street, New ork, NY 10011. No amateur performance may be given without obtaining in advance, e written permission of Helen Merrill.

# CHARACTERS

THE KING, *Ferdinand the First of Castile* [*died 1065*]

THE INFANTA, *his daughter*

COUNT DE GORMAS, *father of Chimena and the King's foremost warrior*

CHIMENA,* *daughter of the Count de Gormas, in love with Rodrigo*

DON DIEGO, *father of Rodrigo, an old man who was once the King's foremost warrior*

RODRIGO, *Don Diego's son, who becomes The Cid**
[*a title deriving from the Arabic El Seid, the Lord*]

DON ARIAS
DON ALONSO } *two Castilian noblemen*

DON SANCHO, *a young Castilian nobleman who is a suitor of Chimena*

LEONORA, *a lady in waiting to the Infanta*

ELVIRA, *a lady in waiting to Chimena*

A PAGE

THE SCENE OF THE PLAY IS LAID IN SEVILLE.

* A somewhat Anglicized pronunciation is recommended: *Shimayna; The Sid* (not Seed).

# ACT I

## Scene 1

### CHIMENA, ELVIRA

CHIMENA. Elvira, you hold back the truth, I swear.
    What did my father say you will not share?

ELVIRA. His words have all my senses quite enthralled.
    He favors Rodrigo whom your heart has called,
    And if I were to guess, I should believe
    His final choice will not cause you to grieve.

CHIMENA. I beg you, tell me more, I will rejoice.
    Why are you certain he'll approve my choice?
    Give me again that hope I long to cherish
    For those sweet words you speak should never perish.
    Oh, why withhold your precious tale? I pray
    Love's flame will soar to light the dark with day.
    Did father heed Don Sancho with good grace,
    Or did he favor my Rodrigo's place?
    You took great care, I hope, not to make clear
    That I am only glad when one is near.

ELVIRA. I painted you indifferent, but tense,
    Granting some hope, yet also cruel suspense,
    And neither stern nor sweet as you await
    Your father's choice of men to be your mate.
    How much this touched him was an easy measure
    In the proud look he gave me, filled with pleasure.
    Since you must linger on his every word
    I shall repeat the phrases which I heard:
    "She does well. Either man is worthy of her.
    Both come of noble stock with loyal valor;
    Young men in whose bold eyes one looks to see
    The prideful spirit of their ancestry.

In Rodrigo's eyes, it's not so hard to trace
The courageous image of a hero's face,
Born to a family whose victorious name
Shines on the pages of our country's fame.
On his father's brow is etched the story
Of the might that was our Spanish glory.
If the son commands an echo of the sire,
Chimena's love for him is my desire."
That moment the King's Council was to meet
And he did leave, his thought cut incomplete.
But his few words on your bold, wooing gallants
Gave your loved one the favorable balance.
The King must choose a tutor for his son
And this post, by your father will be won.
His choice is certain, and his noble spirit
Can have no fear of any rival merit.
Since his exploits have been so far outstanding
The King can find no other claim demanding.
Rodrigo, it seems, has gained his father's aid
To ask your hand after the choice is made.
You must agree that all things seem to bring
The joy which promises love's wedding ring.

CHIMENA. For some dim reason, my distrusting heart
   Accepts no happiness and beats apart
   In fear. Time, suddenly, today, tomorrow,
   Can change the greatest joy to darkest sorrow.

ELVIRA. Soon your silly, childish fears will mend.

CHIMENA. Well, come what may, let us await the end.

*Scene 2*

THE INFANTA, LEONORA, A PAGE

THE INFANTA, *to the* PAGE. Go, tell Chimena, I dislike delay.
   She waits too long in seeing me today.
   Let her know she hurts me, acting this part.

*Exit the* PAGE.

LEONORA. Daily this strange desire moves in your heart,
Madam; you call her here with the demand
To question her about Rodrigo's hand.

THE INFANTA. I have my valid reasons. It is my fault
Chimena's spirit flew into this vault
Of love for Rodrigo. I gave him to her.
It was my will that furnished them the spur,
And now my conscience thinks: Who locks love's chains
Must spare no effort to release love's pains.

LEONORA. But, Madam, as they seek love's richest treasure,
You watch them meet with sorrow and displeasure.
Why should their love, which fills them with such gladness,
Cause in your noble heart this clinging sadness?
Why should the happiness with which they meet
Bring grief that twists their love into deceit?
But I am indiscreet and should not ask.

THE INFANTA. My sorrow would rage higher behind the mask
Of secrecy. If I tell of my soul,
You'll see how love plays a cruel tyrant's role.
This youth, this lover whom I gave away,
Is still my love.

LEONORA. 　　　　For love you still pray?

THE INFANTA. If you placed your soft hand upon mv heart,
It would confess by its impulsive start
How much I love him.

LEONORA. 　　　　　Madam, please excuse me
If I think this is madness that I see.
Can a great lady so forget her place
And love a cavalier to her disgrace?
What would the King proclaim? Or proud Castile?
You have not thought how your father would feel?

THE INFANTA. I know too well, that if my rank were stained
By love, it would be just if death had reigned;
For noble love commands the bloodless fact
Of title joining title as love's act.
But if my passion only sought a ruse,
A thousand legends would serve for excuse.

Yet honor has the strength still to suppress
My strong desire, however hard the stress.
I must recall I am a proud King's daughter
And history must say that great kings sought her.
When I did find my heart had no defense,
I cast off love so warm and so intense.
Instead, I placed Chimena in this net
Of love for Rodrigo, to ease my debt.
Can you still wonder why I must await
Impatiently, their marriage as my fate?
You see the way to death my peace has led;
Love lives by hope and dies when hope is dead.
Its fire fades from lack of nourishment;
Despite all of the pain I have been sent,
Although this marriage will bring bitter bane
To hope, it sets my spirit free again.
Till then my anguish has no boundary;
In dream, Rodrigo hovers close to me.
My will commands I lose, but how to lose?
That's my secret torment: I cannot choose.
With shame I feel my love invite his kiss
And know that all his love can bring no bliss.
My soul must writhe, divided, torn apart,
Into a broken will and a lost heart.
This marriage is death to me! I must fear it,
Yet desire it, though this goal can only split
My life apart; whichever hope may win—
Love or honor—the end is death or sin.

LEONORA. Madam, what can I say to answer you?
I cannot help, although I would be true.
You've won my pity for your sorry plight.
Since with deep grief your spirit must in flight
Depart from love, you will conquer desire
And find in time the peace which calms love's fire.
Have faith in God; His justice is too great
To make you suffer always from this fate.

THE INFANTA. My only hope lies in the loss of hope.

*The* PAGE *returns.*

PAGE. Chimena's here . . .

THE INFANTA.                Ask her to wait. For peace I grope.
*Exit the* PAGE.
LEONORA. Madam, why brood alone in fantasy?
THE INFANTA. Go, give me a time of rest to steady
  Myself. I'll come as soon as I am ready.


## Scene 3

### THE INFANTA

THE INFANTA, *alone.* Oh God, to whom we kneel in prayer and
      sing
  With love, spare me from this endless suffering.
  Grant honor to me and restore my peace
  That giving bliss, my pain may find release.
  For this wedding now, three hearts are praying.
  Bring it to pass and keep my heart from straying!
  Marriage, that will make these lovers one
  Will break my chains, however much it stun.
  I wait too long; Chimena I must see
  And ease my pain by their new love's decree.


## Scene 4

### THE COUNT, DON DIEGO

THE COUNT. You've won what I desired. The King's great hand
  Has conferred on you the honor of the land.
  You are to teach the young Prince of Castile.
DON DIEGO. This adds a luster to my family seal;
  It proves to all the justice of our King
  And the reward old services can bring.

THE COUNT. However great our kings may be, their flaws
    Are like our own and errors mark their laws.
    This choice proves to each member of the court
    That present services gain ill report.

DON DIEGO. Let us say nothing more to vex your mind
    About his choice. Because he is so kind
    He may have chosen me, not just for merit.
    But still we owe too much respect to sit
    In judgment on the King who is supreme;
    So, please, I pray you add another theme:
    You have a daughter, I an only son.
    Give your permission now to make them one
    In marriage, and, suddenly, there'll be no flaw
    To friendship. My son will be your son-in-law.

THE COUNT. Your son should dream of a loftier aim,
    And this new honor given to your claim
    Should build his hopes and cause his heart to swell.
    Perform your duties, Sir. Instruct the Prince well.
    Teach him how a province should be ruled,
    How fear is law before his word has cooled;
    To leave bad men afraid; gain love from good.
    Then add a captain's god-like virtues, whose flood
    Of heavy duties must endure all hardships:
    Fight to triumph; face pain with smiling lips;
    Pass lengthy days and nights on horseback; rattle
    Fully armed in sleep; scale walls in battle
    That victory is his and his alone!
    Teach him by acts, and make his pride like stone.

DON DIEGO. Despite your jealousy, I shall but need
    To teach him what I've learned, and let him read
    The history of my old life. There, long
    Succession of heroic deeds are strong,
    Bright proofs of how to build an army's fame,
    Attack a fortress, win a lasting name.

THE COUNT. Living examples furnish better guides.
    From musty books, princes learn false prides,
    And, to be blunt, what has your ancient praise
    To equal one of my heroic days?
    I hold the power, for your strength is poor,

And my strong arm keeps this kingdom secure.
My sword subdues Granada; Aragon quails,
My fame is in Castile's proudest tales.
Without me you would soon obey the cause
Of foreign kings who would create your laws.
Each moment of each day adds to my glory,
Praise leads to praise and further victory.
If the good Prince rode with me into battle,
Protected by my arm, he'd prove his mettle,
And learn to conquer from my own example.
Soon, his nature's grace would find an ample
Realm . . .

DON DIEGO.    I know. I saw you fight under me.
You've served the King well—thus far I'll agree.
Now that old age fills up my veins with ice
The King favors your courage and advice.
Enough said. It is not difficult to see
That you're today what I was formerly.
However, this honor shows one strong change;
The King seeks to reward my life's rich range.

THE COUNT. You have stolen the honor I deserved!

DON DIEGO. The King's true faith in me has never swerved.

THE COUNT. My loyal deeds have also won his grace.

DON DIEGO. Denial is not grace in your vain case.

THE COUNT. Your old, sly courtier's tricks won you the post!

DON DIEGO. You lie! My reputation counted most.

THE COUNT. You mean the King showed his respect for age.

DON DIEGO. My courage was the King's primary gauge.

THE COUNT. Then he should have favored me with his grace.

DON DIEGO. Who cannot win, does not deserve the place.

THE COUNT. I not deserve it?

DON DIEGO.                     No!

THE COUNT.                          Your impudence,
You rash old man, deserves just recompense!

*He slaps* DON DIEGO *across the face.*

DON DIEGO, *drawing his sword.* Draw and kill me after this cold
    shame,

The first disgrace that ever marked my name.

THE COUNT. Weak as you are, can you fight with a boast?

*He disarms* DON DIEGO.

DON DIEGO. Oh God! My strength's gone when I need it most.

THE COUNT. Your sword is mine, but you might be too vain
If I kept it; false pride whirls in your brain.

*He throws the sword contemptuously at the feet of* DON
DIEGO.

Good-by. Have the Prince read your true story
For his instruction. Though he cheer your glory,
This punishment of aged insolence
Should ornament your words with glittering sense.


*Scene* 5

DON DIEGO

DON DIEGO, *alone*. What senseless fury and impotent rage
One feels at the hard weakness of old age!
Have I lived but to suffer this disgrace?
What does it mean, my courtier's rich lace,
All the laurels of war, when in one day
Reputation fades and withers away?
Look at my arm, once the wonder of Spain,
Which saved the throne from all the world's disdain;
More than the throne, my country did redeem.
Why must my strength fail and a vision seem?
This is a cruel reminder of my deeds.
The flower of my name withers to weeds;
And the King's award, fatal to happiness
Because I lost honor in time of stress.
Must I watch the Count triumph again
And die without revenge, with this dark stain?
No, Count, you be the tutor of my Prince;
Not one who was humiliated since
He won the place. No shame has this office known,

And I stand here unworthy and alone.

*He picks up his sword.*

This sword, that bravely hewed out all my fame,
Is now in my old age a useless claim,
A sword that can my weakness never cure,
Lost symbol of a time when strength was pure.
My son is coming. Revenge demands
That I give you into his youthful hands.


### Scene 6

#### DON DIEGO, DON RODRIGO

DON DIEGO. My son, have you courage?

RODRIGO.                          No man should doubt it.
My father's call will not find me without it.

DON DIEGO. I like your answer and the flame of truth
Which echoes the lost spirit of my youth.
It quickens me and gives me cause to hope
You shall avenge honor for which I grope.
You must avenge me.

RODRIGO.              For what shame?

DON DIEGO.                          For cruelty
To an old man's reputation. He slapped me;
A slap! I tell you that I wished to kill
Him, but my weak arm betrayed my will.
This sword, which I can never use again,
I give to you to still my vengeful brain.
Against his arrogance, your courage prove,
For only blood can this dark act remove.
Kill him or go and die yourself. I know
He is an enemy whose mind will glow
With shrewdness. I've seen him covered with dust
And blood, holding an army at sword's thrust,
And break a hundred squadrons in attack.
No. Courage is a trait he'll never lack.

You must be careful. More than his bravery,
He is . . .

RODRIGO.     Why are you silent? Who is he?

DON DIEGO. Chimena's father.

RODRIGO.                    Her father!

DON DIEGO.                         Can your youthful song
Of love be greater to you than a wrong?
Love the offender, the offense is worse.
You've heard my wrong. Its cure is now your curse.
Enough of this. Avenge yourself and me;
Remember your father was and is the key
To this dark paradox that guides your fate.
I go. Make sure your vengeance is not late.

*Scene 7*

RODRIGO

RODRIGO, *alone*. Into my heart
Cuts the cold steel of a dagger's thrust;
I must avenge a cause that is so just.
A net of fate twists me away from love;
I stand, my heart confused and torn,
                    My soul on fire.
So near at last to find love's healing sense;
                    Oh God, to learn
My father was insulted, and the offense
Done by her father . . . Where shall I turn?

                    In this storm,
My love is mocked whichever way I move.
If I avenge my father, I kill my love;
Honor compels me, yet love holds my arm.
If I marry her, all men will scorn me
                    For this love.

There's evil in each choice that must be made.
                    Oh God, unjust!
How can I leave an insult unrepaid?
How kill Chimena's father? Yet I must.

                    Father, mistress.
My pleasures dead or glory in the tomb,
Soft arms of love or duty that is doom;
One leaves me wretched and the other worthless.

*He stares at his sword.*

And you, my sword, you would betray my heart
                    With your sharp point;
Bright foe of all my dreams of ecstasy,
                    Cause of my pain!
Were you meant to avenge my ancestry,
Or given me my only love to stain?

                    To drink death's chalice?
I owe mistress and father equal debt;
Without revenge with scorn I am beset,
While this dark deed of duty wins her malice.
Oh my sweet love, I must your name deface,
                    Or honor lose.
My anguish grows. My search must end in failure,
                    Rising grief.
My soul accepts my death as the one cure,
For death will bring Chimena's pain relief.

                    Yet die without revenge,
To turn a family's fame to infamy,
Leaving all Spain to mock my memory
As if I were a coward who must cringe;
All this to gain a love I know so well
                    Forever doomed.
Listen no more to this cruel devil's thought
                    Of love star-crossed.
Come, sword, the goal of honor must be sought;
Whatever comes, Chimena's love is lost.

                    Love blinded me.
My father's cause is just, a loyal claim.

Although by sword or grief I die, the same
Blood which he gave, I'll give in purity.
How could a longing dream of love's lost grace
　　　　　Prevent my fate?
Dispel these hopeless, lovesick dreams of pity,
　　　　　That honor stain;
This foul slap revealed no charity,
And love is lost in one short night of pain.

# ACT II

## Scene 1

DON ARIAS, THE COUNT

THE COUNT. Agreed. This quarrel rose with too great heat,
  Sparked by a word which made us indiscreet.
  But the deed is done. There is no remedy.

DON ARIAS. Your pride must yield to your great King's decree.
  For he is deeply moved, and in this cause
  Will use against you his vast power of laws.
  You have no just defense with which to plead.
  The gross act and the victim's age, all lead
  To your indebtedness, to your submission
  Greater than a payment of contrition.

THE COUNT. The King may turn my life as he pleases.

DON ARIAS. After this deed, your sinful pride increases.
  The King still loves you. Appease his rage today.
  When he says, *My desire*, you disobey?

THE COUNT. To keep all that I value in this time,
  A disobedience can't be a crime;
  Yet, were it such, my deeds would overwhelm
  A minor act of shame unto the realm.

DON ARIAS. However great the glory of one's acts,
  The King is not indebted to such facts.
  You flatter pride you've gained from war's rich booty,
  But service to the King is your one duty.
  You'll ruin yourself with this stubbornness.

THE COUNT. Not yet are you a prophet of success.

DON ARIAS. You should consent, and fear the King's stern
  power.

THE COUNT. I shall outlive displeasure of the hour.
  Let the whole state be armed when judgment calls.
  If I should perish, then the kingdom falls.

DON ARIAS. Do you then fear so little the King's might?

THE COUNT. Without me his scepter will fall from light.
  He knows how his fortune would fade, sink down;
  My head in falling would strike off his crown.

DON ARIAS. I beg you by your reason be guided.
  Take counsel.

THE COUNT.      It is no use. I have decided.

DON ARIAS. What shall I tell the King? I must report.

THE COUNT. Say I'll not plead dishonor to the court.

DON ARIAS. A King's great will is always absolute.

THE COUNT. I cannot change. I, too, am resolute.

DON ARIAS. Farewell, then. I came to you in vain. Your path,
  Though laurel-strewn, awaits the lightning's wrath.

THE COUNT. I shall not fear.

DON ARIAS.                The end will be the same.

THE COUNT. Then it shall win Don Diego's acclaim.
  *He is now alone.*
  He who fears not death can fear no threats.
  My heart can bear the worst that life begets.
  Without the King, I'll live in misery,
  But life without honor is death to me.


*Scene 2*

THE COUNT, RODRIGO

RODRIGO. Count, a word.

THE COUNT.            Speak!

RODRIGO.                       First, resolve my doubt.
  You know Don Diego?

THE COUNT.            Yes.

RODRIGO.                    Do not speak out
　　So proudly. Listen to me. Is it true
　　That virtue did this old man's life imbue?

THE COUNT. Perhaps.

RODRIGO.                    In my presence, can you foresee
　　My father's vengeance?

THE COUNT.                    Why say this to me?

RODRIGO. My challenge to a duel should make it plain.

THE COUNT. What young presumption!

RODRIGO.                    You speak with the disdain
　　Of pride; I am young, but more than my few years
　　I have the courage of a race of peers.

THE COUNT. You dare to challenge me? Your words are grand,
　　But have you held a sword within your hand?

RODRIGO. Some men don't require reputation's yoke.
　　Their first sword's thrust can be the final stroke.

THE COUNT. Do you know who I am?

RODRIGO.                    I do not shun
　　Your skill; I know your reputation.
　　The honors you've received for victories
　　Would seem to spell my death in their decrees,
　　But I'll attack the symbol of your arm
　　With courage; faith may save me from great harm.
　　A father's honor should be a strong shield.
　　Unconquered still, you can be made to yield.

THE COUNT. Your fearless heart rings through these words you
　　　　say.
　　My eyes have watched you grow from day to day.
　　I've seen the future hero of Castile.
　　I thought Chimena's marriage soon would seal
　　This hope. I know your love, and I admire
　　The honor which you've shown as your desire.
　　Love hasn't weakened you with hesitation
　　And you are richer in my estimation.
　　I wished a soldier for my son-in-law;
　　It pleases me my choice now shows no flaw.
　　But you arouse my love for open truth.
　　While I admire courage, I pity youth.

Don't let your first duel become your last.
Release me from this most unequal test.
Though I should win, no honor would then follow.
To conquer without peril is most hollow.
That I did kill with ease, men would believe,
And there would only be your death to grieve.

RODRIGO. Your arrogance must lead to further strife.
You take my honor and yet fear my life?

THE COUNT. Leave this room.

RODRIGO.　　　　　　　　　When you will leave with me.

THE COUNT. Are you so tired of life?

RODRIGO.　　　　　　　　　　Or you to die?

THE COUNT. Come, then. You do your duty. A son is base
Who views in silence his proud sire's disgrace.

## Scene 3

### THE INFANTA, CHIMENA, LEONORA

THE INFANTA. Chimena, do not grieve so much. Borrow
Strength to bear the burden of your sorrow.
After this transient storm a calm will come.
Only a small cloud makes your bliss seem numb
And you shall lose nothing though hope's deferred.

CHIMENA. I dare not hope. My heart with pain is stirred.
Upon a placid sea, a smiling face,
This storm brings shipwreck with too swift a pace.
Before I set my sails, my journey's done.
I loved, was loved, our fathers thought as one,
And then, as I told you these joyful tidings,
Disaster sprang from their accursed chidings,
And changed my hope of love that seemed so near
To dreams of woe which I must always fear.
Insane folly, wretched, vain ambition,
Tyrants that bring the noblest to perdition,

When pride must cause desire to be lost
How many sighs and tears shall mark the cost.

THE INFANTA. You are too sure this quarrel merits fear.
Born quickly, it will quickly disappear.
Too many talk of it; it must be mended.
The King has ordered that it be so ended,
And you know my affection for your right
Will do all that it can to ease your plight.

CHIMENA. Too late for reconciliation now.
Insults defeat what reason should avow.
The King's authority will be in vain;
Though wounds are healed, the anguish shall remain.
This hate that's locked by force within the heart
Burns secretly with a cold, searing art.

THE INFANTA. When you are married to Rodrigo, then must
Your father's hatred wither into dust;
And we shall see love silence all discord
When happiness of marriage is your lord.

CHIMENA. I cannot hope although that's my desire.
Don Diego is too proud; I know my sire.
I try to staunch my tears, but I must weep.
The past is torment; the future brings no sleep.

THE INFANTA. What do you fear? An old man's feeble arm?

CHIMENA. Rodrigo's courage.

THE INFANTA.                    He is too young to harm.

CHIMENA. Brave men can be heroes in their first duel.

THE INFANTA. You have no cause to think he'd be so cruel.
He is too much in love to do this deed.
A word from you to halt is all you need.

CHIMENA. If he did not obey, what fatal whim!
Yet if he yields, what would men think of him?
Born great, he cannot suffer such outrage.
If he does yield to love, or to old age,
I'll be ashamed by his so weak compliance
Or crushed by love refusing our alliance.

THE INFANTA. Chimena, in your soul, whatever cost,
The lasting truth of love cannot be lost.
What if I stay your fears of this sad feud,

Command him into prison to ease your mood,
And thus deny all action to his threat?
Would your proud, loving heart be in my debt?
CHIMENA. Oh, Madam, then I would be free from fear.

## Scene 4

### THE INFANTA, CHIMENA, LEONORA, THE PAGE

THE INFANTA. Page, summon Rodrigo. Go, bring him here.
PAGE. He and the Count . . .
CHIMENA.                    Oh, God, I am bereft!
THE INFANTA, *to the* PAGE. What did you see?
PAGE.                         I saw them as they left.
CHIMENA. Alone?
PAGE.          Alone, and deep in argument.
CHIMENA. They fight! All words are now a sad lament.
    Madam, forgive my haste, but I must go.

## Scene 5

### THE INFANTA, LEONORA

THE INFANTA. Alas! My spirit bends like a taut bow.
    I mourn her loss, but love enraptures me.
    Desire tears me; gone is tranquillity.
    The fate that is to part them now, again
    Renews my desperate longing and my pain.
    Their separation causes me to mourn,
    But in my heart an ecstasy is born.
LEONORA. How can the noble virtue of your soul
    So swiftly founder on this darkened shoal?

THE INFANTA. Not dark, but bright, the song my heart must
     sing;
  It makes the laws to which I turn and cling.
  Respect it, as it is a love I cherish.
  Though honor fights, I cannot see it perish,
  And caught in hope that is but vain and senseless,
  My heart in search of his love is defenseless.

LEONORA. Is your great courage lost that grew the stronger?
  Does reason guide and rule your mind no longer?

THE INFANTA. How reason's formal voice does fade, grow faint,
  When heart's inflamed with this sweet poison's taint;
  The patient loves the painful malady
  And lives without a hope for remedy.

LEONORA. Your illness lures you with romantic dreams.
  Rodrigo's lost in such proud, lovesick schemes.

THE INFANTA. Too well I know this, but if pride should yield,
  See how love soothes the heart it seeks to shield.
  If now Rodrigo wins this duel of fate—
  If he defeats a fame so great—
  I shall feel free to love him without shame.
  Think of him with this conquest to his name!
  I dare imagine he will then be free
  To conquer kingdoms, rule them by decree.
  My love tells me I shall see him with time
  The King of all Granada in his prime.
  The vanquished Moors will bow to him in terror,
  Proud Aragon welcome its conqueror,
  And Portugal will fall; across the sea
  His deeds will bear him to his destiny:
  The blood of Africans will mark his laurels;
  Since famous captains make their code of morals,
  He'll rank with heroes of most famous story
  And in his love I'll find my lasting glory.

LEONORA. Madam, your dream of conquests to be won
  Depends upon a duel that's not begun.

THE INFANTA. Rodrigo's with the Count, his father's foe.
  They left together. Is there more to know?

LEONORA. If you insist, I'll grant that they will fight.
  But is his love the same that blinds your sight?

THE INFANTA. Bear with me. I am mad; my dream's a snare.
What evil does my love for him prepare?
Come to my chamber; console me with kindness.
Do not forsake me in my secret blindness.

## Scene 6

### THE KING, DON ARIAS, DON SANCHO

THE KING. Is this Count in his pride bereft of sense?
Does he expect pardon for his offense?

DON ARIAS. I talked to him at length, Sire. He is blind.
Nothing I said could change his stubborn mind.

THE KING. Just Heaven, is this respect for my decrees?
Does he then take so little care to please?
By this insult what does he think to gain?
In my own court, he seeks to mock my reign.
No matter how brave, or how great his role,
I have the means to tame his haughty soul.
Were he the God of Battle here today
He should learn what it means to disobey.
He seeks the insolence he has displayed.
I thought I might by leniency be swayed,
But since he casts off mercy, from this hour
I order him imprisoned by my power.

DON SANCHO. A little time might soothe his raging spurt
Of temper. He is still seething from his hurt.
You know, Sire, such a spirit cannot yield
And wears its first fierce anger like a shield.
He knows his wrong, but caught in this vault
Of rage, his soul cannot confess his fault.

THE KING. Hold your peace, Don Sancho, for you should know
That he who shields the guilty is my foe.

DON SANCHO. I will obey. But, in your gracious way
Permit me just one word . . .

THE KING.                           What is there to say?

DON SANCHO. Who is accustomed to the noblest deeds
  Cannot abase himself before your needs.
  Apologies to him are only masks of shame,
  And this prevents him from accepting blame.
  As your subject, he's troubled by his part,
  But would obey if he had weaker heart.
  Command his strength, as proved in valiant action,
  To heal this deed; he'll give full satisfaction.
  Before then, who dares challenge him to fight,
  I'll answer till the Count speaks for his right.

THE KING. You lack respect to me; but you are young
  And I forgive your youthful, zealous tongue.
  To rule his subjects with consummate care
  A King must never let his temper flare.
  I must respect their lives, conserving them
  As hand is servant of the body's stem.
  My reason's not the same to which you cling.
  You speak as soldier, but I act as King.
  Whatever you may dare think of his plea,
  He loses nothing in obeying me.
  My crown is tarnished by the act he's done.
  He scorned my choice for tutor of my son.
  To strike Don Diego has slandered me,
  Challenged both my command and dignity.
  No more of this . . . Ten vessels have been seen,
  Flying the flag of our enemy's spleen.
  They've sailed up where the river starts to swell.

DON ARIAS. By force the Moors have learned to know you well.
  You've conquered them so often, they fear the wing
  Of hope; they dare not fight so great a King.

THE KING. They'll never see without a jealous frown
  Bright Andalusia ruled by my crown.
  This lovely land, which, once, they did possess,
  They hope again, from envy, to caress.
  That is the reason why I did decide
  My throne should rise here in Seville's rich pride:
  To watch the Moors closely, and thus to break
  Whatever follies they might undertake.

DON ARIAS. At cost of their most valiant soldiers' lives,
Your presence takes the honey from their hives.
You've nothing to fear.

THE KING.                     Only some negligence.
Disaster's bred when courage conquers sense.
You know how easily, since they are near,
The Moors, with changing tide, could sail here.
Yet I'd be guilty of a fatal error
If I aroused my people with this terror.
The fear that would be caused by such alarm
At night would pierce the city with great harm.
Double the guards upon the walls instead.
Enough for now.


### Scene 7

THE KING, DON SANCHO, DON ALONSO

DON ALONSO.          Sire, the Count is dead.
Rodrigo has revenged his father's wrong.

THE KING. I feared his hope for vengeance would be strong
After this deed, and hoped for God's relief.

DON ALONSO. Chimena's coming, seized with bitter grief.
Through tears, for justice she will seek to plead.

THE KING. Although I pity her cause in this deed,
The Count's rash act appears to have deserved
The punishment with which he has been served.
And yet, however just his sudden fate,
I must regret his loss, who was so great.
After such lengthy service to my crown,
His blood for me a thousand times poured down,
Although his arrogance was plain to see,
His sudden death causes me injury.

## Scene 8

THE KING, DON SANCHO, DON ALONSO, CHIMENA,
DON ARIAS, DON DIEGO

CHIMENA. Sire, I plead for justice!

DON DIEGO.                              No, hear my pleas!

CHIMENA. I kneel at your feet.

DON DIEGO.                          I clasp your knees!

CHIMENA. I beg for justice.

DON DIEGO.                      Please hear my defense.

CHIMENA. Punish the crime of this youth's insolence.
    He struck down the support of your proud throne;
    He killed my father.

DON DIEGO.                  He avenged his own.

CHIMENA. Justice is owed to us when we appeal.

DON DIEGO. A just revenge is what she does conceal.

THE KING. Rise, both of you; and speak to me with calm.
    Chimena, I share your sorrow. With qualm
    No less than yours, my heart must now decree.
    *To* DON DIEGO.
    You shall speak later. Do not halt her plea.

CHIMENA. My father, Sire, is dead. No one can hide
    The stream of blood that gushed from his torn side;
    That blood which has so often saved your walls;
    That blood which fought for you at battle's calls;
    That blood which smoked with anger as it flowed
    Because on someone else than you bestowed;
    That blood which many dangers could not thwart,
    Rodrigo spilled within your sacred court.
    Trembling and pale I ran to that grim place.
    I found him dead. Avenge, Sire, this disgrace.
    I cannot speak of it, but only wail.
    My tears can better tell this bitter tale.

THE KING. Have courage, child, for since your father's dead,
Your King will serve as father in his stead.

CHIMENA. Such honor cannot cure my misery.
My father's killed and by his enemy.
His wound lay open and to it I'm bound;
His blood wrote out my duty on the ground;
All of his greatness fallen in the dust
Called for revenge through that wound's fatal crust,
And to be heard by you, most just of kings,
My voice through that sad, twisted mouth now rings.
Sire, do not let the glory of your reign
Be tarnished with the license of this stain,
Exposing your best warriors' defense
To thrusts of every young man's insolence.
Let not this youth defame their glory's plea,
Bathe in their blood, and mock their memory.
If this brave warrior gains no reward,
Then he who serves you will lay down his sword.
Since my father is dead, I demand vengeance
For your sake, Sire, not for my allegiance.
Your loss is great when such a man is killed.
You must rule that Rodrigo's death is willed:
A sacrifice, not mine, Your Majesty,
But yours, that all your subjects justice see;
A sacrifice to honor all your realm,
To show that madness does not guide our helm.

THE KING. Don Diego, answer her.

DON DIEGO.                        How free from strife,
When strength is gone, is he who loses life!
Old age prepares a trap of pain and hate
For noble-minded men who live too late.
I, whose long labors have won me acclaim,
Whom victory has followed with some fame,
Must see myself now doomed by sagging age,
Insulted, vanquished by my body's cage.
What neither combat, lengthy siege, ambush,
Nor jealous rivals, what no foe could crush,
Not even Aragon, this Count has done,
Done in your court; before your throne he's won

Against your choice, with pride in his rash scorn,
Thus leaving me in feeble age forlorn.
Sire, beneath my helmet my hair's turned white;
This blood, so often shed to serve your light—
This arm, which once your enemies did fear—
Would have fallen, been lost, dishonored here
To die, had I not had a son to cling
To honor for his country and his King!
He lent his youth to me; killed for my name,
My dignity, to wash away my shame.
To show such courage as in him was pent,
If to avenge a slap brings punishment,
On me alone should fall the storm of law.
Punish the head whose arm commits some flaw.
Whether or not his action has done harm,
I am the head, Sire; he is but the arm.
Chimena cries that her father is dead.
Had I the strength, for vengeance I'd have bled
To sacrifice my life which age has bowed,
And spare my son for service to you vowed.
Let my blood flow to satisfy her pain.
I won't resist; I will accept its stain,
And far from arguing this stern decree,
I'll die possessing honor, silently.

THE KING. This matter needs a long deliberation
In full council with due consideration.
Don Sancho, guide Chimena home to rest.
Don Diego, here will be my guest
While we decide. Go, fetch his son.

*To* CHIMENA.

                         Justice I'll give.

CHIMENA. His death is just, or justice cannot live.

THE KING. Go, rest, my child, to calm your bitter grief.

CHIMENA. Rest brings a greater anguish, not relief.

# ACT III

## Scene 1

### RODRIGO, ELVIRA

ELVIRA. Rodrigo, why are you here? What have you done?

RODRIGO. I follow my fate as a cursèd son.

ELVIRA. What vanity is yours, this prideful scorning
Of a stricken house you've filled with mourning.
Will you challenge the Count's white, ghostly face?
Did you not kill him?

RODRIGO.                          His life was my disgrace.
My honor forced my hand to do this deed.

ELVIRA. But safety in your victim's house to plead.
What murderer could find asylum there?

RODRIGO. I give myself into my judge's care.
Do not look at me with astonishment.
I search for death, and death for me has sent.
My judge is my Chimena, my belovèd.
My death shall free her since we cannot wed,
And I have come to beg one last request:
Death from her lips and hand will bring me rest.

ELVIRA. No! Flee her sight, flee from her violent hand.
Spare her the anguish of your cruel demand.
Do not add to her present suffering
With all this further grief you seem to bring.

RODRIGO. My dearest love whom I have deeply wronged
Must seek to punish me if life's prolonged.
I shall exchange a hundred deaths for peace,
If she can speed my search for death's release.

ELVIRA. Crushed with her grief, Chimena's gone to plead
Her cause. She is not unaccompanied.

Rodrigo, you must flee and spare my fear.
What would men think if they should find you here?
You'd seek the cry of some false slanderer
That she did hide her father's murderer?
Soon she'll return. You must protect her pride.
I see her! She is coming. You must hide.

### Scene 2

DON SANCHO, CHIMENA, ELVIRA

DON SANCHO. Yes, Madam, blood is sacrificed for blood;
    Your anger and distress a daughter's flood.
    I shall not seek by cunning words or art
    To soothe your anger and console your heart;
    But if I can serve what you must now decree,
    Command my sword to punish him who's free.
    Command my love with vengeance to be troubled;
    In this command my arm's strength will be doubled.

CHIMENA. How miserable I am!

DON SANCHO.                    Accept my sword.

CHIMENA. I'd wrong the King who promised just reward.

DON SANCHO. You know how justice moves so tediously
    That it gives the criminal a chance to flee.
    Its course is often lost in time.
    Permit my sword to save you from this crime.
    That way is certain, justice to assure.

CHIMENA. This is the last resort. If you must cure
    My woe; if that time comes, and you still pity,
    You may defend my cause before this city.

DON SANCHO. For that one happiness, my soul was sent,
    And with the hope of it I go, content.

## Scene 3

CHIMENA, ELVIRA

CHIMENA. At last I'm free to show without restraint,
The burning coldness of my grief's complaint.
To you I need not mask my piercing sadness,
My emptiness of heart, the end of gladness.
My father's dead; it was Rodrigo's sword
That cut away his life from which blood poured.
Weep, weep my eyes! My tears do blind and smother!
Half of my youthful life has killed the other,
And for that stroke of death, I'm forced to cry
Vengeance against the love for which I sigh.

ELVIRA. You must be calm and rest, Madam.

CHIMENA.                                   What use
Is it to talk of rest in pain's abuse?
How shall my sorrow ever be appeased
If I can't hate the hand that did the deed?
What can I hope but torment of the damned
If I avenge, yet love the guilty hand?

ELVIRA. He killed your father and you love him still?

CHIMENA. I do. I worship him with all my will.
My passion fights against what I've been taught;
My lover in my enemy is caught.
Another duel clashes in my soul;
Rodrigo fights my father for love's goal,
Attacks him, drives him back, defends and yields,
Now weak, now strong, his sword in triumph wields;
In this awful war of love and wrath
He wins my heart, but cannot change my path.
Whatever hold my love has over me,
I'll search wherever light of duty be.
Without false step, I'll walk where honor waits.
Rodrigo is my love. I mourn the fates.

My heart will not forsake the hope to wed,
But then I see my father lying dead.

ELVIRA. And you will seek revenge?

CHIMENA.                              Oh cruel chase!
Love torn with duty's hate is always base.
I pray his death, yet hope my prayer is weak.
My death shall follow his, yet his I seek.

ELVIRA. Madam, you must renounce so cruel a task.
Your love is warped by this avenging mask.

CHIMENA. When, almost in my arms, my father dies,
Shall I not hear how blood for vengeance cries?
My heart, deceived by love's call which it hears,
Should give my father only useless tears?
Shall I through love my duty betray
And stifle in such shame, honor's proud way?

ELVIRA. Believe me, Madam, none would expect of you
Revenge against a lover who is true,
One whom you love. You've done all that you should.
You know the King must wear the judge's hood.
Be not so adamant in your strange mood.

CHIMENA. Honor demands that vengeance be pursued.
However love may blind us with desire,
Excuse is shameful to a soul of fire.

ELVIRA. But you love him. You cannot wish him harm.

CHIMENA. That's true.

ELVIRA.                     Then why create this great alarm?

CHIMENA. To save my honor from God's savage whim,
I'll hunt him to his death, die after him!

## Scene 4

### RODRIGO, CHIMENA, ELVIRA

RODRIGO. Take my life now, and grant to us death's grace,
To save you from the anguish of this chase.

CHIMENA. Elvira, where are we? Betrayed by spies?
  Rodrigo in my house, burning my eyes!

RODRIGO. Do not spare me. I won't resist. Enjoy
  The sweetness of my death, revenge's toy.

CHIMENA. Alas.

RODRIGO.          Listen to me.

CHIMENA.                    No.

RODRIGO.                         Please . . .

CHIMENA.                                   Let me die.

RODRIGO. Grant me a word. You know I shall not lie.

  *She turns away.*

  Then speak to me with my despairing sword.

  *He draws his sword and she recoils from it.*

CHIMENA. My father's blood like some dumb beast you've
    gored!

RODRIGO. Chimena.

CHIMENA.          Take that devil's blade away,
  Flashing your bloody crime in sunlit day.

RODRIGO. No, look at it and kill me with your hate.
  Let it increase your wrath and be your fate.

CHIMENA. It's stained with my father's blood.

RODRIGO.                              Plunge it in mine
  And see how it will lose its red design.

CHIMENA. How cruel is God, in one short day we die:
  My father with a sword, his daughter by
  Its sight. Take it away. I cannot stare;
  You wish to speak and kill me with its glare.

ROLRIGO, *sheathing the sword.* I will do as you wish, but I still
    hope
  For mercy. My lost life can only grope
  Through darkness. And yet you must never think
  Because I love you that I hate this link
  With honor. An impossible, gross act
  Dishonored my father and left me racked
  With shame. You know what such a brutal slap
  Does to an old man's pride. This sprung the trap

Of fate in which we're caught. How could I rest
When part of that insult struck at my breast?
I sought your father then. I could not deny
My duty to avenge my father's cry.
Through time of torture, I argued the love due
My father against all of my love for you.
Judge love's great power to endure outrage,
For I still hoped to flee revenge's cage.
My choice was cold disgrace or loss of love,
I thought of you as gentle as a dove.
I told myself I had too hot a temper
And your great beauty almost made the slur
Against me fade away, but then I thought:
Without honor, how could your love be sought?
Even though I have a place in your heart,
Disloyalty would tear our love apart.
To listen to love's lure and heed its voice
Would separate us and condemn your choice.
I told you this, which I must now repeat,
Although it tears my heart out with defeat.
I wronged you greatly, but was forced to act
To earn respect. This is the shameful fact.
To this strange goal of honor I've been true
And now I've come to pay my debt to you.
I paid one debt and for that duty's blame,
I offer you my life as duty's claim;
Your father's death reveals a world of vice.
I cannot save you from a sacrifice.
With courage you must renounce the man
Whose pride caused blood to run against love's ban.
CHIMENA. Oh Rodrigo, how can I ever blame
You as a foe for your refusing shame?
Whichever way my loving grief must flow,
I hate the evil I have learned to know.
With this insult to your proud ancestry,
The call to honor was a simple plea,
And you have done your duty as you saw,
But doing it, have shown me honor's claw.
Your desperate courage marks the way for me.

You avenged your father to pay honor's fee,
And caught in this trap, I'll do the same—
Avenge my father and preserve my name.
Still I have found a reason to despair.
If someone else had robbed me of my care,
My soul would find its joy in seeing you
And you would give the comfort I pursue.
Deep in my grief, I would have found it sweet
For you to kiss my tears and, kissing, meet;
But I must lose you after losing him.
Honor's revealed its dark and bloody whim,
And this duty, which seeks to conquer me,
Bids me kill you to end the mystery.
Despite my love, do not expect my grace,
The force of duty now must line my face.
Though still our love does plead its youthful cause,
My strength, like yours, must follow deadly laws.
By wronging you, you proved to me love's birth,
And, by your death, I must prove my true worth.

RODRIGO. You must not bend to my love any longer.
Honor demands my death. Its law is stronger
And seeks the sacrifice of love, of pity.
My death is welcome. I cannot flee this city
To wait in vain for justice that denies
Your honor, turns our love to mocking lies.
I shall die happy, dying by your hand.

CHIMENA. Please go, I can accuse you where you stand,
Not in an executioner's black shroud.
"She killed her love!" then men would whisper loud.
I must attack, you must defend what's true,
And I must prosecute, not murder you.

RODRIGO. Our love must not destroy your strength to kill
And turn you from fate's deadly, chosen will.
Believe me, dear Chimena, another day
Of vengeance for your father's not my way.
My hand alone avenged my father's shame,
Your hand ought to avenge your father's name.

CHIMENA. Why do you cling so cruelly to your point?
Is honor but a balm you can anoint?

Do not seek to aid me. I am too proud
To wish praise from the righteous, common crowd.
I will not sacrifice my father's care
To your love's urging or your lost despair.

RODRIGO. It is you who cling to your stubborn course.
Whatever happens, show me your remorse.
Kill me for love, if not your father's face,
For pity, if not vengeance, or disgrace.
Killed by your love I would be happier dead
Than with your bitter hate to live instead.

CHIMENA. No, please, I do not hate you.

RODRIGO.                              But you should.

CHIMENA. I cannot.

RODRIGO.               You'll hear dark rumors like a hood
Cover the truth. When men learn of your deed,
Their bitter tongues will spread an evil seed,
But if you kill me, you'll enforce their silence,
And prove by duty's sense their lies of violence.

CHIMENA. The truth shines brighter still if you're not dead;
Then slander will have no false tongue to spread
Its lies to Heaven, but only mourn my woe
Knowing I seek your death, yet love you so.
Leave me alone in my greatest sorrow
And say no more what I must lose tomorrow.
Hide your departure in shadows of night
Or else my honor will not see the light.
Your presence here would only be a reason
For idle tongues to gossip in their season.
Give no one evil cause to blame my virtue.

RODRIGO. Oh, let me die!

CHIMENA.                 Please, go!

RODRIGO.                              What will you do?

CHIMENA. Although my love for you forbids my hate
I must avenge my father's violent fate,
But I confess that deep within my soul,
I hope and pray I shall not gain my goal.

RODRIGO. Your love is a miracle.

CHIMENA.                         Death is near.

RODRIGO. Our fathers caused this curse of pain and fear.

CHIMENA. Rodrigo, who could have thought . . . ?

RODRIGO.                     Who could have known?

CHIMENA. That happiness so close would turn to stone.

RODRIGO. So close; and yet a sudden storm could move
   With fury unforeseen and shatter love.

CHIMENA. Men make their grief.

RODRIGO.                  Remorse burns like a sore.

CHIMENA. Leave now, I cannot listen any more.

RODRIGO. Farewell, until your search frees me from dread
   By killing me, living I'll live as dead.

CHIMENA. If I should win, I promise you my breath
   Shall cease the first moment after your death.
   Farewell, my love. You must not be seen.

   *Exit* RODRIGO.

ELVIRA, *coming forward.* Madam, whatever evil God may
   mean . . .

CHIMENA. Leave me! Do not vex me when my pain is deep.
   I need the silence of the night to weep.


### Scene 5


#### DON DIEGO


DON DIEGO, *alone.* Never can we taste a perfect happiness.
   Our happiest success mingles with sadness.
   Our dream of contentment is always troubled
   By care, like winter fields in shadows stubbled.
   Against my happiness, this shadow nears
   To darken joy and threaten me with fears.
   My enemy is dead who outraged me,
   But my son is lost who has avenged me.
   In vain I seek for him to meet this pity
   For an old, broken man who scours the city.
   What little strength age leaves me to besmirch,

I pour out fruitlessly within my search.
Each hour, each moment caught in this black night,
I think I shall embrace his shadow's flight;
My love for him deceived by this false vision
Forms new shadows of fear and cold suspicion.
I cannot find where my dear son has fled.
I fear the Count's friends since they know he's dead;
Their strength and power suddenly has risen.
Rodrigo may be dead or held in prison.

*He sees a figure approaching.*

Oh God, does my desire still come to mock,
Or have You given me this hopeful shock?
If this is Rodrigo, my prayer's transcended,
My fear dispelled, and my great sorrow ended.


## Scene 6

### DON DIEGO, RODRIGO

DON DIEGO. God has sent you as an answer to my cry.

RODRIGO. Alas.

DON DIEGO.     Do not confound my joy with a sigh,
But let me catch my breath that I may praise;
I cannot disavow you in these days.
You have inherited courage; your daring
Makes our ancestors live through your bold faring.
From them you come; from me springs your design;
Your sword's first thrust has equaled all of mine,
And with a noble ardor, your bold youth
Has claimed renown in this trial of truth.
You are my blessing, the prop of my old age,
Which you have given back to honor's page.
Come, kiss this cheek, and recognize the place
Where fell the slap whose stain you did efface.

RODRIGO. The honor's yours. I could not seek for less
Since I was reared by the conduct you bless.

It was a gift of God, that I defile
My love, and not my father with denial.
But, in your pleasure, please do not be grieved,
If by your joy I cannot be deceived.
Let my despair burst from my aching heart
Where this deed's kept it hidden from the start.
I don't repent my service as your son,
But give me back the happiness I won.
I armed myself against my love for you
And with one stroke I cut my heart in two.
Speak no consolation. I have lost all.
I have repaid my debt, although I fall.

DON DIEGO. The fruit of victory is your reward.
I gave you life, my honor you restored.
And though honor is dearer to me than life,
I owe you more to justify your strife.
But drive this weakness from your mind apart.
Many women will live to soothe your heart.
Love is but passing pleasure; honor is grace.

RODRIGO. What are you saying?

DON DIEGO.              Only what you should face.

RODRIGO. Our sullied honor is avenged by me
And you ask shame of infidelity!
The coward-soldier and the faithless lover
Both find an equal shame on them must hover.
Do not insult my strong will to be loyal.
Let me be noble without thoughts that soil.
My love's too strong by you to be undone;
My love still binds though she cannot be won,
And while Chimena I must leave again,
The death I seek will soon bring end to pain.

DON DIEGO. The time has not yet come to walk death's path,
For now your King and country need your wrath.
The fleet we feared has entered this great river
To sack the startled city with death's shiver.
The Moors are coming and the tide and night
Will bring them silently within our sight.
The court's confused and people shout alarms;
Their cries are everywhere instead of arms.

In this chaos, it was my fortune going
To my house to find some friends, who, knowing
Of my shame, driven on by loyalty,
Had all come there with offers to avenge me.
This you have done, but their swift anger's flood
Will seem the nobler stained with Moorish blood.
Go march at their head at honor's demand.
They wish you to lead them and to command.
Force this attack of enemies to cease,
And then, if you wish death, find noble peace.
Take up this battle fate weaves on its loom
And make the King owe safety to your doom;
Or, for my sake, return with flag on high,
Be not content to serve revenge's eye.
When you subdue the Moor's invading violence,
That act will force Chimena then to silence.
If you love her, the way to her again
Is to return as conqueror, with train.
But time's too precious now for us to waste;
My words delay when we require haste.
You'll fight to show the King that though he lost
When Count de Gormas died, you're worth the cost!

# ACT IV

## Scene 1

### CHIMENA, ELVIRA

CHIMENA. Elvira, is this true, the news you bring?

ELVIRA. It is beyond belief how all men sing
  The praise of glorious deeds by this young knight,
  And raise them in glad song to Heaven's sight.
  The Moors who fought him won a savage death.
  Swift in attack, their retreat drew swifter breath.
  Three hours of battle brought him his reward
  And made two kings surrender to his sword.
  His courage overcame all obstacles.

CHIMENA. Rodrigo's courage did these miracles?

ELVIRA. He conquered them; his leadership was wise,
  The capture of two kings his greatest prize.

CHIMENA. Who came and told you these amazing things?

ELVIRA. Everyone! There is not one who brings
  A word but praise of him who's made us free,
  The guardian angel of our destiny.

CHIMENA. The King, what does he think of these great deeds?

ELVIRA. Rodrigo has not seen the King. He pleads
  For time, but Don Diego has presented
  The captive kings in honor of the Cid,
  And begged the King to grant his conquering son
  A royal pardon for this deed he's done.

CHIMENA. Was he wounded?

ELVIRA.                          I do not know.
  Be calm, I fear the paleness that you show.

CHIMENA. It is my wrath that has been made to falter;
  Through love for him, my duty seems to alter.

In his glory, his praise, my heart is pent,
My duty hesitates, my pride is rent.
Oh love, be gone, let anger grow in peace.
He conquers kings, our love can never cease.
My black raiment of woe is loathsome fee
Caused by his sword's first fatal victory.
Whatever else of him that may be said,
I know that by his hand my father's dead.
You who can fill me full with bitterness—
In this veil and crepe, grief's nightly dress
Which he gave to me when he killed my sire—
Uphold my pride against my heart's desire;
And when my love becomes too strong in me,
Speak to my soul of my sad destiny:
To seek love's death and die in maiden's weeds.

ELVIRA. Be calm. The Princess comes to aid your needs.


### Scene 2

#### THE INFANTA, CHIMENA, LEONORA, ELVIRA

THE INFANTA. I come not to bring your sadness quick relief,
But to join my sighs with your tears of grief.

CHIMENA. You should join in the people's revelment,
Madam, and share their joy which God has sent.
I am the only one who has to sigh.
Rodrigo banished peril. Your hopes are high,
And there is safety in his arm's brave shield.
Today, the only tears are ones I yield.
He has served his King well, as all know;
To me alone his valiant arm brings woe.

THE INFANTA. In truth it is a miracle he's wrought.

CHIMENA. This news leaves me in greater heartbreak caught,
For I shall hear his name by all extolled
As my lost lover who's now the warrior bold.

THE INFANTA. Where do you find such pain in all of this?
This son of Mars once brought a lover's bliss.
He ruled your heart, as you ruled his days.
Your choice is honored by each word of praise.

CHIMENA. Whoever lauds him, grants him what he's due,
But with this praise does torture me anew.
My pain is heightened as they raise him higher.
All that he is, is all that I desire.
Oh, this is cruel to a woman's heart:
To make our love stronger when we must part.
Yet honor shines above love's waiting beauty;
To seek his death can be my only duty.

THE INFANTA. That sense of duty won you yesterday
Approval, for you seemed with love to sway
The sympathy of the entire court,
And all did seek to lend your cause support.
As friend, I have advice for you to heed.

CHIMENA. Not to obey you would be base indeed.

THE INFANTA. Today the justice of your cause is bated
By joyous peace which Rodrigo has created.
He is our greatest hope, by all adored
As Castile's guardian, by the Moors abhorred.
The King himself gives sanction to this truth,
And says your father lives within this youth.
In short, you must listen to words of reason;
To kill this man would be an act of treason.
To revenge a father, can it be lawful
To condemn your country? This is more awful,
In that we're punished as though participants
In a crime of which we are the innocents.
You need not seek, since your great heart refuses,
A marriage which your father's death accuses.
I plead with you to quench this useless strife;
Deprive him of your love, but leave his life.

CHIMENA. Too late; how can I grant him mercy now?
I cannot shame a daughter's sacred vow,
Although my heart cries out in his behalf.
Of King and country he may be the staff,

Surrounded by his Army, but I must blot
His laurels, surround him with a cypress plot.

THE INFANTA. Duty is noble even though it leads
Against the dictates of your heart's deep needs.
But it would be nobler if you withstood
Your pride and sacrificed for public good.
The cruelest punishment you can bestow
Would be denying him your love. I know
Your country calls on you to guard its fame.
You will not act against the King's great name?

CHIMENA. He may refuse, but I cannot keep still.

THE INFANTA. Think well before you seek the death you will.
Farewell, and think of all there is to lose.

CHIMENA. Since Father's death, one way is left to choose.

## Scene 3

THE KING, DON DIEGO, RODRIGO, DON ARIAS, DON SANCHO

THE KING, *to* RODRIGO. Brave son of an illustrious house, whose
   zeal
Has always been the glory of Castile,
Your victory has soared over the train
Of deeds your ancestors have done for Spain.
I have no power to grant a just reward.
Your virtue to my might is overlord.
Our land's deliverance from savage foes,
The glory which on my scepter glows,
The Moor's defeat, before in night's alarm
I could give orders to repulse their harm,
Are exploits that I cannot recompense;
But here the captive kings can grant their sense,
For in my presence they have called you Cid.
This means to them as Lord and King you're bid.
No one can grudge you such a glorious name.
Be henceforth called The Cid, the word a flame

To Granada and Toledo. It shall prove
To all beneath my rule of law, my love
For you, and this proud title then will show
How great you are, how much to you I owe.

RODRIGO. Your Majesty places too high a praise
Upon an act that followed duty's ways.
I blush to hear before my gracious King
The honors that my victory does bring.
I know that to the welfare of your land,
I owe my life whenever you command,
And had I lost it in this sacred cause,
I would have only followed duty's laws.

THE KING. None of my officers, engaged by scores,
Has shown duty and courage such as yours.
When valor goes not to the point of stress,
It cannot bring such rare and great success.
Permit us then to praise you, and tell me
The circumstances of your victory.

RODRIGO. Sire, you know that when the Moorish stranger
Throughout the city sent his chill of danger,
Some friends assembled at my father's home
Compelled my mind which still in love did roam . . .
But, Sire, please pardon my temerity
For I acted without authority.
As danger threatened, I thought of all the dead,
And how at court I would have risked my head,
For if I had to lose it, I would rather
Fight now for you as I fought for my father.

THE KING. I do forgive your vengeance that was just
As you have saved the state from evil's thrust.
When Chimena comes to ask for my decision,
We'll grant her but the grace of pity's vision.
Continue, please.

RODRIGO.                Forward I led our flanks
As a new confidence grew in our ranks.
We were five hundred, but our cause did throng,
And at the port we were three thousand strong.
Even the timid at this final stage,
Drew courage from our Army's massive rage.

Most of my men I then concealed, for shock,
In holds of our vessels lying at the dock.
The rest, whose numbers grew with every hour,
Impatiently grouped near my central power,
Lay noiselessly upon the ground, out of sight,
And so we passed a large part of the night.
The harbor guard, by order, followed suit
To help my stratagem, thus hidden, mute.
Boldly, I pretended that my new orders
Came from my King since Moors had crossed our borders.
At last with darkling light of stars for guide,
We saw their sails floating on the full tide.
The heavy swell bore them up to the land
Where our men lay awaiting my command.
None stayed the Moors; all seemed at peace; no calls
Of guards upon the wharfs or on the walls.
Deceived by silence, they could never doubt
That their surprise attack prepared a rout.
They neared and cast their anchors quickly down,
Rushed forward fearlessly to sack the town.
Our men rose up and a tremendous roar
Exploded to Heaven with the sound of war.
Those in our ships echoed that battle shriek;
They plunged forth armed; the Moors, confused, were weak
With terror, for but half their men had landed.
Before the fight began their cause was stranded.
Bent on swift pillage, they met red slaughter.
We pressed them hard upon the land and water.
Their blood, in rivers, flowed upon the banks
Before they could resist and form in ranks.
But then, despite us, their princes rallied them;
Their courage flamed, and fear they did condemn.
The shame of death without attempt to fight,
Stopped their disorder and restored their might.
Against us, standing firm, their scimitars
Drew blood, that flowed into their bloody scars.
Earth, river, harbor, were all battlegrounds
With death's triumphant screams the only sounds.
How many deeds passed by without the mark
Of glory since they went unseen in dark,

Where each man struck alone his blows of hate
And could not see the hidden shoals of fate.
I encouraged our men on every side,
Made some regroup and some advance in pride,
Sent forth the new arrivals to the fray
And could not know the outcome until day.
At last the dawn showed coming victory,
And, suddenly, the Moors began to flee.
When sounds of our fresh troops drummed quickly near,
The Moorish lust to conquer turned to fear.
They reached their ships and cut their anchor ropes,
Screaming in fear, retreating from their hopes;
In such confusion fled that no one saw
Their two great kings unable to withdraw.
Their panic drove their loyalty astray
And the receding tide swept them away.
Caught in our midst, their kings, with some few men,
Fought fiercely to break from our trap again.
Pierced by our thrusts, they sold their lives too dearly.
"Surrender!" I cried, but they refused to hear me,
And, with their scimitars, they struck instead.
Then, seeing all their soldiers cut down, dead,
And that, alone, they did defend their tender
Lives, they called for me and gave surrender.
I sent them both to you in morning light,
The battle won after that bloody night.
It was in this way, Sire, for your service . . .

### Scene 4

THE KING, DON DIEGO, RODRIGO, DON ARIAS, DON SANCHO,
DON ALONSO

DON ALONSO. Sire, Chimena comes in search of justice.
THE KING. A troubled duty to which I must be true.

*To* RODRIGO.

Go, I shall not force her yet to see you.
I must send you away from Spain's sweet earth.
Let me embrace you and applaud your worth.

*He embraces him. Exit* RODRIGO.

DON DIEGO. Chimena loves, but vengeance does deter.

THE KING. That she loves him, we'll prove by testing her.
Put on a mask of sadness.

## Scene 5

THE KING, DON DIEGO, DON ARIAS, DON SANCHO, DON
ALONSO, CHIMENA, ELVIRA

THE KING.            At last be content,
Chimena, for success to you has bent.
Rodrigo did defeat the Moor's uprise,
But died from savage wounds before our eyes.
Give thanks to God, who has avenged you now.

*To* DON DIEGO.

See how her color drains away her vow!

DON DIEGO. Look, Sire, she swoons and in that swoon supplies
A proof of love beyond all fatal cries.
Her grief betrays her vengeance lives apart;
You can no longer doubt her loving heart.

CHIMENA. It's true he's dead?

THE KING.            No, no, he is alive,
And still for you in lasting love would strive.
Cast off the grief that seized you for his sake.

CHIMENA. Sire, joy does also faintness make.
Too much of pleasure turns us soft and weak,
And must obscure that honor which we seek.

THE KING. You ask us in this falsehood to abstain?
Chimena, your true grief was all too plain.

CHIMENA. Sire, add this then to my misery,
And call my swoon the act of grief's decree.

Misfortune did conspire to make me mute
For death would save his head from my pursuit.
If death for his great country him had greeted,
My vengeance would be lost, my aims defeated.
An end so fair would bring no satisfaction.
I ask his death, but not in glorious action;
Not one so brilliant that it honors him,
No hero's death, but on the scaffold grim;
Death for my father, not for this land of Spain,
A death that will his name forever stain.
To die a hero's death can bring no shame,
But only wins much praise, immortal fame.
I love his victory; this love's no crime;
The State is safe, my victim grows sublime,
Famous, a hero welcomed at gay balls,
And crowned with honors in your palace halls.
It seems his life is worthy then to take
In royal justice for my father's sake . . .
Alas! What dream is this I hope to see?
Rodrigo has nothing to fear from me.
What good are tears which all of you despise?
Your empire gives him freedom for his prize.
Wherever you rule, you heed his plea;
As with the Moors, he triumphs over me.
Justice, whose voice is stifled in war's pain,
Serves as a trophy for this conqueror's gain.
With kings his prisoners and your applause,
He drives his chariot over the laws.

THE KING. Too violently, Chimena, your words call.
A King dispensing justice must weigh all.
A plea for vengeance you've come to uphold,
But justice, without mercy, must grow cold.
Before berating me for clemency,
Consult your heart; let love bend your proud knee.
Then, secretly, your joy shall thank your King,
Whose favor such a love to you can bring.

CHIMENA. To me? My enemy whom I must hate,
Who wrote in blood my lord and father's fate?
My father's death is looked upon so lightly

That it's a favor now to listen rightly!
Since you refuse, Sire, justice to my cause,
Permit me, then, the sword of ancient laws.
He injured me through peril of his sword
And, by a duel, I deserve reward.
From all your cavaliers, I ask his head;
To him who brings this prize, I shall be wed.
Let them fight, Sire, and when blood runs again,
I'll marry the victor if Rodrigo's slain.
Let this be published with your authority.

THE KING. This custom was established anciently.
To punish in a duel, deprives the State
Of all the warriors who've made us great.
Often the sad outcome of this abuse
Serves to ambition as a subtle ruse.
I do exempt Rodrigo from such need;
He is too precious for this fatal creed.
Whatever sins sprang from his sword's bright hilt,
The fleeing Moors have carried off his guilt.

DON DIEGO. What, Sire, you change custom for him alone,
A law which gives your Court its ancient tone?
What will your subjects think? Whom will they shun,
If he find shelter in this hope you've spun?
If he does make a pretext not to go
Where men of honor seek death's final glow?
Such favor would deny his present glory
And shame his deeds, his legendary story.
He slew the Count who had insulted me.
He was a brave man then, and still must be.

THE KING. Since you desire it, I shall let him fight,
But challenges I'll limit to his might;
To win Chimena's hand in marriage pleas
Would make all cavaliers his enemies.
For him to face them all would be too cruel.
Once only, then, shall he be forced to duel.
Choose whom you wish, Chimena, for this score,
But after this combat ask nothing more.

DON DIEGO. Do not excuse those who his sword do fear,
But leave the combat open; none will come near.

After the deeds he has to this day willed,
Who has the senseless courage to be killed?
Who would dare to fight with such a foe,
In this foolhardiness would only show.

DON SANCHO. Open the lists. My challenge you shall hear.
Though it may seem in vain, I shall not fear.

*To* CHIMENA.

Permit this favor as my heart's last fee,
Madam. You know what you have promised me.

THE KING, *to* CHIMENA. Did you accept his offer in your sorrow?

CHIMENA. Sire, I promised.

THE KING.                      Be ready then tomorrow.

DON DIEGO. No, Sire, there is no reason for delay.
One who is brave and just can fight today.

THE KING. How can he fight fresh from this battle's feud?

DON DIEGO. In telling you his tale, his life renewed.

THE KING. Still, he should have a longer time of rest.
To show this duel cannot by me be blessed,
For fear it might become a precedent
To which I've wrongly given my consent,
I shall not witness it, nor shall my Court.

*To* DON ARIAS.

To you as only judge I will resort.
Assure this combat honorably is fought
And that they both acquit them as they ought.
Whoever wins, the prize shall be the same.
With my own hand, I'll pledge Chimena's name,
And his reward shall be her marriage vow.

CHIMENA. How can you, Sire, so cruelly make me bow?

THE KING. You complain, but if your love should win,
You shall accept him as love conquers sin.
Cease murmuring against this mild decree,
For he who triumphs shall your husband be.

# ACT V

## Scene 1

CHIMENA. Rodrigo, here by day! How dare you show
  This boldness against my honor? Go, please go!

RODRIGO. Madam, I go to die, and came to tell
  You of my love before my last farewell,
  The sacred love which binds me to your need
  And takes my life in homage to your creed.

CHIMENA. You go to die?

RODRIGO.                 I hasten toward the end
  Where my blood with your father's then shall blend.

CHIMENA. You go to die! Don Sancho is a foe
  Who strikes into your heart this coward's woe?
  Who has made you so weak or him so strong?
  Rodrigo goes to fight and thinks his wrong
  Already needs his death! You scorned the Moor
  And killed my sire, yet tremble as if poor
  Of heart at Sancho! Your courage is spent.

RODRIGO. I seek no combat, but my punishment.
  When you ask for my death in this strife,
  I am unwilling to defend my life.
  My courage is the same, but not my arm
  Which yearns to hold you as a shield from harm.
  Last night I would have sought death to atone
  Had I been fighting for my cause alone.
  But to betray by death country and King,
  I could not, and so to life I had to cling.
  In my spirit I could not find good reason
  To lose my life by a base act of treason.

Now that I fight for nothing but my name,
You claim my death, and I accept your claim.
You've chosen Sancho's yoke, his hot demand
To fight me. I did not deserve your hand
To cause my death. I shall not strike a blow.
Respect to him who fights for you I owe.
I shall rejoice knowing his thrust is yours,
Since for your gracious honor his blade soars.
I'll meet his challenge with unguarded breast,
For in his hand, your hand will bring me rest.

CHIMENA. If justice and the violence of my task
Force me to wear a prosecutor's mask,
Inflict so harsh a law upon your love
That helpless to this duel you must move,
Remember in your blindness that your fame
Departs with life; and that Rodrigo's name
When dead will bear the stain of a defeat.
Honor is more to you than love's deceit,
For in my father's blood your hands were stained;
The bonds of honor our pure love restrained;
Yet now you think this is so little true
You care not who it is that conquers you.
How inconsistent with yourself you are;
You debase honor, yet place it on a star.
Are you so noble in humility?
Are you so cruel to my sire, then flee
That having conquered him you will submit
To any hand? Forsake this devil's wit.
Though I attack you till your final breath,
Defend your honor though you seek your death.

RODRIGO. The Count is dead. Our enemy, the Moor, bleeds
In defeat. Must I perform yet other deeds?
Chimena, my honor needs no defense.
Men know my courage swept beyond all sense
Of expectation; if honor should die
The world would waste beneath a sunless sky.
No, if I should lose this final duel,
It can but aid your justice of pursual.
No one will dare to think my courage failed,

Or claim my conqueror with joy be hailed;
For men shall only say, "Love was his fate.
He could not live and still endure her hate.
He yielded willingly to fate's dark flood
Which forced his own dear love to seek his blood.
She had to seek his head, and his denial
Would have placed the gift of love on trial.
For honor's sake, in combat he was hurled;
For his sweet mistress, he renounced this world
And died, preferring dreams of her as wife,
His honor to Chimena, her love to life."
Thus you shall see my death in this fight
Will spread the sun of honor in my night,
And by my death proclaim your honor's glory,
That no one's life but mine could end this story.

CHIMENA. Since life and honor have so little power
To keep you from this entrance to death's tower,
Rodrigo, if you love me, fight your foe,
Defend yourself to save me from this woe;
Release me from this compact so forlorn,
And fight to save me from a man I scorn.
What shall I add? Please think of your defense
To force my hand to silent innocence;
And if your love has not hardened to ice,
Defeat him when Chimena is the price.
Farewell! This last word makes me blush with shame.

*Exit* CHIMENA.

RODRIGO, *alone.* Is there an enemy I fear in name?
Castilians, Moors, whoever dares to take
The field against us, now one Army make:
Let all the valiant men whom Spain has nourished
Join together, and their greatness, flourished,
Will shatter against the sweetness of her light;
To gain her love with whom dare I not fight?

## Scene 2

### THE INFANTA

THE INFANTA, *alone.* Shall I consider still my birth and rank
  Which make my love a crime?
Or shall I listen, love, to you whose claim
Makes me rebel against my royal time?
  Unhappy Princess, choose,
  For either choice must lose
The hope of happiness. My royal grace
Would mock me as I kissed Rodrigo's face.

Pitiless fate that sternly separates
  My glory from desire;
Why must the choice of courage that is rare
Bring to my heart this hot, despairing fire?
  Oh God, how many tears
  My heart must blend with fears
Until this long torment can end forever
And either quell my love, or my love sever.

Too long have I been scrupulous.
  Why must I condemn my choice?
Although my birth gives me to kings alone,
To claim Rodrigo's name I can rejoice.
  Striking two kings down,
  He will achieve a crown.
His wondrous name of Cid—does this not prove
That he should rule a princess and her love?

Yet worthy of my birth, he is Chimena's.
  I gave him to her at love's decree.
Not even her father's death could make them hate,
Though from her duty now she cannot flee.
  I dare not hope for bliss tomorrow
  From his crime or from my sorrow,
Since ruthless fate, to punish me, foresees
That they shall keep their love, though enemies.

## Scene 3

### THE INFANTA, LEONORA

THE INFANTA. Why are you here, Leonora?

LEONORA.                              Madam, my heart glows
  With joy to know that you have found repose.

THE INFANTA. How can a heart so filled with grief find rest?

LEONORA. If love requires hope, with hope is blessed,
  Rodrigo can no longer claim your heart.
  You know the duel in which he plays his part.
  Since he must die or else Chimena wed,
  Your soul is cured for then your hope is dead.

THE INFANTA. Ah, if that were true!

LEONORA.                              What do you mean?

THE INFANTA. How kill the hope that in my mind you've seen?
  If under these conditions Rodrigo duels,
  Have I not power to silence tongues of fools?
  Sweet love, who causes cruel suffering,
  Teaches too easily how lovers cling.

LEONORA. How can you breed a discontent between them?
  Her father's death could not their great love stem;
  And by her conduct Chimena clearly shows
  That her pursuit from hatred never flows.
  She asks a trial by combat, and reveres
  As champion the first who volunteers;
  She does not choose an expert for this task;
  A man famous for valor she doesn't ask;
  Instead, Don Sancho satisfies her turn,
  Who never yet in war did merit earn.
  She loves in him his inexperienced hand;
  Thus, her anxiety fears no demand,
  And she fulfills her duty in her aim
  To then permit at last Rodrigo's claim.

THE INFANTA. Well do I know this guile, and yet my heart,
Competing with Chimena, is torn apart.
Unfortunate love; what shall I best decide?

LEONORA. Remember that your lineage you can't hide.
You love a subject, while God grants you a King.

THE INFANTA. My love has changed. No longer does my hope
sing
Of Rodrigo as a simple cavalier.
No, my love now thinks of him as peer.
If I love, it is the Cid whose name atones
For lack of rank, since he has conquered thrones.
Yet I shall give up love, not from a share
Of blame, but for the sacred love they bear.
If he did gain a crown to seal our rift,
I still could not accept his lover's gift.
Since in this duel, he is sure to win,
I'll give him to Chimena to heal my sin;
And you who know the anguish I have won,
Come, see me finish what I have begun.

## Scene 4

### CHIMENA, ELVIRA

CHIMENA. Elvira, how I should be pitied! I hope
And yet there's only fear in which to grope.
I dare not give consent to my desires.
A swift repentance follows their bright fires.
I made two rivals take up arms for me;
The happiest result of fate's decree
Will see my lover slain within this net,
Or else my father still demands my debt.

ELVIRA. You shall be recompensed on either side.
You'll have Rodrigo, or revenge's pride.
Whatever fate ordains this day for you,
It saves your honor, grants a husband true.

CHIMENA. Which husband? He whose love has been my prayer,
Or Sancho whom I hate, Rodrigo's slayer?
In either case I earn a husband stained
With blood of him who in my mind is grained.
My heart rebels whatever the decision.
I fear this quarrel's end more than death's vision.
Go, vengeance, love, you that possess my soul.
You cannot aid me now to reach your goal;
And you, creator of my violent fate,
Decide this combat equally, without hate;
That neither be the victor nor the vanquished.

ELVIRA. Such a cruel end should not by you be wished.
This duel is fresh punishment for you
If it demands again that you must sue
For justice, always in resentment live,
Pursue to death the man you would love give.
Madam, it were better if this violence
Makes him victor and commands your silence,
And that the King who has become your Sire
Should force you to comply with your desire.

CHIMENA. If he is conqueror, how can I yield?
My duty is too strong, too great a shield;
And to command me, even combat's laws
Are not enough; nor even the King's proud cause.
Yet, though Rodrigo break Don Sancho's guard,
Chimena's honor will remain unscarred.
However the King rewards the victor's pleas,
I shall fight him with a thousand enemies.

ELVIRA. Take care lest Heaven punish your strange pride,
And grant you vengeance that you cannot hide.
Will you reject this final happiness
Which your true silence could with honor bless?
What would you then pretend? What could you hope?
You would find one more death with which to cope?
Is one misfortune not enough? Would you heap
Loss upon loss, and greater sorrow reap?
In your pride, you do not deserve in this
The lover who is destined for your kiss,

And Heaven whose anger you wish to provoke,
Instead will bind you to Don Sancho's yoke.

CHIMENA. Elvira, the torment which I seek to flee
Is only swollen by your prophecy.
I would, if possible, avoid them both.
If not, Rodrigo's love was my sworn oath.
No dream of peace inclines my heart to him,
But if he fails I must please Sancho's whim.
This apprehension causes all my hate.

*Enter* DON SANCHO.

Look, Elvira! Oh God! It is too late.


### Scene 5

#### DON SANCHO, CHIMENA, ELVIRA

DON SANCHO. Madam, I must present this sword to you.

CHIMENA. See! Rodrigo's blood! Can this be true?
Traitor, how can you shamefully come here
When you have killed my love and caused my fear?
Cry out, my love, the anguish that I feel.
My father is avenged; love can't conceal
This sword that frees my love to every stare,
Assures my honor, but creates despair.

DON SANCHO. Hear me with calmer . . .

CHIMENA.                                  How dare you speak
When this proud hero's death you wished to seek?
Your triumph was through treachery. Please, go!
Rodrigo never could have felt your blow.
Hope for nothing from me in this cruel strife;
Searching for vengeance, you have taken my life.

DON SANCHO. You are wrong, Madam. Yet further hear me.

CHIMENA. How shall I hear your fatal boast or see
The prideful insolence with which you mime
Your courage, his misfortune, and my crime?

### Scene 6

THE KING, DON DIEGO, DON ARIAS, DON SANCHO,
DON ALONSO, CHIMENA, ELVIRA

CHIMENA. Sire, there is no longer need to hide
The truth which could not be concealed by pride.
For my father, I sought to rise above
My hope, and to condemn the man I love.
Your Majesty has seen with sorrow how
I made my love yield to my duty's vow.
But the shadow of death has come to hover
Over me, change me to a bitter lover.
The vengeance that I to my father owed
Has now upon my lover been bestowed.
By his defense, Sancho has cut love's ties,
Yet for his doing so I'm made his prize.
Sire, if your pity moves you, please withdraw
The cruelty of this barbaric law.
All that I have is his, but to atone
For killing love, let him leave me alone.
Send me to a cloister where I'll mourn
The two from whose great love I have been torn.

DON DIEGO. At last she loves, Sire, and shall no longer claim
It is a crime to speak love's blessèd name.

THE KING. Chimena, you are wrong and speak in error.
Don Sancho has deceived you in your terror.

DON SANCHO. Sire, this is unjust. She speaks from passion's
       sway.
I came here straight to tell her of the way
In which Rodrigo did my sword disarm.
This noble swordsman, with her heart in charm,
Told me to fear nothing. "I mean to leave
This victory uncertain lest she grieve,"
He said. "But since my duty must attend
The King, to her I will this sword now send

Through you as messenger of your defeat."
With these instructions, I came here to greet
Her, but she thought that I had conquered him;
And then her anger turned into this whim
Of grief that did so rob her reason's sense
I could not win a moment's audience.
For my part, though I suffer in defeat,
And though, in love, we shall never meet,
I must bow to the cause of my distress
Which brings a greater love this bright success.

THE KING. You must not be ashamed of such a love,
My daughter, or seek means to disapprove.
Your honor is fulfilled and free from shame;
Your duty paid unto your family's name.
Your father's satisfied, he rests in peace,
While Rodrigo's dangers cannot yet cease.
You see how Heaven has decreed this end:
Since you are free, I have seen fit to send
For Rodrigo; in respect to my command,
Accept your husband with a loving hand.

*Scene 7*

THE KING, DON DIEGO, DON ARIAS, RODRIGO, DON ALONSO,
DON SANCHO, THE INFANTA, CHIMENA, LEONORA, ELVIRA

THE INFANTA. Chimena, dry your tears; from your Princess
Take this hero whom with love you bless.

RODRIGO, *kneeling before Chimena.* Be not offended, Sire, if I
fail to greet
Your regal presence and kneel here at her feet.

*To* CHIMENA.

I came not to demand you for my wife,
But once again to offer you my life.
The law of combat I shall never plead,
Nor ask the King to recognize my deed.

If all that's done cannot appease death's cry,
Tell me what means is left to satisfy.
Must I still fight a thousand enemies,
Extend my deeds across the distant seas,
Defeat an Army, attack a camp alone,
Surpass the greatest heroes, to atone?
If guilt does pass, and we are not deceived,
I dare to hope that this can be achieved;
But if proud honor in its forceful course
Cannot be silent without death's remorse,
No longer seek through others your demands.
My life is yours. Take it with your own hands.
Your hands alone can conquer the unconquered;
For you alone by vengeance can be stirred;
But let my death suffice to punish me
And do not cut me from your memory.
Then righteous death shall keep your honor bright,
And you will hold your dream of love's delight
In lamentation for our hope to wed,
Crying, "He loved and, therefore, he is dead."

CHIMENA. Arise, Rodrigo. I have said too much,
Sire, to deny the truth. My love is such
As I have said, and him I cannot hate.
At your command I must obey my fate;
Your Majesty condemns me to this marriage,
But, Sire, how shall you see the wedding carriage?
And when before the priest we kneel to pray,
Will all your great justice rule there that day?
Rodrigo has become a hero now;
Must I with marriage his reward avow,
And yield myself to an eternal flood
Of guilt, my hands stained with my father's blood?

THE KING. The laws of reason change in course of time
And show the truth of what may seem a crime.
Rodrigo has won you; you must be wise;
But though you are today his valor's prize,
It would insult your honor to decree,
So soon, a wedding for his victory.
Delaying this marriage no law can break;

No date was set when you his hand must take.
You have a year then, if you wish, to mourn.
Meanwhile, Rodrigo still the Moors must scorn,
And having conquered them upon our shores,
Repulsed them and destroyed their Army's stores,
Must take the war into their bloodstained land
And ravage it beneath his sword's command.
They'll tremble when the name of Cid shall ring!
They'll call you Lord, and soon will make you King;
But do from faithful love this mighty deed;
If possible, return with love to plead,
And let your acts create in her such pride
That she shall then no honor lose as bride.

RODRIGO. For my Chimena, Sire, and for your throne,
You need but ask and I'll seek to atone.
Though I shall suffer distant from her face,
Yet I can hope, for in that hope is grace.

THE KING. Rely upon your valor and my word,
And since the pledge of love from her you've heard,
Let time, your courage, and your King remove
The point of honor that obstructs your love.

# THE MISANTHROPE

## A COMEDY

### BY

### MOLIÈRE

*English Version by Richard Wilbur*

...mission for performance and other rights outlined on the copyright page must be ...red from Harcourt Brace Jovanovich, Orlando, Florida 32887, from whom permis- to reprint this play has been granted.

# CHARACTERS

ALCESTE, *in love with Célimène*
PHILINTE, *Alceste's friend*
ORONTE, *in love with Célimène*
CÉLIMÈNE, *Alceste's beloved*
ÉLIANTE, *Célimène's cousin*
ARSINOÉ, *a friend of Célimène's*
ACASTE
CLITANDRE } *marquesses*
BASQUE, *Célimène's servant*
A GUARD *of the Marshalsea*
DUBOIS, *Alceste's valet*

THE SCENE THROUGHOUT IS IN CÉLIMÈNE'S HOUSE AT PARIS.

# ACT I

## Scene 1

### PHILINTE, ALCESTE

PHILINTE. Now, what's got into you?

ALCESTE, *seated.*　　　　　　　Kindly leave me alone.

PHILINTE. Come, come, what is it? This lugubrious tone . . .

ALCESTE. Leave me, I said; you spoil my solitude.

PHILINTE. Oh, listen to me, now, and don't be rude.

ALCESTE. I choose to be rude, Sir, and to be hard of hearing.

PHILINTE. These ugly moods of yours are not endearing;
　Friends though we are, I really must insist . . .

ALCESTE, *abruptly rising.* Friends? Friends, you say? Well,
　　　cross me off your list.
　I've been your friend till now, as you well know;
　But after what I saw a moment ago
　I tell you flatly that our ways must part.
　I wish no place in a dishonest heart.

PHILINTE. Why, what have I done, Alceste? Is this quite just?

ALCESTE. My God, you ought to die of self-disgust.
　I call your conduct inexcusable, Sir,
　And every man of honor will concur.
　I see you almost hug a man to death,
　Exclaim for joy until you're out of breath,
　And supplement these loving demonstrations
　With endless offers, vows, and protestations;
　Then when I ask you "Who was that?" I find
　That you can barely bring his name to mind!
　Once the man's back is turned, you cease to love him,
　And speak with absolute indifference of him!
　By God, I say it's base and scandalous

To falsify the heart's affections thus;
If I caught myself behaving in such a way,
I'd hang myself for shame, without delay.

PHILINTE. It hardly seems a hanging matter to me;
I hope that you will take it graciously
If I extend myself a slight reprieve,
And live a little longer, by your leave.

ALCESTE. How dare you joke about a crime so grave?

PHILINTE. What crime? How else are people to behave?

ALCESTE. I'd have them be sincere, and never part
With any word that isn't from the heart.

PHILINTE. When someone greets us with a show of pleasure,
It's but polite to give him equal measure,
Return his love the best that we know how,
And trade him offer for offer, vow for vow.

ALCESTE. No, no, this formula you'd have me follow,
However fashionable, is false and hollow,
And I despise the frenzied operations
Of all these barterers of protestations,
These lavishers of meaningless embraces,
These utterers of obliging commonplaces,
Who court and flatter everyone on earth
And praise the fool no less than the man of worth.
Should you rejoice that someone fondles you,
Offers his love and service, swears to be true,
And fills your ears with praises of your name,
When to the first damned fop he'll say the same?
No, no: no self-respecting heart would dream
Of prizing so promiscuous an esteem;
However high the praise, there's nothing worse
Than sharing honors with the universe.
Esteem is founded on comparison:
To honor all men is to honor none.
Since you embrace this indiscriminate vice,
Your friendship comes at far too cheap a price;
I spurn the easy tribute of a heart
Which will not set the worthy man apart:
I choose, Sir, to be chosen; and in fine,
The friend of mankind is no friend of mine.

PHILINTE. But in polite society, custom decrees
   That we show certain outward courtesies. . . .

ALCESTE. Ah, no! we should condemn with all our force
   Such false and artificial intercourse.
   Let men behave like men; let them display
   Their inmost hearts in everything they say;
   Let the heart speak, and let our sentiments
   Not mask themselves in silly compliments.

PHILINTE. In certain cases it would be uncouth
   And most absurd to speak the naked truth;
   With all respect for your exalted notions,
   It's often best to veil one's true emotions.
   Wouldn't the social fabric come undone
   If we were wholly frank with everyone?
   Suppose you met with someone you couldn't bear;
   Would you inform him of it then and there?

ALCESTE. Yes.

PHILINTE.     Then you'd tell old Emilie it's pathetic
   The way she daubs her features with cosmetic
   And plays the gay coquette at sixty-four?

ALCESTE. I would.

PHILINTE.     And you'd call Dorilas a bore,
   And tell him every ear at court is lame
   From hearing him brag about his noble name?

ALCESTE. Precisely.

PHILINTE.     Ah, you're joking.

ALCESTE.                         *Au contraire:*
   In this regard there's none I'd choose to spare.
   All are corrupt; there's nothing to be seen
   In court or town but aggravates my spleen.
   I fall into deep gloom and melancholy
   When I survey the scene of human folly,
   Finding on every hand base flattery,
   Injustice, fraud, self-interest, treachery. . . .
   Ah, it's too much; mankind has grown so base,
   I mean to break with the whole human race.

PHILINTE. This philosophic rage is a bit extreme;
   You've no idea how comical you seem;

Indeed, we're like those brothers in the play
Called *School for Husbands,* one of whom was prey . . .

ALCESTE. Enough, now! None of your stupid similes.

PHILINTE. Then let's have no more tirades, if you please.
The world won't change, whatever you say or do;
And since plain speaking means so much to you,
I'll tell you plainly that by being frank
You've earned the reputation of a crank,
And that you're thought ridiculous when you rage
And rant against the manners of the age.

ALCESTE. So much the better; just what I wish to hear.
No news could be more grateful to my ear.
All men are so detestable in my eyes,
I should be sorry if they thought me wise.

PHILINTE. Your hatred's very sweeping, is it not?

ALCESTE. Quite right: I hate the whole degraded lot.

PHILINTE. Must all poor human creatures be embraced,
Without distinction, by your vast distaste?
Even in these bad times, there are surely a few . . .

ALCESTE. No, I include all men in one dim view:
Some men I hate for being rogues; the others
I hate because they treat the rogues like brothers,
And, lacking a virtuous scorn for what is vile,
Receive the villain with a complaisant smile.
Notice how tolerant people choose to be
Toward that bold rascal who's at law with me.
His social polish can't conceal his nature;
One sees at once that he's a treacherous creature;
No one could possibly be taken in
By those soft speeches and that sugary grin.
The whole world knows the shady means by which
The low-brow's grown so powerful and rich,
And risen to a rank so bright and high
That virtue can but blush, and merit sigh.
Whenever his name comes up in conversation,
None will defend his wretched reputation;
Call him knave, liar, scoundrel, and all the rest,
Each head will nod, and no one will protest.
And yet his smirk is seen in every house,

He's greeted everywhere with smiles and bows,
And when there's any honor that can be got
By pulling strings, he'll get it, like as not.
My God! It chills my heart to see the ways
Men come to terms with evil nowadays;
Sometimes, I swear, I'm moved to flee and find
Some desert land unfouled by humankind.

PHILINTE. Come, let's forget the follies of the times
And pardon mankind for its petty crimes;
Let's have an end of rantings and of railings,
And show some leniency toward human failings.
This world requires a pliant rectitude;
Too stern a virtue makes one stiff and rude;
Good sense views all extremes with detestation,
And bids us to be noble in moderation.
The rigid virtues of the ancient days
Are not for us; they jar with all our ways
And ask of us too lofty a perfection.
Wise men accept their times without objection,
And there's no greater folly, if you ask me,
Than trying to reform society.
Like you, I see each day a hundred and one
Unhandsome deeds that might be better done,
But still, for all the faults that meet my view,
I'm never known to storm and rave like you.
I take men as they are, or let them be,
And teach my soul to bear their frailty;
And whether in court or town, whatever the scene,
My phlegm's as philosophic as your spleen.

ALCESTE. This phlegm which you so eloquently commend,
Does nothing ever rile it up, my friend?
Suppose some man you trust should treacherously
Conspire to rob you of your property,
And do his best to wreck your reputation?
Wouldn't you feel a certain indignation?

PHILINTE. Why, no. These faults of which you so complain
Are part of human nature, I maintain,
And it's no more a matter for disgust
That men are knavish, selfish and unjust,

Than that the vulture dines upon the dead,
And wolves are furious, and apes ill-bred.

ALCESTE. Shall I see myself betrayed, robbed, torn to bits,
And not . . . Oh, let's be still and rest our wits.
Enough of reasoning, now. I've had my fill.

PHILINTE. Indeed, you would do well, Sir, to be still.
Rage less at your opponent, and give some thought
To how you'll win this lawsuit that he's brought.

ALCESTE. I assure you I'll do nothing of the sort.

PHILINTE. Then who will plead your case before the court?

ALCESTE. Reason and right and justice will plead for me.

PHILINTE. Oh, Lord. What judges do you plan to see?

ALCESTE. Why, none. The justice of my cause is clear.

PHILINTE. Of course, man; but there's politics to fear. . . .

ALCESTE. No, I refuse to lift a hand. That's flat.
I'm either right, or wrong.

PHILINTE.                          Don't count on that.

ALCESTE. No, I'll do nothing.

PHILINTE.                          Your enemy's influence
Is great, you know . . .

ALCESTE.                          That makes no difference.

PHILINTE. It will; you'll see.

ALCESTE.                          Must honor bow to guile?
If so, I shall be proud to lose the trial.

PHILINTE. Oh, really . . .

ALCESTE.                          I'll discover by this case
Whether or not men are sufficiently base
And impudent and villainous and perverse
To do me wrong before the universe.

PHILINTE. What a man!

ALCESTE.                          Oh, I could wish, whatever the cost,
Just for the beauty of it, that my trial were lost.

PHILINTE. If people heard you talking so, Alceste,
They'd split their sides. Your name would be a jest.

ALCESTE. So much the worse for jesters.

PHILINTE.                    May I enquire
  Whether this rectitude you so admire,
  And these hard virtues you're enamored of
  Are qualities of the lady whom you love?
  It much surprises me that you, who seem
  To view mankind with furious disesteem,
  Have yet found something to enchant your eyes
  Amidst a species which you so despise.
  And what is more amazing, I'm afraid,
  Is the most curious choice your heart has made.
  The honest Éliante is fond of you,
  Arsinoé, the prude, admires you too;
  And yet your spirit's been perversely led
  To choose the flighty Célimène instead,
  Whose brittle malice and coquettish ways
  So typify the manners of our days.
  How is it that the traits you most abhor
  Are bearable in this lady you adore?
  Are you so blind with love that you can't find them?
  Or do you contrive, in her case, not to mind them?

ALCESTE. My love for that young widow's not the kind
  That can't perceive defects; no, I'm not blind.
  I see her faults, despite my ardent love,
  And all I see I fervently reprove.
  And yet I'm weak; for all her falsity,
  That woman knows the art of pleasing me,
  And though I never cease complaining of her,
  I swear I cannot manage not to love her.
  Her charm outweighs her faults; I can but aim
  To cleanse her spirit in my love's pure flame.

PHILINTE. That's no small task; I wish you all success.
  You think then that she loves you?

ALCESTE.                  Heavens, yes!
  I wouldn't love her did she not love me.

PHILINTE. Well, if her taste for you is plain to see,
  Why do these rivals cause you such despair?

ALCESTE. True love, Sir, is possessive, and cannot bear
  To share with all the world. I'm here today
  To tell her she must send that mob away.

PHILINTE. If I were you, and had your choice to make,
    Éliante, her cousin, would be the one I'd take;
    That honest heart, which cares for you alone,
    Would harmonize far better with your own.

ALCESTE. True, true: each day my reason tells me so;
    But reason doesn't rule in love, you know.

PHILINTE. I fear some bitter sorrow is in store;
    This love . . .

### Scene 2

#### ORONTE, ALCESTE, PHILINTE

ORONTE, *to* ALCESTE. The servants told me at the door
    That Éliante and Célimène were out,
    But when I heard, dear Sir, that you were about,
    I came to say, without exaggeration,
    That I hold you in the vastest admiration,
    And that it's always been my dearest desire
    To be the friend of one I so admire.
    I hope to see my love of merit requited,
    And you and I in friendship's bond united.
    I'm sure you won't refuse—if I may be frank—
    A friend of my devotedness—and rank.

*During this speech of* ORONTE'S, ALCESTE *is abstracted, and
seems unaware that he is being spoken to. He only breaks
off his reverie when* ORONTE *says:*

It was for you, if you please, that my words were intended.

ALCESTE. For me, Sir?

ORONTE.               Yes, for you. You're not offended?

ALCESTE. By no means. But this much surprises me. . . .
    The honor comes most unexpectedly. . . .

ORONTE. My high regard should not astonish you;
    The whole world feels the same. It is your due.

ALCESTE. Sir . . .

ORONTE.                Why, in all the State there isn't one
   Can match your merits; they shine, Sir, like the sun.

ALCESTE. Sir . . .

ORONTE.                You are higher in my estimation
   Than all that's most illustrious in the nation.

ALCESTE. Sir . . .

ORONTE.                If I lie, may heaven strike me dead!
   To show you that I mean what I have said,
   Permit me, Sir, to embrace you most sincerely,
   And swear that I will prize our friendship dearly.
   Give me your hand. And now, Sir, if you choose,
   We'll make our vows.

ALCESTE.                    Sir . . .

ORONTE.                          What! You refuse?

ALCESTE. Sir, it's a very great honor you extend:
   But friendship is a sacred thing, my friend;
   It would be profanation to bestow
   The name of friend on one you hardly know.
   All parts are better played when well-rehearsed;
   Let's put off friendship, and get acquainted first.
   We may discover it would be unwise
   To try to make our natures harmonize.

ORONTE. By heaven! You're sagacious to the core;
   This speech has made me admire you even more.
   Let time, then, bring us closer day by day;
   Meanwhile, I shall be yours in every way.
   If, for example, there should be anything
   You wish at court, I'll mention it to the King.
   I have his ear, of course; it's quite well known
   That I am much in favor with the throne.
   In short, I am your servant. And now, dear friend,
   Since you have such fine judgment, I intend
   To please you, if I can, with a small sonnet
   I wrote not long ago. Please comment on it,
   And tell me whether I ought to publish it.

ALCESTE. You must excuse me, Sir; I'm hardly fit
   To judge such matters.

ORONTE.                    Why not?

ALCESTE.                              I am, I fear,
  Inclined to be unfashionably sincere.

ORONTE. Just what I ask; I'd take no satisfaction
  In anything but your sincere reaction.
  I beg you not to dream of being kind.

ALCESTE. Since you desire it, Sir, I'll speak my mind.

ORONTE. *Sonnet*. It's a sonnet. . . . *Hope* . . . The poem's
    addressed
  To a lady who wakened hopes within my breast.
  *Hope* . . . this is not the pompous sort of thing,
  Just modest little verses, with a tender ring.

ALCESTE. Well, we shall see.

ORONTE.                          *Hope* . . . I'm anxious to hear
  Whether the style seems properly smooth and clear,
  And whether the choice of words is good or bad.

ALCESTE. We'll see, we'll see.

ORONTE.                          Perhaps I ought to add
  That it took me only a quarter-hour to write it.

ALCESTE. The time's irrelevant, Sir: kindly recite it.

ORONTE, *reading*.
          *Hope comforts us awhile, 'tis true,*
            *Lulling our cares with careless laughter,*
          *And yet such joy is full of rue,*
            *My Phyllis, if nothing follows after.*

PHILINTE. I'm charmed by this already; the style's delightful.

ALCESTE, *sotto voce, to* PHILINTE. How can you say that? Why,
    the thing is frightful.

ORONTE.   *Your fair face smiled on me awhile,*
            *But was it kindness so to enchant me?*
          *'Twould have been fairer not to smile,*
            *If hope was all you meant to grant me.*

PHILINTE. What a clever thought! How handsomely you
    phrase it!

ALCESTE, *sotto voce, to* PHILINTE. You know the thing is trash.
    How dare you praise it?

ORONTE.   *If it's to be my passion's fate*
            *Thus everlastingly to wait,*

*Then death will come to set me free:*
*For death is fairer than the fair;*
*Phyllis, to hope is to despair*
*When one must hope eternally.*

PHILINTE. The close is exquisite—full of feeling and grace.

ALCESTE, *sotto voce, aside.* Oh, blast the close; you'd better close your face
Before you send your lying soul to hell.

PHILINTE. I can't remember a poem I've liked so well.

ALCESTE, *sotto voce, aside.* Good Lord!

ORONTE, *to* PHILINTE.                    I fear you're flattering
me a bit.

PHILINTE. Oh, no!

ALCESTE, *sotto voce, aside.*
                    What else d'you call it, you hypocrite?

ORONTE, *to* ALCESTE. But you, Sir, keep your promise now: don't shrink
From telling me sincerely what you think.

ALCESTE. Sir, these are delicate matters; we all desire
To be told that we've the true poetic fire.
But once, to one whose name I shall not mention,
I said, regarding some verse of his invention,
That gentlemen should rigorously control
That itch to write which often afflicts the soul;
That one should curb the heady inclination
To publicize one's little avocation;
And that in showing off one's works of art
One often plays a very clownish part.

ORONTE. Are you suggesting in a devious way
That I ought not . . .

ALCESTE.                    Oh, that I do not say.
Further, I told him that no fault is worse
Than that of writing frigid, lifeless verse,
And that the merest whisper of such a shame
Suffices to destroy a man's good name.

ORONTE. D'you mean to say my sonnet's dull and trite?

ALCESTE. I don't say that. But I went on to cite
  Numerous cases of once-respected men
  Who came to grief by taking up the pen.

ORONTE. And am I like them? Do I write so poorly?

ALCESTE. I don't say that. But I told this person, "Surely
  You're under no necessity to compose;
  Why you should wish to publish, heaven knows.
  There's no excuse for printing tedious rot
  Unless one writes for bread, as you do not.
  Resist temptation, then, I beg of you;
  Conceal your pastimes from the public view;
  And don't give up, on any provocation,
  Your present high and courtly reputation,
  To purchase at a greedy printer's shop
  The name of silly author and scribbling fop."
  These were the points I tried to make him see.

ORONTE. I sense that they are also aimed at me;
  But now—about my sonnet—I'd like to be told . . .

ALCESTE. Frankly, that sonnet should be pigeonholed.
  You've chosen the worst models to imitate.
  The style's unnatural. Let me illustrate:

  For example, *Your fair face smiled on me awhile,*
  Followed by, *'Twould have been fairer not to smile!*
  Or this: *such joy is full of rue;*
  Or this: *For death is fairer than the fair;*
  Or, *Phyllis, to hope is to despair*
    *When one must hope eternally!*

This artificial style, that's all the fashion,
Has neither taste, nor honesty, nor passion;
It's nothing but a sort of wordy play,
And nature never spoke in such a way.
What, in this shallow age, is not debased?
Our fathers, though less refined, had better taste;
I'd barter all that men admire today
For one old love song I shall try to say:

    *If the King had given me for my own*
    *Paris, his citadel,*
    *And I for that must leave alone*

*Her whom I love so well,*
*I'd say then to the Crown,*
*Take back your glittering town;*
*My darling is more fair, I swear,*
*My darling is more fair.*

The rhyme's not rich, the style is rough and old,
But don't you see that it's the purest gold
Beside the tinsel nonsense now preferred,
And that there's passion in its every word?

*If the King had given me for my own*
*Paris, his citadel,*
*And I for that must leave alone*
*Her whom I love so well,*
*I'd say then to the Crown,*
*Take back your glittering town;*
*My darling is more fair, I swear,*
*My darling is more fair.*

There speaks a loving heart. (*To* PHILINTE) You're laugh-
ing, eh?
Laugh on, my precious wit. Whatever you say,
I hold that song's worth all the bibelots
That people hail today with ah's and oh's.

ORONTE. And I maintain my sonnet's very good.

ALCESTE. It's not at all surprising that you should.
You have your reasons; permit me to have mine
For thinking that you cannot write a line.

ORONTE. Others have praised my sonnet to the skies.

ALCESTE. I lack their art of telling pleasant lies.

ORONTE. You seem to think you've got no end of wit.

ALCESTE. To praise your verse, I'd need still more of it.

ORONTE. I'm not in need of your approval, Sir.

ALCESTE. That's good; you couldn't have it if you were.

ORONTE. Come now, I'll lend you the subject of my sonnet;
I'd like to see you try to improve upon it.

ALCESTE. I might, by chance, write something just as shoddy;
But then I wouldn't show it to everybody.

ORONTE. You're most opinionated and conceited.

ALCESTE. Go find your flatterers, and be better treated.

ORONTE. Look here, my little fellow, pray watch your tone.

ALCESTE. My great big fellow, you'd better watch your own.

PHILINTE, *stepping between them.* Oh, please, please, gentlemen! This will never do.

ORONTE. The fault is mine, and I leave the field to you.
I am your servant, Sir, in every way.

ALCESTE. And I, Sir, am your most abject valet.


## Scene 3

### PHILINTE, ALCESTE

PHILINTE. Well, as you see, sincerity in excess
Can get you into a very pretty mess;
Oronte was hungry for appreciation. . . .

ALCESTE. Don't speak to me.

PHILINTE.                         What?

ALCESTE.                                   No more conversation.

PHILINTE. Really, now . . .

ALCESTE.                         Leave me alone.

PHILINTE.                                             If I . . .

ALCESTE.                                                       Out of my sight!

PHILINTE. But what . . .

ALCESTE.         I won't listen.

PHILINTE.                             But . . .

ALCESTE.                                 Silence!

PHILINTE.                                             Now, is it polite . . .

ALCESTE. By heaven, I've had enough. Don't follow me.

PHILINTE. Ah, you're just joking. I'll keep you company.

# ACT II

## Scene 1

### ALCESTE, CÉLIMÈNE

ALCESTE. Shall I speak plainly, Madam? I confess
    Your conduct gives me infinite distress,
    And my resentment's grown too hot to smother.
    Soon, I foresee, we'll break with one another.
    If I said otherwise, I should deceive you;
    Sooner or later, I shall be forced to leave you,
    And if I swore that we shall never part,
    I should misread the omens of my heart.
CÉLIMÈNE. You kindly saw me home, it would appear,
    So as to pour invectives in my ear.
ALCESTE. I've no desire to quarrel. But I deplore
    Your inability to shut the door
    On all these suitors who beset you so.
    There's what annoys me, if you care to know.
CÉLIMÈNE. Is it my fault that all these men pursue me?
    Am I to blame if they're attracted to me?
    And when they gently beg an audience,
    Ought I to take a stick and drive them hence?
ALCESTE. Madam, there's no necessity for a stick;
    A less responsive heart would do the trick.
    Of your attractiveness I don't complain;
    But those your charms attract, you then detain
    By a most melting and receptive manner,
    And so enlist their hearts beneath your banner.
    It's the agreeable hopes which you excite
    That keep these lovers round you day and night;
    Were they less liberally smiled upon,

That sighing troop would very soon be gone.
But tell me, Madam, why it is that lately
This man Clitandre interests you so greatly?
Because of what high merits do you deem
Him worthy of the honor of your esteem?
Is it that your admiring glances linger
On the splendidly long nail of his little finger?
Or do you share the general deep respect
For the blond wig he chooses to affect?
Are you in love with his embroidered hose?
Do you adore his ribbons and his bows?
Or is it that this paragon bewitches
Your tasteful eye with his vast German breeches?
Perhaps his giggle, or his falsetto voice,
Makes him the latest gallant of your choice?

CÉLIMÈNE. You're much mistaken to resent him so.
Why I put up with him you surely know:
My lawsuit's very shortly to be tried,
And I must have his influence on my side.

ALCESTE. Then lose your lawsuit, Madam, or let it drop;
Don't torture me by humoring such a fop.

CÉLIMÈNE. You're jealous of the whole world, Sir.

ALCESTE.                                          That's true,
Since the whole world is well-received by you.

CÉLIMÈNE. That my good nature is so unconfined
Should serve to pacify your jealous mind;
Were I to smile on one, and scorn the rest,
Then you might have some cause to be distressed.

ALCESTE. Well, if I mustn't be jealous, tell me, then,
Just how I'm better treated than other men.

CÉLIMÈNE. You know you have my love. Will that not do?

ALCESTE. What proof have I that what you say is true?

CÉLIMÈNE. I would expect, Sir, that my having said it
Might give the statement a sufficient credit.

ALCESTE. But how can I be sure that you don't tell
The selfsame thing to other men as well?

CÉLIMÈNE. What a gallant speech! How flattering to me!
What a sweet creature you make me out to be!

Well then, to save you from the pangs of doubt,
All that I've said I hereby cancel out;
Now, none but yourself shall make a monkey of you:
Are you content?

ALCESTE.                    Why, why am I doomed to love you?
I swear that I shall bless the blissful hour
When this poor heart's no longer in your power!
I make no secret of it: I've done my best
To exorcise this passion from my breast;
But thus far all in vain; it will not go;
It's for my sins that I must love you so.

CÉLIMÈNE. Your love for me is matchless, Sir; that's clear.

ALCESTE. Indeed, in all the world it has no peer;
Words can't describe the nature of my passion,
And no man ever loved in such a fashion.

CÉLIMÈNE. Yes, it's a brand-new fashion, I agree:
You show your love by castigating me,
And all your speeches are enraged and rude.
I've never been so furiously wooed.

ALCESTE. Yet you could calm that fury, if you chose.
Come, shall we bring our quarrels to a close?
Let's speak with open hearts, then, and begin . . .

### Scene 2

CÉLIMÈNE, ALCESTE, BASQUE

CÉLIMÈNE. What is it?

BASQUE.                    Acaste is here.

CÉLIMÈNE.                                        Well, send him in.

## Scene 3

### CÉLIMÈNE, ALCESTE

ALCESTE. What! Shall we never be alone at all?
  You're always ready to receive a call,
  And you can't bear, for ten ticks of the clock,
  Not to keep open house for all who knock.
CÉLIMÈNE. I couldn't refuse him: he'd be most put out.
ALCESTE. Surely that's not worth worrying about.
CÉLIMÈNE. Acaste would never forgive me if he guessed
  That I consider him a dreadful pest.
ALCESTE. If he's a pest, why bother with him then?
CÉLIMÈNE. Heavens! One can't antagonize such men;
  Why, they're the chartered gossips of the court,
  And have a say in things of every sort.
  One must receive them, and be full of charm;
  They're no great help, but they can do you harm,
  And though your influence be ever so great,
  They're hardly the best people to alienate.
ALCESTE. I see, dear lady, that you could make a case
  For putting up with the whole human race;
  These friendships that you calculate so nicely . . .

## Scene 4

### ALCESTE, CÉLIMÈNE, BASQUE

BASQUE. Madam, Clitandre is here as well.
ALCESTE.                                        Precisely.
CÉLIMÈNE. Where are you going?
ALCESTE.                                        Elsewhere.

CÉLIMÈNE.                                    Stay.
ALCESTE.                                              No, no.
CÉLIMÈNE. Stay, Sir.
ALCESTE.                    I can't.
CÉLIMÈNE.                        I wish it.
ALCESTE.                                  No, I must go.
  I beg you, Madam, not to press the matter;
  You know I have no taste for idle chatter.
CÉLIMÈNE. Stay: I command you.
ALCESTE.                                  No, I cannot stay.
CÉLIMÈNE. Very well; you have my leave to go away.

### Scene 5

ÉLIANTE, PHILINTE, ACASTE, CLITANDRE, ALCESTE,
CÉLIMÈNE, BASQUE

ÉLIANTE, *to* CÉLIMÈNE. The Marquesses have kindly come
    to call.
  Were they announced?
CÉLIMÈNE.                        Yes. Basque, bring chairs for all.
  BASQUE *provides the chairs, and exits.*
  *To* ALCESTE. You haven't gone?
ALCESTE.                                  No; and I shan't depart
  Till you decide who's foremost in your heart.
CÉLIMÈNE. Oh, hush.
ALCESTE.                      It's time to choose; take them, or me.
CÉLIMÈNE. You're mad.
ALCESTE.                        I'm not, as you shall shortly see.
CÉLIMÈNE. Oh?
ALCESTE.          You'll decide.
CÉLIMÈNE.                            You're joking now, dear friend.
ALCESTE. No, no; you'll choose; my patience is at an end.

CLITANDRE. Madam, I come from court, where poor Cléonte
Behaved like a perfect fool, as is his wont.
Has he no friend to counsel him, I wonder,
And teach him less unerringly to blunder?

CÉLIMÈNE. It's true, the man's a most accomplished dunce;
His gauche behavior charms the eye at once;
And every time one sees him, on my word,
His manner's grown a trifle more absurd.

ACASTE. Speaking of dunces, I've just now conversed
With old Damon, who's one of the very worst;
I stood a lifetime in the broiling sun
Before his dreary monologue was done.

CÉLIMÈNE. Oh, he's a wondrous talker, and has the power
To tell you nothing hour after hour:
If, by mistake, he ever came to the point,
The shock would put his jawbone out of joint.

ÉLIANTE, *to* PHILINTE. The conversation takes its usual turn,
And all our dear friends' ears will shortly burn.

CLITANDRE. Timante's a character, Madam.

CÉLIMÈNE.                         Isn't he, though?
A man of mystery from top to toe,
Who moves about in a romantic mist
On secret missions which do not exist.
His talk is full of eyebrows and grimaces;
How tired one gets of his momentous faces;
He's always whispering something confidential
Which turns out to be quite inconsequential;
Nothing's too slight for him to mystify;
He even whispers when he says "good-by."

ACASTE. Tell us about Géralde.

CÉLIMÈNE.                     That tiresome ass.
He mixes only with the titled class,
And fawns on dukes and princes, and is bored
With anyone who's not at least a lord.
The man's obsessed with rank, and his discourses
Are all of hounds and carriages and horses;
He uses Christian names with all the great,
And the word Milord, with him, is out of date.

CLITANDRE. He's very taken with Bélise, I hear.

CÉLIMÈNE. She is the dreariest company, poor dear.
  Whenever she comes to call, I grope about
  To find some topic which will draw her out,
  But, owing to her dry and faint replies,
  The conversation wilts, and droops, and dies.
  In vain one hopes to animate her face
  By mentioning the ultimate commonplace;
  But sun or shower, even hail or frost
  Are matters she can instantly exhaust.
  Meanwhile her visit, painful though it is,
  Drags on and on through mute eternities,
  And though you ask the time, and yawn, and yawn,
  She sits there like a stone and won't be gone.

ACASTE. Now for Adraste.

CÉLIMÈNE.                    Oh, that conceited elf
  Has a gigantic passion for himself;
  He rails against the court, and cannot bear it
  That none will recognize his hidden merit;
  All honors given to others give offense
  To his imaginary excellence.

CLITANDRE. What about young Cléon? His house, they say,
  Is full of the best society, night and day.

CÉLIMÈNE. His cook has made him popular, not he:
  It's Cléon's table that people come to see.

ÉLIANTE. He gives a splendid dinner, you must admit.

CÉLIMÈNE. But must he serve himself along with it?
  For my taste, he's a most insipid dish
  Whose presence sours the wine and spoils the fish.

PHILINTE. Damis, his uncle, is admired no end.
  What's your opinion, Madam?

CÉLIMÈNE.                        Why, he's my friend.

PHILINTE. He seems a decent fellow, and rather clever.

CÉLIMÈNE. He works too hard at cleverness, however.
  I hate to see him sweat and struggle so
  To fill his conversation with bons mots.
  Since he's decided to become a wit
  His taste's so pure that nothing pleases it;

He scolds at all the latest books and plays,
Thinking that wit must never stoop to praise,
That finding fault's a sign of intellect,
That all appreciation is abject,
And that by damning everything in sight
One shows oneself in a distinguished light.
He's scornful even of our conversations:
Their trivial nature sorely tries his patience;
He folds his arms, and stands above the battle,
And listens sadly to our childish prattle.

ACASTE. Wonderful, Madam! You've hit him off precisely.

CLITANDRE. No one can sketch a character so nicely.

ALCESTE. How bravely, Sirs, you cut and thrust at all
These absent fools, till one by one they fall:
But let one come in sight, and you'll at once
Embrace the man you lately called a dunce,
Telling him in a tone sincere and fervent
How proud you are to be his humble servant.

CLITANDRE. Why pick on us? *Madame's* been speaking, Sir,
And you should quarrel, if you must, with her.

ALCESTE. No, no, by God, the fault is yours, because
You lead her on with laughter and applause,
And make her think that she's the more delightful
The more her talk is scandalous and spiteful.
Oh, she would stoop to malice far, far less
If no such claque approved her cleverness.
It's flatterers like you whose foolish praise
Nourishes all the vices of these days.

PHILINTE. But why protest when someone ridicules
Those you'd condemn, yourself, as knaves or fools?

CÉLIMÈNE. Why, Sir? Because he loves to make a fuss.
You don't expect him to agree with us,
When there's an opportunity to express
His heaven-sent spirit of contrariness?
What other people think, he can't abide;
Whatever they say, he's on the other side;
He lives in deadly terror of agreeing;
'Twould make him seem an ordinary being.
Indeed, he's so in love with contradiction,

He'll turn against his most profound conviction
And with a furious eloquence deplore it,
If only someone else is speaking for it.

ALCESTE. Go on, dear lady, mock me as you please;
You have your audience in ecstasies.

PHILINTE. But what she says is true: you have a way
Of bridling at whatever people say;
Whether they praise or blame, your angry spirit
Is equally unsatisfied to hear it.

ALCESTE. Men, Sir, are always wrong, and that's the reason
That righteous anger's never out of season;
All that I hear in all their conversation
Is flattering praise or reckless condemnation.

CÉLIMÈNE. But . . .

ALCESTE.              No, no, Madam, I am forced to state
That you have pleasures which I deprecate,
And that these others, here, are much to blame
For nourishing the faults which are your shame.

CLITANDRE. I shan't defend myself, Sir; but I vow
I'd thought this lady faultless until now.

ACASTE. I see her charms and graces, which are many;
But as for faults, I've never noticed any.

ALCESTE. I see them, Sir; and rather than ignore them,
I strenuously criticize her for them.
The more one loves, the more one should object
To every blemish, every least defect.
Were I this lady, I would soon get rid
Of lovers who approved of all I did,
And by their slack indulgence and applause
Endorsed my follies and excused my flaws.

CÉLIMÈNE. If all hearts beat according to your measure,
The dawn of love would be the end of pleasure;
And love would find its perfect consummation
In ecstasies of rage and reprobation.

ÉLIANTE. Love, as a rule, affects men otherwise,
And lovers rarely love to criticize.
They see their lady as a charming blur,
And find all things commendable in her.

If she has any blemish, fault, or shame,
They will redeem it by a pleasing name.
The pale-faced lady's lily-white, perforce;
The swarthy one's a sweet brunette, of course;
The spindly lady has a slender grace;
The fat one has a most majestic pace;
The plain one, with her dress in disarray,
They classify as *beauté négligée;*
The hulking one's a goddess in their eyes,
The dwarf, a concentrate of Paradise;
The haughty lady has a noble mind;
The mean one's witty, and the dull one's kind;
The chatterbox has liveliness and verve,
The mute one has a virtuous reserve.
So lovers manage, in their passion's cause,
To love their ladies even for their flaws.

ALCESTE. But I still say . . .

CÉLIMÈNE.                I think it would be nice
To stroll around the gallery once or twice.
What! You're not going, Sirs?

CLITANDRE AND ACASTE.        No, Madam, no.

ALCESTE. You seem to be in terror lest they go.
Do what you will, Sirs; leave, or linger on,
But I shan't go till after you are gone.

ACASTE. I'm free to linger, unless I should perceive
*Madame* is tired, and wishes me to leave.

CLITANDRE. And as for me, I needn't go today
Until the hour of the King's *coucher.*

CÉLIMÈNE, *to* ALCESTE. You're joking, surely?

ALCESTE.                    Not in the least; we'll see
Whether you'd rather part with them, or me.

## Scene 6

ALCESTE, CÉLIMÈNE, ÉLIANTE, ACASTE, PHILINTE,
CLITANDRE, BASQUE

BASQUE, *to* ALCESTE. Sir, there's a fellow here who bids me state
That he must see you, and that it can't wait.

ALCESTE. Tell him that I have no such pressing affairs.

BASQUE. It's a long tailcoat that this fellow wears,
With gold all over.

CÉLIMÈNE, *to* ALCESTE. You'd best go down and see.
Or—have him enter.

## Scene 7

ALCESTE, CÉLIMÈNE, ÉLIANTE, ACASTE, PHILINTE,
CLITANDRE, GUARD

ALCESTE, *confronting the* GUARD.        Well, what do you want
with me?
Come in, Sir.

GUARD.        I've a word, Sir, for your ear.

ALCESTE. Speak it aloud, Sir; I shall strive to hear.

GUARD. The Marshals have instructed me to say
You must report to them without delay.

ALCESTE. Who? Me, Sir?

GUARD.                Yes, Sir; you.

ALCESTE.                        But what do they want?

PHILINTE, *to* ALCESTE. To scotch your silly quarrel with Oronte.

CÉLIMÈNE, *to* PHILINTE. What quarrel?

PHILINTE.                        Oronte and he have
fallen out

Over some verse he spoke his mind about;
The Marshals wish to arbitrate the matter.

ALCESTE. Never shall I equivocate or flatter!

PHILINTE. You'd best obey their summons; come, let's go.

ALCESTE. How can they mend our quarrel, I'd like to know?
Am I to make a cowardly retraction,
And praise those jingles to his satisfaction?
I'll not recant; I've judged that sonnet rightly.
It's bad.

PHILINTE. But you might say so more politely. . . .

ALCESTE. I'll not back down; his verses make me sick.

PHILINTE. If only you could be more politic!
But come, let's go.

ALCESTE.            I'll go, but I won't unsay
A single word.

PHILINTE.          Well, let's be on our way.

ALCESTE. Till I am ordered by my lord the King
To praise that poem, I shall say the thing
Is scandalous, by God, and that the poet
Ought to be hanged for having the nerve to show it.

*To* CLITANDRE *and* ACASTE, *who are laughing.*

By heaven, Sirs, I really didn't know
That I was being humorous.

CÉLIMÈNE.                    Go, Sir, go;
Settle your business.

ALCESTE.               I shall, and when I'm through,
I shall return to settle things with you.

# ACT III

## Scene 1

CLITANDRE, ACASTE

CLITANDRE. Dear Marquess, how contented you appear;
  All things delight you, nothing mars your cheer.
  Can you, in perfect honesty, declare
  That you've a right to be so debonair?

ACASTE. By Jove, when I survey myself, I find
  No cause whatever for distress of mind.
  I'm young and rich; I can in modesty
  Lay claim to an exalted pedigree;
  And owing to my name and my condition
  I shall not want for honors and position.
  Then as to courage, that most precious trait,
  I seem to have it, as was proved of late
  Upon the field of honor, where my bearing,
  They say, was very cool and rather daring.
  I've wit, of course; and taste in such perfection
  That I can judge without the least reflection,
  And at the theater, which is my delight,
  Can make or break a play on opening night,
  And lead the crowd in hisses or bravos,
  And generally be known as one who knows.
  I'm clever, handsome, gracefully polite;
  My waist is small, my teeth are strong and white;
  As for my dress, the world's astonished eyes
  Assure me that I bear away the prize.
  I find myself in favor everywhere,
  Honored by men, and worshiped by the fair;
  And since these things are so, it seems to me
  I'm justified in my complacency.

CLITANDRE. Well, if so many ladies hold you dear,
Why do you press a hopeless courtship here?

ACASTE. Hopeless, you say? I'm not the sort of fool
That likes his ladies difficult and cool.
Men who are awkward, shy, and peasantish
May pine for heartless beauties, if they wish,
Grovel before them, bear their cruelties,
Woo them with tears and sighs and bended knees,
And hope by dogged faithfulness to gain
What their poor merits never could obtain.
For men like me, however, it makes no sense
To love on trust, and foot the whole expense.
Whatever any lady's merits be,
I think, thank God, that I'm as choice as she;
That if my heart is kind enough to burn
For her, she owes me something in return;
And that in any proper love affair
The partners must invest an equal share.

CLITANDRE. You think, then, that our hostess favors you?

ACASTE. I've reason to believe that that is true.

CLITANDRE. How did you come to such a mad conclusion?
You're blind, dear fellow. This is sheer delusion.

ACASTE. All right, then: I'm deluded and I'm blind.

CLITANDRE. Whatever put the notion in your mind?

ACASTE. Delusion.

CLITANDRE.            What persuades you that you're right?

ACASTE. I'm blind.

CLITANDRE.            But have you any proofs to cite?

ACASTE. I tell you I'm deluded.

CLITANDRE.                        Have you, then,
Received some secret pledge from Célimène?

ACASTE. Oh, no: she scorns me.

CLITANDRE.                        Tell me the truth, I beg.

ACASTE. She just can't bear me.

CLITANDRE.                        Ah, don't pull my leg.
Tell me what hope she's given you, I pray.

ACASTE. I'm hopeless, and it's you who win the day.
  She hates me thoroughly, and I'm so vexed
  I mean to hang myself on Tuesday next.

CLITANDRE. Dear Marquess, let us have an armistice
  And make a treaty. What do you say to this?
  If ever one of us can plainly prove
  That Célimène encourages his love,
  The other must abandon hope, and yield,
  And leave him in possession of the field.

ACASTE. Now, there's a bargain that appeals to me;
  With all my heart, dear Marquess, I agree.
  But hush.

### Scene 2

#### CÉLIMÈNE, ACASTE, CLITANDRE

CÉLIMÈNE. Still here?

CLITANDRE.　　　　　'Twas love that stayed our feet.

CÉLIMÈNE. I think I heard a carriage in the street.
  Whose is it? D'you know?

### Scene 3

#### CÉLIMÈNE, ACASTE, CLITANDRE, BASQUE

BASQUE.　　　　　Arsinoé is here,
  *Madame.*

CÉLIMÈNE. Arsinoé, you say? Oh, dear.

BASQUE. Éliante is entertaining her below.

CÉLIMÈNE. What brings the creature here, I'd like to know?

ACASTE. They say she's dreadfully prudish, but in fact
  I think her piety . . .

CÉLIMÈNE.                It's all an act.
At heart she's worldly, and her poor success
In snaring men explains her prudishness.
It breaks her heart to see the beaux and gallants
Engrossed by other women's charms and talents,
And so she's always in a jealous rage
Against the faulty standards of the age.
She lets the world believe that she's a prude
To justify her loveless solitude,
And strives to put a brand of moral shame
On all the graces that she cannot claim.
But still she'd love a lover; and Alceste
Appears to be the one she'd love the best.
His visits here are poison to her pride;
She seems to think I've lured him from her side;
And everywhere, at court or in the town,
The spiteful, envious woman runs me down.
In short, she's just as stupid as can be,
Vicious and arrogant in the last degree,
And . . .

### Scene 4

ARSINOÉ, CÉLIMÈNE, CLITANDRE, ACASTE

CÉLIMÈNE. Ah! What happy chance has brought you here?
    I've thought about you ever so much, my dear.
ARSINOÉ. I've come to tell you something you should know.
CÉLIMÈNE. How good of you to think of doing so!
    CLITANDRE *and* ACASTE *go out, laughing.*

## Scene 5

### ARSINOÉ, CÉLIMÈNE

ARSINOÉ. It's just as well those gentlemen didn't tarry.
CÉLIMÈNE. Shall we sit down?
ARSINOÉ.                                    That won't be necessary.
 Madam, the flame of friendship ought to burn
 Brightest in matters of the most concern,
 And as there's nothing which concerns us more
 Than honor, I have hastened to your door
 To bring you, as your friend, some information
 About the status of your reputation.
 I visited, last night, some virtuous folk,
 And, quite by chance, it was of you they spoke;
 There was, I fear, no tendency to praise
 Your light behavior and your dashing ways.
 The quantity of gentlemen you see
 And your by now notorious coquetry
 Were both so vehemently criticized
 By everyone, that I was much surprised.
 Of course, I needn't tell you where I stood;
 I came to your defense as best I could,
 Assured them you were harmless, and declared
 Your soul was absolutely unimpaired.
 But there are some things, you must realize,
 One can't excuse, however hard one tries,
 And I was forced at last into conceding
 That your behavior, Madam, is misleading,
 That it makes a bad impression, giving rise
 To ugly gossip and obscene surmise,
 And that if you were more *overtly* good,
 You wouldn't be so much misunderstood.
 Not that I think you've been unchaste—no! no!
 The saints preserve me from a thought so low!
 But mere good conscience never did suffice:
 One must avoid the outward show of vice.

Madam, you're too intelligent, I'm sure,
To think my motives anything but pure
In offering you this counsel—which I do
Out of a zealous interest in you.

CÉLIMÈNE. Madam, I haven't taken you amiss;
I'm very much obliged to you for this;
And I'll at once discharge the obligation
By telling you about *your* reputation.
You've been so friendly as to let me know
What certain people say of me, and so
I mean to follow your benign example
By offering you a somewhat similar sample.
The other day, I went to an affair
And found some most distinguished people there
Discussing piety, both false and true.
The conversation soon came round to you.
Alas! Your prudery and bustling zeal
Appeared to have a very slight appeal.
Your affectation of a grave demeanor,
Your endless talk of virtue and of honor,
The aptitude of your suspicious mind
For finding sin where there is none to find,
Your towering self-esteem, that pitying face
With which you contemplate the human race,
Your sermonizings and your sharp aspersions
On people's pure and innocent diversions—
All these were mentioned, Madam, and, in fact,
Were roundly and concertedly attacked.
"What good," they said, "are all these outward shows,
When everything belies her pious pose?
She prays incessantly; but then, they say,
She beats her maids and cheats them of their pay;
She shows her zeal in every holy place,
But still she's vain enough to paint her face;
She holds that naked statues are immoral,
But with a naked *man* she'd have no quarrel."
Of course, I said to everybody there
That they were being viciously unfair;
But still they were disposed to criticize you,
And all agreed that someone should advise you

To leave the morals of the world alone,
And worry rather more about your own.
They felt that one's self-knowledge should be great
Before one thinks of setting others straight;
That one should learn the art of living well
Before one threatens other men with hell,
And that the Church is best equipped, no doubt,
To guide our souls and root our vices out.
Madam, you're too intelligent, I'm sure,
To think my motives anything but pure
In offering you this counsel—which I do
Out of a zealous interest in you.

ARSINOÉ. I dared not hope for gratitude, but I
Did not expect so acid a reply;
I judge, since you've been so extremely tart,
That my good counsel pierced you to the heart.

CÉLIMÈNE. Far from it, Madam. Indeed, it seems to me
We ought to trade advice more frequently.
One's vision of oneself is so defective
That it would be an excellent corrective.
If you are willing, Madam, let's arrange
Shortly to have another frank exchange
In which we'll tell each other, *entre nous*,
What you've heard tell of me, and I of you.

ARSINOÉ. Oh, people never censure you, my dear;
It's me they criticize. Or so I hear.

CÉLIMÈNE. Madam, I think we either blame or praise
According to our taste and length of days.
There is a time of life for coquetry,
And there's a season, too, for prudery.
When all one's charms are gone, it is, I'm sure,
Good strategy to be devout and pure:
It makes one seem a little less forsaken.
Some day, perhaps, I'll take the road you've taken:
Time brings all things. But I have time aplenty,
And see no cause to be a prude at twenty.

ARSINOÉ. You give your age in such a gloating tone
That one would think I was an ancient crone;
We're not so far apart, in sober truth,

That you can mock me with a boast of youth!
Madam, you baffle me. I wish I knew
What moves you to provoke me as you do.

CÉLIMÈNE. For my part, Madam, I should like to know
Why you abuse me everywhere you go.
Is it my fault, dear lady, that your hand
Is not, alas, in very great demand?
If men admire me, if they pay me court
And daily make me offers of the sort
You'd dearly love to have them make to you,
How can I help it? What would you have me do?
If what you want is lovers, please feel free
To take as many as you can from me.

ARSINOÉ. Oh, come. D'you think the world is losing sleep
Over that flock of lovers which you keep,
Or that we find it difficult to guess
What price you pay for their devotedness?
Surely you don't expect us to suppose
Mere merit could attract so many beaux?
It's not your virtue that they're dazzled by;
Nor is it virtuous love for which they sigh.
You're fooling no one, Madam; the world's not blind;
There's many a lady heaven has designed
To call men's noblest, tenderest feelings out,
Who has no lovers dogging her about;
From which it's plain that lovers nowadays
Must be acquired in bold and shameless ways,
And only pay one court for such reward
As modesty and virtue can't afford.
Then don't be quite so puffed up, if you please,
About your tawdry little victories;
Try, if you can, to be a shade less vain,
And treat the world with somewhat less disdain.
If one were envious of your amours,
One soon could have a following like yours;
Lovers are no great trouble to collect
If one prefers them to one's self-respect.

CÉLIMÈNE. Collect them then, my dear; I'd love to see
You demonstrate that charming theory;

Who knows, you might . . .

ARSINOÉ.                             Now, Madam, that will do;
  It's time to end this trying interview.
  My coach is late in coming to your door,
  Or I'd have taken leave of you before.

CÉLIMÈNE. Oh, please don't feel that you must rush away;
  I'd be delighted, Madam, if you'd stay.
  However, lest my conversation bore you,
  Let me provide some better company for you;
  This gentleman, who comes most apropos,
  Will please you more than I could do, I know.

## Scene 6

### ALCESTE, CÉLIMÈNE, ARSINOÉ

CÉLIMÈNE. Alceste, I have a little note to write
  Which simply must go out before tonight;
  Please entertain *Madame;* I'm sure that she
  Will overlook my incivility.

## Scene 7

### ALCESTE, ARSINOÉ

ARSINOÉ. Well, Sir, our hostess graciously contrives
  For us to chat until my coach arrives;
  And I shall be forever in her debt
  For granting me this little tête-à-tête.
  We women very rightly give our hearts
  To men of noble character and parts,
  And your especial merits, dear Alceste,
  Have roused the deepest sympathy in my breast.

Oh, how I wish they had sufficient sense
At court, to recognize your excellence!
They wrong you greatly, Sir. How it must hurt you
Never to be rewarded for your virtue!

ALCESTE. Why, Madam, what cause have I to feel aggrieved?
What great and brilliant thing have I achieved?
What service have I rendered to the King
That I should look to him for anything?

ARSINOÉ. Not everyone who's honored by the State
Has done great services. A man must wait
Till time and fortune offer him the chance.
Your merit, Sir, is obvious at a glance,
And . . .

ALCESTE.    Ah, forget my merit; I'm not neglected.
The court, I think, can hardly be expected
To mine men's souls for merit, and unearth
Our hidden virtues and our secret worth.

ARSINOÉ. *Some* virtues, though, are far too bright to hide;
Yours are acknowledged, Sir, on every side.
Indeed, I've heard you warmly praised of late
By persons of considerable weight.

ALCESTE. This fawning age has praise for everyone,
And all distinctions, Madam, are undone.
All things have equal honor nowadays,
And no one should be gratified by praise.
To be admired, one only need exist,
And every lackey's on the honors list.

ARSINOÉ. I only wish, Sir, that you had your eye
On some position at court, however high;
You'd only have to hint at such a notion
For me to set the proper wheels in motion;
I've certain friendships I'd be glad to use
To get you any office you might choose.

ALCESTE. Madam, I fear that any such ambition
Is wholly foreign to my disposition.
The soul God gave me isn't of the sort
That prospers in the weather of a court.
It's all too obvious that I don't possess
The virtues necessary for success.

My one great talent is for speaking plain;
I've never learned to flatter or to feign;
And anyone so stupidly sincere
Had best not seek a courtier's career.
Outside the court, I know, one must dispense
With honors, privilege, and influence;
But still one gains the right, foregoing these,
Not to be tortured by the wish to please.
One needn't live in dread of snubs and slights,
Nor praise the verse that every idiot writes,
Nor humor silly Marquesses, nor bestow
Politic sighs on Madam So-and-So.

ARSINOÉ. Forget the court, then; let the matter rest.
But I've another cause to be distressed
About your present situation, Sir.
It's to your love affair that I refer.
She whom you love, and who pretends to love you,
Is, I regret to say, unworthy of you.

ALCESTE. Why, Madam! Can you seriously intend
To make so grave a charge against your friend?

ARSINOÉ. Alas, I must. I've stood aside too long
And let that lady do you grievous wrong;
But now my debt to conscience shall be paid:
I tell you that your love has been betrayed.

ALCESTE. I thank you, Madam; you're extremely kind.
Such words are soothing to a lover's mind.

ARSINOÉ. Yes, though she *is* my friend, I say again
You're very much too good for Célimène.
She's wantonly misled you from the start.

ALCESTE. You may be right; who knows another's heart?
But ask yourself if it's the part of charity
To shake my soul with doubts of her sincerity.

ARSINOÉ. Well, if you'd rather be a dupe than doubt her,
That's your affair. I'll say no more about her.

ALCESTE. Madam, you know that doubt and vague suspicion
Are painful to a man in my position;
It's most unkind to worry me this way
Unless you've some real proof of what you say.

ARSINOÉ. Sir, say no more: all doubt shall be removed,
And all that I've been saying shall be proved.
You've only to escort me home, and there
We'll look into the heart of this affair.
I've ocular evidence which will persuade you
Beyond a doubt, that Célimène's betrayed you.
Then, if you're saddened by that revelation,
Perhaps I can provide some consolation.

# ACT IV

## Scene 1

### ÉLIANTE, PHILINTE

PHILINTE. Madam, he acted like a stubborn child;
  I thought they never would be reconciled;
  In vain we reasoned, threatened, and appealed;
  He stood his ground and simply would not yield.
  The Marshals, I feel sure, have never heard
  An argument so splendidly absurd.
  "No, gentlemen," said he, "I'll not retract.
  His verse is bad: extremely bad, in fact.
  Surely it does the man no harm to know it.
  Does it disgrace him, not to be a poet?
  A gentleman may be respected still,
  Whether he writes a sonnet well or ill.
  That I dislike his verse should not offend him;
  In all that touches honor, I commend him;
  He's noble, brave, and virtuous—but I fear
  He can't in truth be called a sonneteer.
  I'll gladly praise his wardrobe; I'll endorse
  His dancing, or the way he sits a horse;
  But, gentlemen, I cannot praise his rhyme.
  In fact, it ought to be a capital crime
  For anyone so sadly unendowed
  To write a sonnet, and read the thing aloud."
  At length he fell into a gentler mood
  And, striking a concessive attitude,
  He paid Oronte the following courtesies:
  "Sir, I regret that I'm so hard to please,
  And I'm profoundly sorry that your lyric
  Failed to provoke me to a panegyric."

After these curious words, the two embraced,
And then the hearing was adjourned—in haste.

ÉLIANTE. His conduct has been very singular lately;
Still, I confess that I respect him greatly.
The honesty in which he takes such pride
Has—to my mind—its noble, heroic side.
In this false age, such candor seems outrageous;
But I could wish that it were more contagious.

PHILINTE. What most intrigues me in our friend Alceste
Is the grand passion that rages in his breast.
The sullen humors he's compounded of
Should not, I think, dispose his heart to love;
But since they do, it puzzles me still more
That he should choose your cousin to adore.

ÉLIANTE. It does, indeed, belie the theory
That love is born of gentle sympathy,
And that the tender passion must be based
On sweet accords of temper and of taste.

PHILINTE. Does she return his love, do you suppose?

ÉLIANTE. Ah, that's a difficult question, Sir. Who knows?
How can we judge the truth of her devotion?
Her heart's a stranger to its own emotion.
Sometimes it thinks it loves, when no love's there;
At other times it loves quite unaware.

PHILINTE. I rather think Alceste is in for more
Distress and sorrow than he's bargained for;
Were he of my mind, Madam, his affection
Would turn in quite a different direction,
And we would see him more responsive to
The kind regard which he receives from you.

ÉLIANTE. Sir, I believe in frankness, and I'm inclined,
In matters of the heart, to speak my mind.
I don't oppose his love for her; indeed,
I hope with all my heart that he'll succeed,
And were it in my power, I'd rejoice
In giving him the lady of his choice.
But if, as happens frequently enough
In love affairs, he meets with a rebuff—

If Célimène should grant some rival's suit—
I'd gladly play the role of substitute;
Nor would his tender speeches please me less
Because they'd once been made without success.

PHILINTE. Well, Madam, as for me, I don't oppose
Your hopes in this affair; and heaven knows
That in my conversations with the man
I plead your cause as often as I can.
But if those two should marry, and so remove
All chance that he will offer you his love,
Then I'll declare my own, and hope to see
Your gracious favor pass from him to me.
In short, should you be cheated of Alceste,
I'd be most happy to be second best.

ÉLIANTE. Philinte, you're teasing.

PHILINTE.                          Ah, Madam, never fear;
No words of mine were ever so sincere,
And I shall live in fretful expectation
Till I can make a fuller declaration.

### Scene 2

ALCESTE, ÉLIANTE, PHILINTE

ALCESTE. Avenge me, Madam! I must have satisfaction,
Or this great wrong will drive me to distraction!

ÉLIANTE. Why, what's the matter? What's upset you so?

ALCESTE. Madam, I've had a mortal, mortal blow.
If Chaos repossessed the universe,
I swear I'd not be shaken any worse.
I'm ruined. . . . I can say no more. . . . My soul . . .

ÉLIANTE. Do try, Sir, to regain your self-control.

ALCESTE. Just heaven! Why were so much beauty and grace
Bestowed on one so vicious and so base?

ÉLIANTE. Once more, Sir, tell us. . . .

ALCESTE.            My world has gone to wrack;
I'm—I'm betrayed; she's stabbed me in the back:
Yes, Célimène (who would have thought it of her?)
Is false to me, and has another lover.

ÉLIANTE. Are you quite certain? Can you prove these things?

PHILINTE. Lovers are prey to wild imaginings
And jealous fancies. No doubt there's some mistake. . . .

ALCESTE. Mind your own business, Sir, for heaven's sake.

     *To* ÉLIANTE.

Madam, I have the proof that you demand
Here in my pocket, penned by her own hand.
Yes, all the shameful evidence one could want
Lies in this letter written to Oronte—
Oronte! whom I felt sure she couldn't love,
And hardly bothered to be jealous of.

PHILINTE. Still, in a letter, appearances may deceive;
This may not be so bad as you believe.

ALCESTE. Once more I beg you, Sir, to let me be;
Tend to your own affairs; leave mine to me.

ÉLIANTE. Compose yourself; this anguish that you feel . . .

ALCESTE. Is something, Madam, you alone can heal.
My outraged heart, beside itself with grief,
Appeals to you for comfort and relief.
Avenge me on your cousin, whose unjust
And faithless nature has deceived my trust;
Avenge a crime your pure soul must detest.

ÉLIANTE. But how, Sir?

ALCESTE.            Madam, this heart within my breast
Is yours; pray take it; redeem my heart from her,
And so avenge me on my torturer.
Let her be punished by the fond emotion,
The ardent love, the bottomless devotion,
The faithful worship which this heart of mine
Will offer up to yours as to a shrine.

ÉLIANTE. You have my sympathy, Sir, in all you suffer;
Nor do I scorn the noble heart you offer;
But I suspect you'll soon be mollified,     /
And this desire for vengeance will subside.

When some belovèd hand has done us wrong
We thirst for retribution—but not for long;
However dark the deed that she's committed,
A lovely culprit's very soon acquitted.
Nothing's so stormy as an injured lover,
And yet no storm so quickly passes over.

ALCESTE. No, Madam, no—this is no lovers' spat;
I'll not forgive her; it's gone too far for that;
My mind's made up; I'll kill myself before
I waste my hopes upon her any more.
Ah, here she is. My wrath intensifies.
I shall confront her with her tricks and lies,
And crush her utterly, and bring you then
A heart no longer slave to Célimène.

### Scene 3

#### CÉLIMÈNE, ALCESTE

ALCESTE, *aside*. Sweet heaven, help me to control my passion.
CÉLIMÈNE, *aside*. Oh, Lord.

   *To* ALCESTE.

               Why stand there staring in that fashion?
And what d'you mean by those dramatic sighs,
And that malignant glitter in your eyes?

ALCESTE. I mean that sins which cause the blood to freeze
Look innocent beside your treacheries;
That nothing Hell's or Heaven's wrath could do
Ever produced so bad a thing as you.

CÉLIMÈNE. Your compliments were always sweet and pretty.

ALCESTE. Madam, it's not the moment to be witty.
No, blush and hang your head; you've ample reason,
Since I've the fullest evidence of your treason.
Ah, this is what my sad heart prophesied;
Now all my anxious fears are verified;
My dark suspicion and my gloomy doubt

Divined the truth, and now the truth is out.
For all your trickery, I was not deceived;
It was my bitter stars that I believed.
But don't imagine that you'll go scot-free;
You shan't misuse me with impunity.
I know that love's irrational and blind;
I know the heart's not subject to the mind,
And can't be reasoned into beating faster;
I know each soul is free to choose its master;
Therefore had you but spoken from the heart,
Rejecting my attentions from the start,
I'd have no grievance, or at any rate
I could complain of nothing but my fate.
Ah, but so falsely to encourage me—
That was a treason and a treachery
For which you cannot suffer too severely,
And you shall pay for that behavior dearly.
Yes, now I have no pity, not a shred;
My temper's out of hand; I've lost my head;
Shocked by the knowledge of your double-dealings,
My reason can't restrain my savage feelings;
A righteous wrath deprives me of my senses,
And I won't answer for the consequences.

CÉLIMÈNE. What does this outburst mean? Will you please
 explain?
Have you, by any chance, gone quite insane?

ALCESTE. Yes, yes, I went insane the day I fell
A victim to your black and fatal spell,
Thinking to meet with some sincerity
Among the treacherous charms that beckoned me.

CÉLIMÈNE. Pooh. Of what treachery can you complain?

ALCESTE. How sly you are, how cleverly you feign!
But you'll not victimize me any more.
Look: here's a document you've seen before.
This evidence, which I acquired today,
Leaves you, I think, without a thing to say.

CÉLIMÈNE. Is this what sent you into such a fit?

ALCESTE. You should be blushing at the sight of it.

CÉLIMÈNE. Ought I to blush? I truly don't see why.

ALCESTE. Ah, now you're being bold as well as sly;
Since there's no signature, perhaps you'll claim . . .

CÉLIMÈNE. I wrote it, whether or not it bears my name.

ALCESTE. And you can view with equanimity
This proof of your disloyalty to me!

CÉLIMÈNE. Oh, don't be so outrageous and extreme.

ALCESTE. You take this matter lightly, it would seem.
Was it no wrong to me, no shame to you,
- That you should send Oronte this billet-doux?

CÉLIMÈNE. Oronte! Who said it was for him?

ALCESTE.                                    Why, those
Who brought me this example of your prose.
But what's the difference? If you wrote the letter
To someone else, it pleases me no better.
My grievance and your guilt remain the same.

CÉLIMÈNE. But need you rage, and need I blush for shame,
If this was written to a *woman* friend?

ALCESTE. Ah! Most ingenious. I'm impressed no end;
And after that incredible evasion
Your guilt is clear. I need no more persuasion.
How dare you try so clumsy a deception?
D'you think I'm wholly wanting in perception?
Come, come, let's see how brazenly you'll try
To bolster up so palpable a lie:
Kindly construe this ardent closing section
As nothing more than sisterly affection!
Here, let me read it. Tell me, if you dare to,
That this is for a woman . . .

CÉLIMÈNE.                        I don't care to.
What right have you to badger and berate me,
And so highhandedly interrogate me?

ALCESTE. Now, don't be angry; all I ask of you
Is that you justify a phrase or two . . .

CÉLIMÈNE. No, I shall not. I utterly refuse,
And you may take those phrases as you choose.

ALCESTE. Just show me how this letter could be meant
For a woman's eyes, and I shall be content.

CÉLIMÈNE. No, no, it's for Oronte; you're perfectly right.
  I welcome his attentions with delight,
  I prize his character and his intellect,
  And everything is just as you suspect.
  Come, do your worst now; give your rage free rein;
  But kindly cease to bicker and complain.

ALCESTE, *aside*. Good God! Could anything be more inhuman?
  Was ever a heart so mangled by a woman?
  When I complain of how she has betrayed me,
  She bridles, and commences to upbraid me!
  She tries my tortured patience to the limit;
  She won't deny her guilt; she glories in it!
  And yet my heart's too faint and cowardly
  To break these chains of passion, and be free,
  To scorn her as it should, and rise above
  This unrewarded, mad, and bitter love.

*To* CÉLIMÈNE.

  Ah, traitress, in how confident a fashion
  You take advantage of my helpless passion,
  And use my weakness for your faithless charms
  To make me once again throw down my arms!
  But do at least deny this black transgression;
  Take back that mocking and perverse confession;
  Defend this letter and your innocence,
  And I, poor fool, will aid in your defense.
  Pretend, pretend, that you are just and true,
  And I shall make myself believe in you.

CÉLIMÈNE. Oh, stop it. Don't be such a jealous dunce,
  Or I shall leave off loving you at once.
  Just why should I *pretend?* What could impel me
  To stoop so low as that? And kindly tell me
  Why, if I loved another, I shouldn't merely
  Inform you of it, simply and sincerely!
  I've told you where you stand, and that admission
  Should altogether clear me of suspicion;
  After so generous a guarantee,
  What right have you to harbor doubts of me?
  Since women are (from natural reticence)
  Reluctant to declare their sentiments,

And since the honor of our sex requires
That we conceal our amorous desires,
Ought any man for whom such laws are broken
To question what the oracle has spoken?
Should he not rather feel an obligation
To trust that most obliging declaration?
Enough, now. Your suspicions quite disgust me;
Why should I love a man who doesn't trust me?
I cannot understand why I continue,
Fool that I am, to take an interest in you.
I ought to choose a man less prone to doubt,
And give you something to be vexed about.

ALCESTE. Ah, what a poor enchanted fool I am;
These gentle words, no doubt, were all a sham;
But destiny requires me to entrust
My happiness to you, and so I must.
I'll love you to the bitter end, and see
How false and treacherous you dare to be.

CÉLIMÈNE. No, you don't really love me as you ought.

ALCESTE. I love you more than can be said or thought;
Indeed, I wish you were in such distress
That I might show my deep devotedness.
Yes, I could wish that you were wretchedly poor,
Unloved, uncherished, utterly obscure;
That fate had set you down upon the earth
Without possessions, rank, or gentle birth;
Then, by the offer of my heart, I might
Repair the great injustice of your plight;
I'd raise you from the dust, and proudly prove
The purity and vastness of my love.

CÉLIMÈNE. This is a strange benevolence indeed!
God grant that I may never be in need. . . .
Ah, here's Monsieur Dubois, in quaint disguise.

## Scene 4

CÉLIMÈNE, ALCESTE, DUBOIS

ALCESTE. Well, why this costume? Why those frightened eyes?
  What ails you?

DUBOIS.        Well, Sir, things are most mysterious.

ALCESTE. What do you mean?

DUBOIS.               I fear they're very serious.

ALCESTE. What?

DUBOIS.       Shall I speak more loudly?

ALCESTE.                Yes; speak out.

DUBOIS. Isn't there someone here, Sir?

ALCESTE.            Speak, you lout!
  Stop wasting time.

DUBOIS.       Sir, we must slip away.

ALCESTE. How's that?

DUBOIS.        We must decamp without delay.

ALCESTE. Explain yourself.

DUBOIS.         I tell you we must fly.

ALCESTE. What for?

DUBOIS.      We mustn't pause to say good-by.

ALCESTE. Now what d'you mean by all of this, you clown?

DUBOIS. I mean, Sir, that we've got to leave this town.

ALCESTE. I'll tear you limb from limb and joint from joint
  If you don't come more quickly to the point.

DUBOIS. Well, Sir, today a man in a black suit,
  Who wore a black and ugly scowl to boot,
  Left us a document scrawled in such a hand
  As even Satan couldn't understand.
  It bears upon your lawsuit, I don't doubt;
  But all hell's devils couldn't make it out.

ALCESTE. Well, well, go on. What then? I fail to see
   How this event obliges us to flee.

DUBOIS. Well, Sir: an hour later, hardly more,
   A gentleman who's often called before
   Came looking for you in an anxious way.
   Not finding you, he asked me to convey
   (Knowing I could be trusted with the same)
   The following message. . . . Now, what *was* his name?

ALCESTE. Forget his name, you idiot. What did he say?

DUBOIS. Well, it was one of your friends, Sir, anyway.
   He warned you to begone, and he suggested
   That if you stay, you may well be arrested.

ALCESTE. What? Nothing more specific? Think, man, think!

DUBOIS. No, Sir. He had me bring him pen and ink,
   And dashed you off a letter which, I'm sure,
   Will render things distinctly less obscure.

ALCESTE. Well—let me have it!

CÉLIMÈNE.                    What *is* this all about?

ALCESTE. God knows; but I have hopes of finding out.
   How long am I to wait, you blitherer?

DUBOIS, *after a protracted search for the letter*. I must have
      left it on your table, Sir.

ALCESTE. I ought to . . .

CÉLIMÈNE.              No, no, keep your self-control;
   Go find out what's behind his rigmarole.

ALCESTE. It seems that fate, no matter what I do,
   Has sworn that I may not converse with you;
   But, Madam, pray permit your faithful lover
   To try once more before the day is over.

# ACT V

## Scene 1

### ALCESTE, PHILINTE

ALCESTE. No, it's too much. My mind's made up, I tell you.

PHILINTE. Why should this blow, however hard, compel
   you . . .

ALCESTE. No, no, don't waste your breath in argument;
   Nothing you say will alter my intent;
   This age is vile, and I've made up my mind
   To have no further commerce with mankind.
   Did not truth, honor, decency, and the laws
   Oppose my enemy and approve my cause?
   My claims were justified in all men's sight;
   I put my trust in equity and right;
   Yet, to my horror and the world's disgrace,
   Justice is mocked, and I have lost my case!
   A scoundrel whose dishonesty is notorious
   Emerges from another lie victorious!
   Honor and right condone his brazen fraud,
   While rectitude and decency applaud!
   Before his smirking face, the truth stands charmed,
   And virtue conquered, and the law disarmed!
   His crime is sanctioned by a court decree!
   And not content with what he's done to me,
   The dog now seeks to ruin me by stating
   That I composed a book now circulating,
   A book so wholly criminal and vicious
   That even to speak its title is seditious!
   Meanwhile Oronte, my rival, lends his credit
   To the same libelous tale, and helps to spread it!
   Oronte! a man of honor and of rank,

With whom I've been entirely fair and frank;
Who sought me out and forced me, willy-nilly,
To judge some verse I found extremely silly;
And who, because I properly refused
To flatter him, or see the truth abused,
Abets my enemy in a rotten slander!
There's the reward of honesty and candor!
The man will hate me to the end of time
For failing to commend his wretched rhyme!
And not this man alone, but all humanity
Do what they do from interest and vanity;
They prate of honor, truth, and righteousness,
But lie, betray, and swindle nonetheless.
Come then: man's villainy is too much to bear;
Let's leave this jungle and this jackal's lair.
Yes! treacherous and savage race of men,
You shall not look upon my face again.

PHILINTE. Oh, don't rush into exile prematurely;
Things aren't as dreadful as you make them, surely.
It's rather obvious, since you're still at large,
That people don't believe your enemy's charge.
Indeed, his tale's so patently untrue
That it may do more harm to him than you.

ALCESTE. Nothing could do that scoundrel any harm:
His frank corruption is his greatest charm,
And, far from hurting him, a further shame
Would only serve to magnify his name.

PHILINTE. In any case, his bald prevarication
Has done no injury to your reputation,
And you may feel secure in that regard.
As for your lawsuit, it should not be hard
To have the case reopened, and contest
This judgment . . .

ALCESTE.                No, no, let the verdict rest.
Whatever cruel penalty it may bring,
I wouldn't have it changed for anything.
It shows the times' injustice with such clarity
That I shall pass it down to our posterity
As a great proof and signal demonstration

Of the black wickedness of this generation.
It may cost twenty thousand francs; but I
Shall pay their twenty thousand, and gain thereby
The right to storm and rage at human evil,
And send the race of mankind to the devil.

PHILINTE. Listen to me. . . .

ALCESTE.                 Why? What can you possibly say?
Don't argue, Sir; your labor's thrown away.
Do you propose to offer lame excuses
For men's behavior and the times' abuses?

PHILINTE. No, all you say I'll readily concede:
This is a low, conniving age indeed;
Nothing but trickery prospers nowadays,
And people ought to mend their shabby ways.
Yes, man's a beastly creature; but must we then
Abandon the society of men?
Here in the world, each human frailty
Provides occasion for philosophy,
And that is virtue's noblest exercise;
If honesty shone forth from all men's eyes,
If every heart were frank and kind and just,
What could our virtues do but gather dust
(Since their employment is to help us bear
The villainies of men without despair)?
A heart well-armed with virtue can endure. . . .

ALCESTE. Sir, you're a matchless reasoner, to be sure;
Your words are fine and full of cogency;
But don't waste time and eloquence on me.
*My* reason bids me go, for my own good.
My tongue won't lie and flatter as it should;
God knows what frankness it might next commit,
And what I'd suffer on account of it.
Pray let me wait for Célimène's return
In peace and quiet. I shall shortly learn,
By her response to what I have in view,
Whether her love for me is feigned or true.

PHILINTE. Till then, let's visit Éliante upstairs.

ALCESTE. No, I am too weighed down with somber cares.

Go to her, do; and leave me with my gloom
Here in the darkened corner of this room.

PHILINTE. Why, that's no sort of company, my friend;
I'll see if Éliante will not descend.

*Scene 2*

CÉLIMÈNE, ORONTE, ALCESTE

ORONTE. Yes, Madam, if you wish me to remain
Your true and ardent lover, you must deign
To give me some more positive assurance.
All this suspense is quite beyond endurance.
If your heart shares the sweet desires of mine,
Show me as much by some convincing sign;
And here's the sign I urgently suggest:
That you no longer tolerate Alceste,
But sacrifice him to my love, and sever
All your relations with the man forever.

CÉLIMÈNE. Why do you suddenly dislike him so?
You praised him to the skies not long ago.

ORONTE. Madam, that's not the point. I'm here to find
Which way your tender feelings are inclined.
Choose, if you please, between Alceste and me,
And I shall stay or go accordingly.

ALCESTE, *emerging from the corner*. Yes, Madam, choose; this
            gentleman's demand
Is wholly just, and I support his stand.
I too am true and ardent; I too am here
To ask you that you make your feelings clear.
No more delays, now; no equivocation;
The time has come to make your declaration.

ORONTE. Sir, I've no wish in any way to be
An obstacle to your felicity.

ALCESTE. Sir, I've no wish to share her heart with you;
That may sound jealous, but at least it's true.

ORONTE. If, weighing us, she leans in your direction . . .

ALCESTE. If she regards you with the least affection . . .

ORONTE. I swear I'll yield her to you there and then.

ALCESTE. I swear I'll never see her face again.

ORONTE. Now, Madam, tell us what we've come to hear.

ALCESTE. Madam, speak openly and have no fear.

ORONTE. Just say which one is to remain your lover.

ALCESTE. Just name one name, and it will all be over.

ORONTE. What! Is it possible that you're undecided?

ALCESTE. What! Can your feelings possibly be divided?

CÉLIMÈNE. Enough: this inquisition's gone too far:
    How utterly unreasonable you are!
    Not that I couldn't make the choice with ease;
    My heart has no conflicting sympathies;
    I know full well which one of you I favor,
    And you'd not see me hesitate or waver.
    But how can you expect me to reveal
    So cruelly and bluntly what I feel?
    I think it altogether too unpleasant
    To choose between two men when both are present;
    One's heart has means more subtle and more kind
    Of letting its affections be divined,
    Nor need one be uncharitably plain
    To let a lover know he loves in vain.

ORONTE. No, no, speak plainly; I for one can stand it.
    I beg you to be frank.

ALCESTE.                And I demand it.
    The simple truth is what I wish to know,
    And there's no need for softening the blow.
    You've made an art of pleasing everyone,
    But now your days of coquetry are done:
    You have no choice now, Madam, but to choose,
    For I'll know what to think if you refuse;
    I'll take your silence for a clear admission
    That I'm entitled to my worst suspicion.

ORONTE. I thank you for this ultimatum, Sir,
    And I may say I heartily concur.

CÉLIMÈNE. Really, this foolishness is very wearing:
  Must you be so unjust and overbearing?
  Haven't I told you why I must demur?
  Ah, here's Éliante; I'll put the case to her.

## Scene 3

ÉLIANTE, PHILINTE, CÉLIMÈNE, ORONTE, ALCESTE

CÉLIMÈNE. Cousin, I'm being persecuted here
  By these two persons, who, it would appear,
  Will not be satisfied till I confess
  Which one I love the more, and which the less,
  And tell the latter to his face that he
  Is henceforth banished from my company.
  Tell me, has ever such a thing been done?
ÉLIANTE. You'd best not turn to me; I'm not the one
  To back you in a matter of this kind:
  I'm all for those who frankly speak their mind.
ORONTE. Madam, you'll search in vain for a defender.
ALCESTE. You're beaten, Madam, and may as well surrender.
ORONTE. Speak, speak, you must; and end this awful strain.
ALCESTE. Or don't, and your position will be plain.
ORONTE. A single word will close this painful scene.
ALCESTE. But if you're silent, I'll know what you mean.

## Scene 4

ARSINOÉ, CÉLIMÈNE, ÉLIANTE, ALCESTE, PHILINTE,
ACASTE, CLITANDRE, ORONTE

ACASTE, *to* CÉLIMÈNE. Madam, with all due deference, we two
  Have come to pick a little bone with you.

CLITANDRE, *to* ORONTE *and* ALCESTE. I'm glad you're present,
    Sirs; as you'll soon learn,
Our business here is also your concern.

ARSINOÉ, *to* CÉLIMÈNE. Madam, I visit you so soon again
Only because of these two gentlemen,
Who came to me indignant and aggrieved
About a crime too base to be believed.
Knowing your virtue, having such confidence in it,
I couldn't think you guilty for a minute,
In spite of all their telling evidence;
And, rising above our little difference,
I've hastened here in friendship's name to see
You clear yourself of this great calumny.

ACASTE. Yes, Madam, let us see with what composure
You'll manage to respond to this disclosure.
You lately sent Clitandre this tender note.

CLITANDRE. And this one, for Acaste, you also wrote.

ACASTE, *to* ORONTE *and* ALCESTE. You'll recognize this writing,
    Sirs, I think;
The lady is so free with pen and ink
That you must know it all too well, I fear.
But listen: this is something you should hear.

"How absurd you are to condemn my lightheartedness in society, and to accuse me of being happiest in the company of others. Nothing could be more unjust; and if you do not come to me instantly and beg pardon for saying such a thing, I shall never forgive you as long as I live. Our big bumbling friend the Viscount . . ."

What a shame that he's not here.

"Our big bumbling friend the Viscount, whose name stands first in your complaint, is hardly a man to my taste; and ever since the day I watched him spend three-quarters of an hour spitting into a well, so as to make circles in the water, I have been unable to think highly of him. As for the little Marquess . . ."

In all modesty, gentlemen, that is I.

"As for the little Marquess, who sat squeezing my hand for such a long while yesterday, I find him in all respects the most trifling creature alive; and the only things of value about him are his cape and his sword. As for the man with the green ribbons . . ."

*To* ALCESTE.

It's your turn now, Sir.

"As for the man with the green ribbons, he amuses me now and then with his bluntness and his bearish ill-humor; but there are many times indeed when I think him the greatest bore in the world. And as for the sonneteer . . ."

*To* ORONTE.

Here's your helping.

"And as for the sonneteer, who has taken it into his head to be witty, and insists on being an author in the teeth of opinion, I simply cannot be bothered to listen to him, and his prose wearies me quite as much as his poetry. Be assured that I am not always so well-entertained as you suppose; that I long for your company, more than I dare to say, at all these entertainments to which people drag me; and that the presence of those one loves is the true and perfect seasoning to all one's pleasures."

CLITANDRE. And now for me.

"Clitandre, whom you mention, and who so pesters me with his saccharine speeches, is the last man on earth for whom I could feel any affection. He is quite mad to suppose that I love him, and so are you, to doubt that you are loved. Do come to your senses; exchange your suppositions for his; and visit me as often as possible, to help me bear the annoyance of his unwelcome attentions."

It's a sweet character that these letters show,
And what to call it, Madam, you well know.
Enough. We're off to make the world acquainted
With this sublime self-portrait that you've painted.

ACASTE. Madam, I'll make you no farewell oration;
No, you're not worthy of my indignation.
Far choicer hearts than yours, as you'll discover,
Would like this little Marquess for a lover.

## Scene 5

CÉLIMÈNE, ÉLIANTE, ARSINOÉ, ALCESTE,
ORONTE, PHILINTE

ORONTE. So! After all those loving letters you wrote,
You turn on me like this, and cut my throat!
And your dissembling, faithless heart, I find,
Has pledged itself by turns to all mankind!
How blind I've been! But now I clearly see;
I thank you, Madam, for enlightening me.
My heart is mine once more, and I'm content;
The loss of it shall be your punishment.

*To* ALCESTE.

Sir, she is yours; I'll seek no more to stand
Between your wishes and this lady's hand.

## Scene 6

CÉLIMÈNE, ÉLIANTE, ARSINOÉ, ALCESTE, PHILINTE

ARSINOÉ, *to* CÉLIMÈNE. Madam, I'm forced to speak. I'm far
    too stirred
To keep my counsel, after what I've heard.
I'm shocked and staggered by your want of morals.
It's not my way to mix in others' quarrels;
But really, when this fine and noble spirit,
This man of honor and surpassing merit,
Laid down the offering of his heart before you,
How *could* you . . .

ALCESTE.         Madam, permit me, I implore you,
To represent myself in this debate.
Don't bother, please, to be my advocate.

My heart, in any case, could not afford
To give your services their due reward;
And if I chose, for consolation's sake,
Some other lady, 'twould not be you I'd take.

ARSINOÉ. What makes you think you could, Sir? And how dare
    you
Imply that I've been trying to ensnare you?
If you can for a moment entertain
Such flattering fancies, you're extremely vain.
I'm not so interested as you suppose
In Célimène's discarded gigolos.
Get rid of that absurd illusion, do.
Women like me are not for such as you.
Stay with this creature, to whom you're so attached;
I've never seen two people better matched.


### Scene 7

CÉLIMÈNE, ÉLIANTE, ALCESTE, PHILINTE

ALCESTE, *to* CÉLIMÈNE. Well, I've been still throughout this
    exposé,
Till everyone but me has said his say.
Come, have I shown sufficient self-restraint?
And may I now . . .
CÉLIMÈNE.              Yes, make your just complaint.
Reproach me freely, call me what you will;
You've every right to say I've used you ill.
I've wronged you, I confess it; and in my shame
I'll make no effort to escape the blame.
The anger of those others I could despise;
My guilt toward you I sadly recognize.
Your wrath is wholly justified, I fear;
I know how culpable I must appear,
I know all things bespeak my treachery,
And that, in short, you've grounds for hating me.
Do so; I give you leave.

ALCESTE.                    Ah, traitress—how,
How should I cease to love you, even now?
Though mind and will were passionately bent
On hating you, my heart would not consent.

*To* ÉLIANTE *and* PHILINTE.

Be witness to my madness, both of you;
See what infatuation drives one to;
But wait; my folly's only just begun,
And I shall prove to you before I'm done
How strange the human heart is, and how far
From rational we sorry creatures are.

*To* CÉLIMÈNE.

Woman, I'm willing to forget your shame,
And clothe your treacheries in a sweeter name;
I'll call them youthful errors, instead of crimes,
And lay the blame on these corrupting times.
My one condition is that you agree
To share my chosen fate, and fly with me
To that wild, trackless, solitary place
In which I shall forget the human race.
Only by such a course can you atone
For those atrocious letters; by that alone
Can you remove my present horror of you,
And make it possible for me to love you.

CÉLIMÈNE. What! *I* renounce the world at my young age,
And die of boredom in some hermitage?

ALCESTE. Ah, if you really loved me as you ought,
You wouldn't give the world a moment's thought;
Must you have me, and all the world beside?

CÉLIMÈNE. Alas, at twenty one is terrified
Of solitude. I fear I lack the force
And depth of soul to take so stern a course.
But if my hand in marriage will content you,
Why, there's a plan which I might well consent to,
And . . .

ALCESTE.    No, I detest you now. I could excuse
Everything else, but since you thus refuse
To love me wholly, as a wife should do,

And see the world in me, as I in you,
Go! I reject your hand, and disenthrall
My heart from your enchantments, once for all.

## Scene 8

### ÉLIANTE, ALCESTE, PHILINTE

ALCESTE, *to* ÉLIANTE. Madam, your virtuous beauty has no
    peer;
  Of all this world, you only are sincere;
  I've long esteemed you highly, as you know;
  Permit me ever to esteem you so,
  And if I do not now request your hand,
  Forgive me, Madam, and try to understand.
  I feel unworthy of it; I sense that fate
  Does not intend me for the married state,
  That I should do you wrong by offering you
  My shattered heart's unhappy residue,
  And that in short . . .
ÉLIANTE.            Your argument's well taken:
  Nor need you fear that I shall feel forsaken.
  Were I to offer him this hand of mine,
  Your friend Philinte, I think, would not decline.
PHILINTE. Ah, Madam, that's my heart's most cherished goal,
  For which I'd gladly give my life and soul.
ALCESTE, *to* ÉLIANTE *and* PHILINTE. May you be true to all you
    now profess,
  And so deserve unending happiness.
  Meanwhile, betrayed and wronged in everything,
  I'll flee this bitter world where vice is king,
  And seek some spot unpeopled and apart
  Where I'll be free to have an honest heart.
PHILINTE. Come, Madam, let's do everything we can
  To change the mind of this unhappy man.

# PHAEDRA

## A TRAGEDY

### BY

## JEAN RACINE

*English Version by Robert Lowell*

for
Miss Harriet Winslow

...ission for performance and other rights outlined on the copyright page must be
·ed from Farrar Straus & Giroux, 19 Union Square West, New York, NY 10003,
whom permission to reprint this play has be n granted.

# BACKGROUND OF THE ACTION

The story of Racine's *Phèdre* is a Greek myth. Phaedra, the wife of Theseus, the hero and king of Athens, is the daughter of Minos and Pasiphaë, the rulers of Crete. Pasiphaë coupled with a bull, and bore the Minotaur, half bull and half man, who was slain by Theseus in the maze at Crete. Phaedra falls madly in love with her stepson, Hippolytus. She is rejected by him, and falsely accuses him of trying to assault her. Theseus prays to Poseidon, the sea-god, to destroy Hippolytus; Hippolytus is destroyed. Phaedra confesses and kills herself. *Phèdre* is in some ways a miraculous translation and adaptation of Euripides' *Hippolytos*. Racine quite alters and to my mind even surpasses his wonderful original.

# CHARACTERS

THESEUS, *son of Aegeus and King of Athens*
PHAEDRA, *wife of Theseus and daughter of Minos and Pasiphaë*
HIPPOLYTUS, *son of Theseus and Antiope, Queen of the Amazons*
ARICIA, *princess of the royal blood of Athens*
OENONE, *nurse of Phaedra*
THERAMENES, *tutor of Hippolytus*
ISMENE, *friend of Aricia*
PANOPE, *waiting-woman of Phaedra*
GUARDS

THE SCENE IS LAID IN TROEZEN, A CITY ABOUT FORTY MILES FROM ATHENS, ON THE OPPOSITE SIDE OF THE GULF OF AEGINA.

*Pronunciation:*
Phaedra = Pheédra
Oenone = Eenónee
Ismene = Ismeénee
Pasiphaë = Pásiphá-ee
Aricia = Arísha
Theramenes = Therámeneés
Panope = Pánopée

# ACT I

## Scene 1

### HIPPOLYTUS, THERAMENES

HIPPOLYTUS. No no, my friend, we're off! Six months have passed
　since Father heard the ocean howl and cast
　his galley on the Aegean's skull-white froth.
　Listen! The blank sea calls us—off, off, off!
　I'll follow Father to the fountainhead
　and marsh of hell. We're off. Alive or dead,
　I'll find him.

THERAMENES. Where, my lord? I've sent a host
　of veteran seamen up and down the coast;
　each village, creek and cove from here to Crete
　has been ransacked and questioned by my fleet;
　my flagship skirted Hades' rapids, furled
　sail there a day, and scoured the underworld.
　Have you fresh news? New hopes? One even doubts
　if noble Theseus wants his whereabouts
　discovered. Does he need his helpers to share
　the plunder of his latest love affair;
　a shipload of spectators and his son
　to watch him ruin his last Amazon—
　some creature, taller than a man, whose tanned
　and single bosom slithers from his hand,
　when he leaps to crush her like a waterfall
　of honeysuckle?

HIPPOLYTUS. You are cynical,
　my friend. Your insinuations wrong a king,
　sick as myself of his philandering.
　His heart is Phaedra's and no rivals dare

to challenge Phaedra's sole possession there.
I sail to find my father. The command
of duty calls me from this stifling land.

THERAMENES. This stifling land? Is that how you deride
this gentle province where you used to ride
the bridle-paths, pursuing happiness?
You cured your orphaned childhood's loneliness
and found a peace here you preferred to all
the blaze of Athens' brawling protocol.
A rage for exploits blinds you. Your disease
is boredom.

HIPPOLYTUS. Friend, this kingdom lost its peace,
when Father left my mother, for defiled
bull-serviced Pasiphaë's child. The child
of homicidal Minos is our queen!

THERAMENES. Yes, Phaedra reigns and rules here. I have seen
you crouch before her outbursts like a cur.
When she first met you, she refused to stir
until your father drove you out of court.
The news is better now; our friends report
the queen is dying. Will you cross the seas,
desert your party and abandon Greece?
Why flee from Phaedra? Phaedra fears the night
less than she fears the day that strives to light
the universal ennui of her eyes—
this dying woman, who desires to die!

HIPPOLYTUS. No, I despise her Cretan vanity,
hysteria and idle cruelty.
I fear Aricia; she alone survives
the blood-feud that destroyed her brothers' lives.

THERAMENES. Prince, Prince, forgive my laughter. Must you fly
beyond the limits of the world and die,
floating in flotsam, friendless, far from help,
and clubbed to death by Tartars in the kelp?
Why arm the shrinking violet with a knife?
Do you hate Aricia, and fear for your life,
Prince?

HIPPOLYTUS. If I hated her, I'd trust myself
and stay.

THERAMENES. Shall I explain you to yourself?
Prince, you have ceased to be that hard-mouthed, proud
and pure Hippolytus, who scorned the crowd
of common lovers once and rose above
your wayward father by despising love.
Now you justify your father, and you feel
love's poison running through you, now you kneel
and breathe the heavy incense, and a god
possesses you and revels in your blood!
Are you in love?
HIPPOLYTUS.          Theramenes, when I call
and cry for help, you push me to the wall.
Why do you plague me, and try to make me fear
the qualities you taught me to revere?
I sucked in prudence with my mother's milk.
Antiope, no harlot draped in silk,
first hardened me. I was my mother's son
and not my father's. When the Amazon,
my mother, was dethroned, my mind approved
her lessons more than ever. I still loved
her bristling chastity. Later, you told
stories about my father's deeds that made me hold
back judgment—how he stood for Hercules,
a second Hercules who cleared the Cretan seas
of pirates, throttled Scirron, Cercyon,
Procrustes, Sinnis, and the giant man
of Epidaurus writhing in his gore.
He pierced the maze and killed the Minotaur.
Other things turned my stomach: that long list
of women, all refusing to resist.
Helen, caught up with all her honeyed flesh
from Sparta; Periboea, young and fresh,
in tears in Salamis. A hundred more,
their names forgotten by my father—whore
and virgin, child and mother, all deceived,
if their protestations can be believed!
Ariadne declaiming to the rocks,
her sister, Phaedra, kidnapped. Phaedra locks
the gate at last! You know how often I
would weary, fall to nodding and deny

the possibility of hearing the whole
ignoble, dull, insipid boast unroll.
And now I too must fall. The gods have made me creep.
How can I be in love? I have no specious heap
of honors, friend. No mastered monsters drape
my shoulders—Theseus' excuse to rape
at will. Suppose I chose a woman. Why
choose an orphan? Aricia is eternally
cut off from marriage, lest she breed
successors to her fierce brothers, and seed
the land with treason. Father only grants
her life on one condition. This—he wants
no bridal torch to burn for her. Unwooed
and childless, she must answer for the blood
her brothers shed. How can I marry her,
gaily subvert our kingdom's character,
and sail on the high seas of love?

THERAMENES.                              You'll prove
nothing by reason, for you are in love.
Theseus' injustice to Aricia throws
her in the light; your eyes he wished to close
are open. She dazzles you. Her pitiful
seclusion makes her doubly terrible.
Does this innocent passion freeze your blood?
There's sweetness in it. Is your only good
the dismal famine of your chastity?
You shun your father's path? Where would you be,
Prince, if Antiope had never burned
chastely for Theseus? Love, my lord, has turned
the head of Hercules, and thousands—fired
the forge of Vulcan! All your uninspired, cold
moralizing is nothing, Prince. You have changed!
Now no one sees you riding, half-deranged
along the sand-bars, where you drove your horse
and foaming chariot with all your force,
tilting and staggering upright through the surf—
far from their usual course across the turf.
The woods are quiet. . . . How your eyes hang down!
You often murmur and forget to frown.
All's out, Prince. You're in love, you burn. Flames, flames,

Prince! A dissimulated sickness maims
the youthful quickness of your daring. Does
lovely Aricia haunt you?

HIPPOLYTUS.                Friend, spare us.
I sail to find my father.

THERAMENES.               Will you see
Phaedra before you go?

HIPPOLYTUS.               I mean to be
here when she comes. Go, tell her. I will do
my duty. Wait, I see her nurse. What new
troubles torment her?

### Scene 2

HIPPOLYTUS, THERAMENES, OENONE

OENONE. Who has griefs like mine,
my lord? I cannot help the queen in her decline.
Although I sit beside her day and night,
she shuts her eyes and withers in my sight.
An eternal tumult roisters through her head,
panics her sleep, and drags her from her bed.
Just now she fled me at the prime
of day to see the sun for the last time.
She's coming.

HIPPOLYTUS.    So! I'll steal away. My flight
removes a hateful object from her sight.

### Scene 3

PHAEDRA, OENONE

PHAEDRA. Dearest, we'll go no further. I must rest.
I'll sit here. My emotions shake my breast,

the sunlight throws black bars across my eyes.
My knees give. If I fall, why should I rise,
Nurse?

*She sits down.*

OENONE. Heaven help us! Let me comfort you.

PHAEDRA. Tear off these gross, official rings, undo
these royal veils. They drag me to the ground.
Why have you frilled me, laced me, crowned me, and wound
my hair in turrets? All your skill torments
and chokes me. I am crushed by ornaments.
Everything hurts me, and drags me to my knees!

OENONE. Now this, now that, Madam. You never cease
commanding us, then cancelling your commands.
You feel your strength return, summon all hands
to dress you like a bride, then say you choke!
We open all the windows, fetch a cloak,
rush you outdoors. It's no use, you decide
that sunlight kills you, and only want to hide.

PHAEDRA. I feel the heaven's royal radiance cool
and fail, as if it feared my terrible
shame has destroyed its right to shine on men.
I'll never look upon the sun again.

OENONE. Renunciation on renunciation!
Now you slander the source of your creation.
Why do you run to death and tear your hair?

PHAEDRA. Oh God, take me to some sunless forest lair . . .
There hoof-beats raise a dust-cloud, and my eye
follows a horseman outlined on the sky!

OENONE. What's this, my lady?

PHAEDRA.                          I have lost my mind.
Where am I? O forget my words! I find
I've lost the habit now of talking sense.
My face is red and guilty—evidence
of treason! I've betrayed my darkest fears,
Nurse, and my eyes, despite me, fill with tears.

OENONE. Lady, if you must weep, weep for your silence
that filled your days and mine with violence.
Ah deaf to argument and numb to care,

you have no mercy on us. Spare me, spare
yourself. Your blood is like polluted water,
fouling a mind desiring its own slaughter.
The sun has died and shadows filled the skies
thrice now, since you have closed your eyes;
the day has broken through the night's content
thrice now, since you have tasted nourishment.
Is your salvation from your terrified
conscience this passive, servile suicide?
Lady, your madness harms the gods who gave
you life, betrays your husband. Who will save
your children? Your downfall will orphan them,
deprive them of their kingdom, and condemn
their lives and future to the discipline
of one who abhors you and all your kin,
a tyrant suckled by an Amazon,
Hippolytus . . .

PHAEDRA.        Oh God!

OENONE.                You still hate someone;
thank heaven for that, Madam!

PHAEDRA.                You spoke his name!

OENONE. Hippolytus, Hippolytus! There's hope
in hatred, Lady. Give your anger rope.
I love your anger. If the winds of love
and fury stir you, you will live. Above
your children towers this foreigner, this child
of Scythian cannibals, now wild
to ruin the kingdom, master Greece, and choke
the children of the gods beneath his yoke.
Why dawdle? Why deliberate at length?
Oh, gather up your dissipated strength.

PHAEDRA. I've lived too long.

OENONE.                Always, always agonized!
Is your conscience still stunned and paralyzed?
Do you think you have washed your hands in blood?

PHAEDRA. Thank God, my hands are clean still. Would to God
my heart were innocent!

OENONE.                         Your heart, your heart!
  What have you done that tears your soul apart?

PHAEDRA. I've said too much. Oenone, let me die;
  by dying I shall escape blasphemy.

OENONE. Search for another hand to close your eyes.
  Oh cruel Queen, I see that you despise
  my sorrow and devotion. I'll die first,
  and end the anguish of this service cursed
  by your perversity. A thousand roads
  always lie open to the killing gods.
  I'll choose the nearest. Lady, tell me how
  Oenone's love has failed you. Will you allow
  your nurse to die, your nurse, who gave up all—
  nation, parents, children, to serve in thrall.
  I saved you from your mother, King Minos' wife!
  Will your death pay me for giving up my life?

PHAEDRA. What I could tell you, I have told you. Nurse,
  only my silence saves me from the curse
  of heaven.

OENONE.     How could you tell me anything
  worse than watching you dying?

PHAEDRA.                         I would bring
  my life and rank dishonor. What can I say
  to save myself, or put off death a day?

OENONE. Ah Lady, I implore you by my tears,
  and by your suffering body. Heaven hears,
  and knows the truth already. Let me see.

PHAEDRA. Stand up.

OENONE.             Your hesitation's killing me!

PHAEDRA. What can I tell you? How the gods reprove
  me!

OENONE. Speak!

PHAEDRA.       Oh Venus, murdering Venus! love
  gored Pasiphaë with the bull.

OENONE.                     Forget
  your mother! When she died she paid her debt.

PHAEDRA. Oh Ariadne, oh my Sister, lost
  for love of Theseus on that rocky coast.

OENONE. Lady, what nervous languor makes you rave
against your family; they are in the grave.

PHAEDRA. Remorseless Aphrodite drives me. I,
my race's last and worst love-victim, die.

OENONE. Are you in love?

PHAEDRA.                    I am with love!

OENONE.                                    Who
is he?

PHAEDRA. I'll tell you. Nothing love can do
could equal . . . Nurse, I am in love. The shame
kills me. I love the. . . . Do not ask his name.

OENONE. Who?

PHAEDRA.      Nurse, you know my old loathing for the son
of Theseus and the barbarous Amazon?

OENONE. Hippolytus! My God, oh my God!

PHAEDRA.                                  You,
not I, have named him.

OENONE.                  What can you do,
but die? Your words have turned my blood to ice.
Oh righteous heavens, must the blasphemies
of Pasiphaë fall upon her daughter?
Her Furies strike us down across the water.
Why did we come here?

PHAEDRA. My evil comes from farther off. In May,
in brilliant Athens, on my marriage day,
I turned aside for shelter from the smile
of Theseus. Death was frowning in an aisle—
Hippolytus! I saw his face, turned white!
My lost and dazzled eyes saw only night,
capricious burnings flickered through my bleak
abandoned flesh. I could not breathe or speak.
I faced my flaming executioner,
Aphrodite, my mother's murderer!
I tried to calm her wrath by flowers and praise,
I built her a temple, fretted months and days
on decoration. I even hoped to find
symbols and stays for my distracted mind,
searching the guts of sacrificial steers.

Yet when my erring passions, mutineers
to virtue, offered incense at the shrine
of love, I failed to silence the malign
Goddess. Alas, my hungry open mouth,
thirsting with adoration, tasted drouth—
Venus resigned her altar to my new lord—
and even while I was praying, I adored
Hippolytus above the sacred flame,
now offered to his name I could not name.
I fled him, yet he stormed me in disguise,
and seemed to watch me with his father's eyes.
I even turned against myself, screwed up
my slack courage to fury, and would not stop
shrieking and raging, till half-dead with love
and the hatred of a stepmother, I drove
Hippolytus in exile from the rest
and strenuous wardship of his father's breast.
Then I could breathe, Oenone; he was gone;
my lazy, nerveless days meandered on
through dreams and daydreams, like a stately carriage
touring the level landscape of my marriage.
Yet nothing worked. My husband sent me here
to Troezen, far from Athens; once again the dear
face shattered me; I saw Hippolytus
each day, and felt my ancient, venomous
passion tear my body limb from limb;
naked, Venus was clawing down her victim.
What could I do? Each moment, terrified
by loose diseased emotions, now I cried
for death to save my glory and expel
my gloomy frenzy from this world, my hell.
And yet your tears and words bewildered me,
and so endangered my tranquillity,
at last I spoke. Nurse, I shall not repent,
if you will leave me the passive content
of dry silence and solitude.

## Scene 4

#### PHAEDRA, OENONE, PANOPE

PANOPE. My heart breaks. Would to God, I could refuse
 to tell your majesty my evil news.
 The King is dead! Listen, the heavens ring
 with shouts and lamentations for the King.

OENONE. The King is dead? What's this?

PANOPE.         In vain
 you beg the gods to send him back again.
 Hippolytus has heard the true report,
 he is already heading for the port.

PHAEDRA. Oh God!

PANOPE.     They've heard in Athens. Everyone
 is joining factions—some salute your son,
 others are calling for Hippolytus;
 they want him to reform and harden us—
 even Aricia claims the loyalty
 of a fanatical minority.
 The Prince's captains have recalled their men.
 His flag is up, and now he sails again
 for Athens. Queen, if he appear there now,
 he'll drag the people with him!

OENONE.        Stop, allow
 the Queen a little respite for her grief.
 She hears you, and will act for our relief.

## Scene 5

#### PHAEDRA, OENONE

OENONE. I'd given up persuading you to live;
 death was your refuge, only death could give

you peace and save your troubled glory. I
myself desired to follow you, and die.
But this catastrophe prescribes new laws:
the king is dead, and for the king who was,
fate offers you his kingdom. You have a son;
he should be king! If you abandon
him, he'll be a slave. The gods, his ancestors,
will curse and drive you on your fatal course.
Live! Who'll condemn you if you love and woo
the Prince? Your stepson is no kin to you,
now that your royal husband's death has cut
and freed you from the throttling marriage-knot.
Do not torment the Prince with persecution,
and give a leader to the revolution;
no, win his friendship, bind him to your side.
Give him this city and its countryside.
He will renounce the walls of Athens, piled
stone on stone by Minerva for your child.
Stand with Hippolytus, annihilate
Aricia's faction, and possess the state!

PHAEDRA. So be it! Your superior force has won.
I will live if compassion for my son,
devotion to the Prince, and love of power
can give me courage in this fearful hour.

# ACT II

## Scene 1

### ARICIA, ISMENE

ARICIA. What's this? The Prince has sent a messenger?
The Prince begs me to wait and meet him here?
The Prince begs! Goose, you've lost your feeble wits!

ISMENE. Lady, be calm. These are the benefits
of Theseus' death: first Prince Hippolytus
comes courting favors; soon the populous
cities of Greece will follow—they will eat
out of your hand, Princess, and kiss your feet.

ARICIA. This felon's hand, this slave's! My dear, your news
is only frivolous gossip, I refuse
to hope.

ISMENE. Ah Princess, the just powers of hell
Have struck. Theseus has joined your brothers!

ARICIA.                   Tell
me how he died.

ISMENE.            Princess, fearful tales
are circulating. Sailors saw his sails,
his infamous black sails, spin round and round
in Charybdis' whirlpool; all hands were drowned.
Yet others say on better evidence
that Theseus and Pirithoüs passed the dense
darkness of hell to rape Persephone.
Pirithoüs was murdered by the hound;
Theseus, still living, was buried in the ground.

ARICIA. This is an old wives' tale. Only the dead
enter the underworld, and see the bed
of Queen Persephone. What brought him there?

ISMENE. Princess, the King is dead—dead! Everywhere
men know and mourn. Already our worshipping
townsmen acclaim Hippolytus for their king;
in her great palace, Phaedra, the self-styled
regent, rages and trembles for her child.

ARICIA. What makes you think the puritanical
son of Theseus is human? Will he recall
my sentence and relent?

ISMENE.                        I know he will.

ARICIA. You know nothing about him. He would kill
a woman, rather than be kind to one.
That wolf-cub of a fighting Amazon
hates me above all women. He would walk
from here to hell, rather than hear me talk.

ISMENE. Do you know Hippolytus? Listen to me.
His famous, blasphemous frigidity,
what is it, when you've seen him close at hand?
I've watched him like a hawk, and seen him stand
shaking beside you—all his reputation
for hating womenkind bears no relation
to what I saw. He couldn't take his eyes
off you! His eyes speak what his tongue denies.

ARICIA. I can't believe you. Your story's absurd!
How greedily I listen to each word!
Ismene, you know me, you know how my heart
was reared on death and always set apart
from what it cherished—can this plaything of
the gods and furies feel the peace of love?
What sights I've seen, Ismene! "Heads will roll,"
my brothers told me, "we will rule." I, the sole
survivor of those fabulous kings, who tilled
the soil of Greece, have seen my brothers killed,
six brothers murdered! In a single hour,
the tyrant, Theseus, lopped them in their flower.
The monster spared my life, and yet decreed
the torments of this childless life I lead
in exile, where no Greek can look on me;
my forced, perpetual virginity
preserves his crown; no son shall bear my name

or blow my brothers' ashes into flame.
Ismene, you know how well his tyranny
favors my temperament and strengthens me
to guard the honor of my reputation;
his rigor fortified my inclination.
How could I test his son's civilities?
I'd never even seen him with my eyes!
I'd never seen him. I'd restrained my eye,
that giddy nerve, from dwelling thoughtlessly
upon his outward grace and beauty—on mere
embellishments of nature, a veneer
the Prince himself despises and ignores.
My heart loves nobler virtues, and adores
in him his father's hard intelligence.
He has his father's daring and a sense
of honor his father lacks. Let me confess,
I love him for his lofty haughtiness
never submitted to a woman's yoke.
How could Phaedra's splendid marriage provoke
my jealousy? Have I so little pride,
I'd snatch at a rake's heart, a heart denied
to none—all riddled, opened up to let
thousands pass in like water through a net?
To carry sorrows to a heart, alone
untouched by passion, inflexible as stone,
to fasten my dominion on a force
as nervous as a never-harnessed horse—
this stirs me, this enflames me. Devilish Zeus
is easier mastered than Hippolytus;
heaven's love-infatuated emperor
confers less glory on his conqueror!
Ismene, I'm afraid. Why should I boast?
His very virtues I admire the most
threaten to rise and throw me from the brink
of hope. What girlish folly made me think
Hippolytus could love Aricia?

ISMENE.                              Here
he is. He loves you, Princess. Have no fear.

## Scene 2

### ARICIA, ISMENE, HIPPOLYTUS

HIPPOLYTUS.                    Princess, before
I leave here, I must tell you what's in store
for you in Greece. Alas, my father's dead.
The fierce forebodings that disquieted
my peace are true. Death, only death, could hide
his valor from this world he pacified.
The homicidal Fates will not release
the comrade, friend and peer of Hercules.
Princess, I trust your hate will not resent
honors whose justice is self-evident.
A single hope alleviates my grief,
Princess, I hope to offer you relief.
I now revoke a law whose cruelty
has pained my conscience. Princess, you are free
to marry. Oh enjoy this province, whose
honest, unhesitating subjects choose
Hippolytus for king. Live free as air,
here, free as I am, much more free!

ARICIA.                           I dare
not hope. You are too gracious. Can you free
Aricia from your father's stern decree?

HIPPOLYTUS. Princess, the Athenian people, torn in two
between myself and Phaedra's son, want you.

ARICIA. Want me, my lord!

HIPPOLYTUS.                    I've no illusions. Lame
Athenian precedents condemn my claim,
because my mother was a foreigner.
But what is that? If my only rival were
my younger brother, his minority
would clear my legal disability.
However, a better claim than his or mine
now favors you, ennobled by the line

of great Erectheus. Your direct descent
sets you before my father; he was only lent
this kingdom by adoption. Once the common
Athenian, dazed by Theseus' superhuman
energies, had no longing to exhume
the rights that rushed your brothers to their doom.
Now Athens calls you home; the ancient feud
too long has stained the sacred olive wood;
blood festers in the furrows of our soil
to blight its fruits and scorch the farmer's toil.
This province suits me, let the vines of Crete
offer my brother a secure retreat.
The rest is yours. All Attica is yours;
I go to win you what your right assures.

ARICIA. Am I awake, my lord? Your sayings seem
like weird phantasmagoria in a dream.
How can your sparkling promises be true?
Some god, my lord, some god, has entered you!
How justly you are worshipped in this town;
oh how the truth surpasses your renown!
You wish to endow me with your heritage!
I only hoped you would not hate me. This rage
your father felt, how can you put it by
and treat me kindly?

HIPPOLYTUS.            Princess, is my eye
blind to beauty? Am I a bear, a bull, a boar,
some abortion fathered by the Minotaur?
Some one-eyed Cyclops, able to resist
Aricia's loveliness and still exist?
How can a man stand up against your grace?

ARICIA. My lord, my lord!

HIPPOLYTUS.            I cannot hide my face,
Princess! I'm driven. Why does my violence
so silence reason and intelligence?
Must I be still, and let my adoration
simmer away in silent resignation?
Princess, I've lost all power to restrain
myself. You see a madman, whose insane
pride hated love, and hoped to sit ashore,

watching the galleys founder in the war;
I was Diana's liegeman, dressed in steel.
I hoped to trample love beneath my heel—
alas, the flaming Venus burns me down,
I am the last dependent on her crown.
What left me charred and writhing in her clutch?
A single moment and a single touch.
Six months now, bounding like a wounded stag,
I've tried to shake this poisoned dart, and drag
myself to safety from your eyes that blind
when present, and when absent leave behind
volleys of burning arrows in my mind.
Ah Princess, shall I dive into the sea,
or steal the wings of Icarus to flee
love's Midas' touch that turns my world to gold?
Your image drives me stumbling through the cold,
floods my deserted forest caves with light,
darkens the day and dazzles through my night.
I'm grafted to your side by all I see;
all things unite us and imprison me.
I have no courage for the Spartan exercise
that trained my hand and steeled my energies.
Where are my horses? I forget their names.
My triumphs with my chariot at the games
no longer give me strength to mount a horse.
The ocean drives me shuddering from its shores.
Does such a savage conquest make you blush?
My boorish gestures, headlong cries that rush
at you like formless monsters from the sea?
Ah, Princess, hear me! Your serenity
must pardon the distortions of a weak
and new-born lover, forced by you to speak
love's foreign language, words that snarl and yelp . . .
I never could have spoken without your help.

## Scene 3

ARICIA, ISMENE, HIPPOLYTUS, THERAMENES

THERAMENES. I announce the Queen. She comes hurriedly,
  looking for you.

HIPPOLYTUS.       For me!

THERAMENES.              Don't ask me why;
  she insisted. I promised I'd prevail
  on you to speak with her before you sail.

HIPPOLYTUS. What can she want to hear? What can I say?

ARICIA. Wait for her, here! You cannot turn away.
  Forget her malice. Hating her will serve
  no purpose. Wait for her! Her tears deserve
  your pity.

HIPPOLYTUS. You're going, Princess? And I must go
  to Athens, far from you. How shall I know
  if you accept my love?

ARICIA.              My Lord, pursue
  your gracious promise. Do what you must do,
  make Athens tributary to my rule.
  Nothing you offer is unacceptable,
  yet this empire, so great, so glorious,
  is the least precious of your gifts to us.

## Scene 4

HIPPOLYTUS, THERAMENES

HIPPOLYTUS. We're ready. Wait, the Queen's here. I need you.
  You must interrupt this tedious interview.
  Hurry down to the ship, then rush back, pale
  and breathless. Say the wind's up and we must sail.

## Scene 5

HIPPOLYTUS, OENONE, PHAEDRA

PHAEDRA, *to* OENONE. He's here! Why does he scowl and look
    away from me? What shall I do? What shall I say?

OENONE. Speak for your son, he has no other patron.

PHAEDRA. Why are you so impatient to be gone
    from us, my lord? Stay! we will weep together.
    Pity my son; he too has lost his father.
    My own death's near. Rebellion, sick with wrongs,
    now like a sea-beast, lifts its slimey prongs,
    its muck, its jelly. You alone now stand
    to save the state. Who else can understand
    a mother? I forget. You will not hear
    me! An enemy deserves no pity. I fear
    your anger. Must my son, your brother, Prince,
    be punished for his cruel mother's sins?

HIPPOLYTUS. I've no such thoughts.

PHAEDRA.                              I persecuted you
    blindly, and now you have good reason to
    return my impudence. How could you find
    the motivation of this heart and mind
    that scourged and tortured you, till you began
    to lose the calm composure of a man,
    and dwindle to a harsh and sullen boy,
    a thing of ice, unable to enjoy
    the charms of any civilized resource
    except the heavy friendship of your horse,
    that whirled you far from women, court and throne,
    to course the savage woods for wolves alone?
    You have good reason, yet if pain's a measure,
    no one has less deserved your stern displeasure.
    My lord, no one has more deserved compassion.

HIPPOLYTUS. Lady, I understand a mother's passion,
    a mother jealous for her children's rights.

How can she spare a first wife's son? Long nights
of plotting, devious days of quarrelling—
a madhouse! What else can remarriage bring?
Another would have shown equal hostility,
pushed her advantage more outrageously.

PHAEDRA. My lord, if you had known how far my love
and yearning have exalted me above
this usual weakness . . . Our afflicting kinship
is ending . . .

HIPPOLYTUS. Madam, the precious minutes slip
by, I fatigue you. Fight against your fears.
Perhaps Poseidon has listened to our tears,
perhaps your husband's still alive. He hears
us, he is surging home—only a short
day's cruise conceals him, as he scuds for port.

PHAEDRA. That's folly, my lord. Who has twice visited
black Hades and the river of the dead
and returned? No, the poisonous Acheron
never lets go. Theseus drifts on and on,
a gutted galley on that clotted waste—
he woos, he wins Persephone, the chaste . . .
What am I saying? Theseus is not dead.
He lives in you. He speaks, he's taller by a head.
I see him, touch him, and my heart—a reef . . .
Ah Prince, I wander. Love betrays my grief . . .

HIPPOLYTUS. No, no, my father lives. Lady, the blind
furies release him; in your loyal mind,
love's fullness holds him, and he cannot die.

PHAEDRA. I hunger for Theseus. Always in my eye
he wanders, not as he appeared in hell,
lascivious eulogist of any belle
he found there, from the lowest to the Queen;
no, faithful, airy, just a little mean
through virtue, charming all, yet young and new,
as we would paint a god—as I now see you!
Your valiant shyness would have graced his speech,
he would have had your stature, eyes, and reach,
Prince, when he flashed across our Cretan waters,
the loved enslaver of King Minos' daughters.

Where were you? How could he conscript the flower
of Athens' youth against my father's power,
and ignore you? You were too young, they say;
you should have voyaged as a stowaway.
No dawdling bypath would have saved our bull,
when your just vengeance thundered through its skull.
There, light of foot, and certain of your goal,
you would have struck my brother's monstrous soul,
and pierced our maze's slow meanders, led
by Ariadne and her subtle thread.
By Ariadne? Prince, I would have fought
for precedence; my every flaming thought,
love-quickened, would have shot you through the dark,
straight as an arrow to your quaking mark.
Could I have waited, panting, perishing,
entrusting your survival to a string,
like Ariadne, when she skulked behind,
there at the portal, to bemuse her mind
among the solemn cloisters of the porch?
No, Phaedra would have snatched your burning torch,
and lunged before you, reeling like a priest
of Dionysus to distract the beast.
I would have reached the final corridor
a lap before you, and killed the Minotaur!
Lost in the labyrinth, and at your side,
would it have mattered, if I lived or died?

HIPPOLYTUS. What are you saying, Madam? You forget
my father is your husband!

PHAEDRA.                        I have let
you see my grief for Theseus! How could I
forget my honor and my majesty,
Prince?

HIPPOLYTUS. Madam, forgive me! My foolish youth
conjectured hideous untruths from your truth.
I cannot face my insolence. Farewell . . .

PHAEDRA. You monster! You understood me too well!
Why do you hang there, speechless, petrified,
polite! My mind whirls. What have I to hide?
Phaedra in all her madness stands before you.

I love you! Fool, I love you, I adore you!
Do not imagine that my mind approved
my first defection, Prince, or that I loved
your youth light-heartedly, and fed my treason
with cowardly compliance, till I lost my reason.
I wished to hate you, but the gods corrupt
us; though I never suffered their abrupt
seductions, shattering advances, I
too bear their sensual lightnings in my thigh.
I too am dying. I have felt the heat
that drove my mother through the fields of Crete,
the bride of Minos, dying for the full
magnetic April thunders of the bull.
I struggled with my sickness, but I found
no grace or magic to preserve my sound
intelligence and honor from this lust,
plowing my body with its horny thrust.
At first I fled you, and when this fell short
of safety, Prince, I exiled you from court.
Alas, my violence to resist you made
my face inhuman, hateful. I was afraid
to kiss my husband lest I love his son.
I made you fear me (this was easily done);
you loathed me more, I ached for you no less.
Misfortune magnified your loveliness.
I grew so wrung and wasted, men mistook
me for the Sibyl. If you could bear to look
your eyes would tell you. Do you believe my passion
is voluntary? That my obscene confession
is some dark trick, some oily artifice?
I came to beg you not to sacrifice
my son, already uncertain of his life.
Ridiculous, mad embassy, for a wife
who loves her stepson! Prince, I only spoke
about myself! Avenge yourself, invoke
your father; a worse monster threatens you
than any Theseus ever fought and slew.
The wife of Theseus loves Hippolytus!
See, Prince! Look, this monster, ravenous
for her execution, will not flinch.

I want your sword's spasmodic final inch.

OENONE. Madam, put down this weapon. Your distress
attracts the people. Fly these witnesses.
Hurry! Stop kneeling! What a time to pray!

## Scene 6

### THERAMENES, HIPPOLYTUS

THERAMENES. Is this Phaedra, fleeing, or rather dragged away
sobbing? Where is your sword? Who tore
this empty scabbard from your belt?

HIPPOLYTUS.                                   No more!
Oh let me get away! I face disaster.
Horrors unnerve me. Help! I cannot master
my terror. Phaedra . . . No, I won't expose
her. No! Something I do not dare disclose . . .

THERAMENES. Our ship is ready, but before you leave,
listen! Prince, what we never would believe
has happened: Athens has voted for your brother.
The citizens have made him king. His mother
is regent.

HIPPOLYTUS. Phaedra is in power!

THERAMENES. An envoy sent from Athens came this hour
to place the scepter in her hands. Her son
is king.

HIPPOLYTUS. Almighty gods, you know this woman!
Is it her spotless virtue you reward?

THERAMENES. I've heard a rumor. Someone swam aboard
a ship off Epirus. He claims the King
is still alive. I've searched. I know the thing
is nonsense.

HIPPOLYTUS.  Search! Nothing must be neglected.
If the king's dead, I'll rouse the disaffected
people, crown Aricia, and place our lands,
our people, and our lives in worthy hands.

# ACT III

PHAEDRA, OENONE

PHAEDRA. Why do my people rush to crown me queen?
Who can even want to see me? They have seen
my downfall. Will their praise deliver me?
Oh bury me at the bottom of the sea!
Nurse, I have said too much! Led on by you,
I've said what no one should have listened to.
*He* listened. How could he pretend my drift
was hidden? Something held him, and made him shift
his ground . . . He only wanted to depart
and hide, while I was pouring out my heart.
Oh how his blushing multiplied my shame!
Why did you hold me back? You are to blame,
Oenone. But for you, I would have killed
myself. Would he have stood there, iron-willed
and merciless, while I fell upon his sword?
He would have snatched it, touched me, and restored
my life! No, no!

OENONE.                  Control yourself! No peace
comes from surrendering to your disease,
Madam. Oh daughter of the kings of Crete,
why are you weeping and fawning at the feet
of this barbarian, less afraid of fate
than of a woman? You must rule the state.

PHAEDRA. Can I, who have no courage to restrain
the insurrection of my passions, reign?
Will the Athenians trust their sovereignty
to me? Love's despotism is crushing me,
I am ruined.

OENONE.          Fly!

PHAEDRA.          How can I leave him?

OENONE. Lady, you have already banished him;
can't you take flight?

PHAEDRA.              The time for flight has passed.
He knows me now. I rushed beyond the last
limits of modesty, when I confessed.
Hope was no longer blasting through my breast;
I was resigned to hopelessness and death,
and gasping out my last innocent breath,
Oenone, when you forced me back to life.
You thought I was no longer Theseus' wife,
and let me feel that I was free to love.

OENONE. I would have done anything to remove
your danger. Whether I'm guilty or innocent
is all the same to me. Your punishment
should fall on one who tried to kill you, not
on poor Oenone. Lady, you must plot
and sacrifice this monster, whose unjust
abhorrence left you dying in the dust.
Oh humble him, undo him, oh despise
him! Lady, you must see him with my eyes.

PHAEDRA. Oenone, he was nourished in the woods;
he is all shyness and ungracious moods
because the forests left him half-inhuman.
He's never heard love spoken by a woman!
We've gone too far. Oenone, we're unwise;
perhaps the young man's silence was surprise.

OENONE. His mother, the Amazon, was never moved
by men.

PHAEDRA. The boy exists. She must have loved!

OENONE. He has a sullen hatred for our sex.

PHAEDRA. Oh, all the better; rivals will not vex
my chances. Your advice is out of season;
now you must serve my frenzy, not my reason!
You tell me love has never touched his heart;
we'll look, we'll find an undefended part.
He's turned his bronze prows seaward; look, the wind

already blows like a trumpeter behind
his bulging canvas! The Acropolis
of Athens and its empire shall be his!
Hurry, Oenone, hunt the young man down,
blind him with dazzling visions of the crown.
Go tell him I relinquish my command,
I only want the guidance of his hand.
Let him assume these powers that weary me;
he will instruct my son in sovereignty.
Perhaps he will adopt my son, and be
the son's and mother's one divinity!
Oenone, rush to him, use every means
to bend and win him; if he fears the Queen's
too proud, he'll listen to her slave. Plead, groan
insist . . . say I am giving him my throne. . . .
No, say I'm dying!

## Scene 2

### PHAEDRA

PHAEDRA. Implacable Aphrodite, now you see
the depths to which your tireless cruelty
has driven Phaedra—here is my bosom;
every thrust and arrow has struck home!
Oh Goddess, if you hunger for renown,
rise now, and shoot a worthier victim down!
Conquer the barbarous Hippolytus,
who mocks the graces and the power of Venus,
and gazes on your godhead with disgust.
Avenge me, Venus! See, my cause is just,
my cause is yours. Oh bend him to my will! . .
You're back, Oenone? Does he hate me still?

## Scene 3

PHAEDRA, OENONE

OENONE. Your love is folly, dash it from your soul,
gather your scattered pride and self-control,
Madam! I've seen the royal ship arrive.
Theseus is back, Theseus is still alive!
Thousands of voices thunder from the docks.
People are waving flags and climbing rocks.
While I was looking for Hippolytus . . .

PHAEDRA. My husband's living! Must you trouble us
by talking? What am I living for?
He lives, Oenone, let me hear no more
about it.

OENONE.    Why?

PHAEDRA.         I told you, but my fears
were stilled, alas, and smothered by your tears.
Had I died this morning, I might have faced
the gods. I heeded you and die disgraced!

OENONE. You are disgraced!

PHAEDRA.                        Oh Gods of wrath,
how far I've travelled on my dangerous path!
I go to meet my husband; at his side
will stand Hippolytus. How shall I hide
my thick adulterous passion for this youth,
who has rejected me, and knows the truth?
Will the stern Prince stand smiling and approve
the labored histrionics of my love
for Theseus, see my lips, still languishing
for his, betray his father and his King?
Will he not draw his sword and strike me dead?
Suppose he spares me? What if nothing's said?
Am I a gorgon, or Circe, or the infidel
Medea, stifled by the flames of hell,
yet rising like Aphrodite from the sea,

refreshed and radiant with indecency?
Can I kiss Theseus with dissembled poise?
I think each stone and pillar has a voice.
The very dust rises to disabuse
my husband—to defame me and accuse!
Oenone, I want to die. Death will give
me freedom; oh it's nothing not to live;
death to the unhappy's no catastrophe!
I fear the name that must live after me,
and crush my son until the end of time.
Is his inheritance his mother's crime?
his right to curse me, when my pollution stains
the blood of heaven bubbling in his veins?
The day will come, alas, the day will come,
when nothing will be left to save him from
the voices of despair. If he should live
he'll flee his subjects like a fugitive.

OENONE. He has my pity. Who has ever built
firmer foundations to expose her guilt?
But why expose your son? Is your contribution
for his defense to serve the prosecution?
Suppose you kill yourself? The world will say
you fled your outraged husband in dismay.
Could there be stronger evidence and proof
than Phaedra crushed beneath the horse's hoof
of blasphemous self-destruction to convince
the crowds who'll dance attendance on the Prince?
The crowds will mob your children when they hear
their defamation by a foreigner!
Wouldn't you rather see earth bury us?
Tell me, do you still love Hippolytus?

PHAEDRA. I see him as a beast, who'd murder us.

OENONE. Madam, let the positions be reversed!
You fear the Prince; you must accuse him first.
Who'll dare assert your story is untrue,
if all the evidence shall speak for you:
your present grief, your past despair of mind,
the Prince's sword so luckily left behind?

Do you think Theseus will oppose his son's
second exile? He has consented once!

PHAEDRA. How dare I take this murderous, plunging course?

OENONE. I tremble, Lady, I too feel remorse.
If death could rescue you from infamy,
Madam, I too would follow you and die.
Help me by being silent. I will speak
in such a way the King will only seek
a bloodless exile to assert his rights.
A father is still a father when he smites.
You shudder at this evil sacrifice,
but nothing's evil or too high a price
to save your menaced honor from defeat.
Ah Minos, Minos, you defended Crete
by killing young men! Help us! If the cost
for saving Phaedra is a holocaust
of virtue, Minos, you must sanctify
our undertaking, or watch your daughter die.
I see the King.

PHAEDRA.                    Hippolytus I see:
His insolent eyes are my dark destiny.
Bewildered, lost, I know not what to do.
Do as you wish, then. I leave it to you.


*Scene 4*

PHAEDRA, THESEUS, HIPPOLYTUS, OENONE, THERAMENES

THESEUS. Fate's heard me, Phaedra, and removed the bar
that kept me from your arms.

PHAEDRA.                              Theseus, stop where you are!
Your raptures and endearments are profane.
Your arm must never comfort me again.
You have been wronged, the gods who spared your life
have used your absence to disgrace your wife,
unworthy now to please you or come near.
My only refuge is to disappear.

## Scene 5

#### THESEUS, HIPPOLYTUS, THERAMENES

THESEUS. What a strange welcome! This bewilders me.
  My son, what's happened?

HIPPOLYTUS.                Phaedra holds the key.
  Ask Phaedra. If you love me, let me leave
  this kingdom. I'm determined to achieve
  some action that will show my strength. I fear
  Phaedra. I am afraid of living here.

THESEUS. My son, you want to leave me?

HIPPOLYTUS.                    I never sought
  her grace or favor. Your decision brought
  her here from Athens. Your desires prevailed
  against my judgment, Father, when you sailed
  leaving Phaedra and Aricia in my care.
  I've done my duty, now I must prepare
  for sterner actions, I must test my skill
  on monsters far more dangerous to kill
  than any wolf or eagle in this wood.
  Release me, I too must prove my manhood!
  Oh Father, you were hardly half my age,
  when herds of giants writhed before your rage—
  you were already famous as the scourge
  of insolence. Our people saw you purge
  the pirates from the shores of Greece and Thrace,
  the harmless merchantman was free to race
  the winds, and weary Hercules could pause
  from slaughter, knowing you upheld his cause.
  The world revered you. I am still unknown;
  even my mother's deeds surpass my own.
  Some tyrants have escaped you; let me meet
  with them and throw their bodies at your feet.
  I'll drag them from their wolf-holes; if I die,
  my death will show I struggled worthily.

Oh, Father, raise me from oblivion;
my deeds shall tell the universe I am your son.

THESEUS. What do I see? Oh gods, what horror drives
my queen and children fleeing for their lives
before me? If so little warmth remains,
oh why did you release me from my chains?
Why am I hated, and so little loved?
I had a friend, just one. His folly moved
me till I aided his conspiracy
to ravish Queen Persephone.
The gods, tormented by our blasphemous
designs, befogged our minds and blinded us—
we invaded Epirus instead of hell.
There a diseased and subtle tyrant fell
upon us as we slept, and while I stood
by, helpless, monsters crazed for human blood
consumed Pirithoüs. I myself was chained
fast in a death-deep dungeon. I remained
six months there, then the gods had pity,
and put me in possession of the city.
I killed the tyrant; now his body feasts
the famished, pampered bellies of his beasts.
At last, I voyaged home, cast anchor, furled
my sails. When I was rushing to my world—
what am I saying? When my heart and soul
were mine again, unable to control
themselves for longing—who receives me? All run
and shun me, as if I were a skeleton.
Now I myself begin to feel the fear
I inspire. I wish I were a prisoner
again or dead. Speak! Phaedra says my home
was outraged. Who betrayed me? Someone come
and tell me. I have fought for Greece. Will Greece,
sustained by Theseus, give my enemies
asylum in my household? Tell me why
I've no avenger? Is my son a spy?
You will not answer. I must know my fate.
Suspicion chokes me, while I hesitate
and stand here pleading. Wait, let no one stir.
Phaedra shall tell me what has troubled her.

### Scene 6

HIPPOLYTUS, THERAMENES

HIPPOLYTUS. What now? His anger turns my blood to ice.
Will Phaedra, always uncertain, sacrifice
herself? What will she tell the King? How hot
the air's becoming here! I feel the rot
of love seeping like poison through this house.
I feel the pollution. I cannot rouse
my former loyalties. When I try to gather
the necessary strength to face my father,
my mind spins with some dark presentiment . . .
How can such terror touch the innocent?
I LOVE ARICIA! Father, I confess
my treason to you is my happiness!
I LOVE ARICIA! Will this bring you joy,
our love you have no power to destroy?

# ACT IV

## Scene 1

### THESEUS, OENONE

THESEUS. What's this, you tell me he dishonors me,
  and has assaulted Phaedra's chastity?
  Oh heavy fortune, I no longer know
  who loves me, who I am, or where I go.
  Who has ever seen such disloyalty
  after such love? Such sly audacity?
  His youth made no impression on her soul,
  so he fell back on force to reach his goal!
  I recognize this perjured sword; I gave
  him this myself to teach him to be brave!
  Oh Zeus, are blood-ties no impediment?
  Even Phaedra to save him from punishment!
  Why did her silence spare this parricide?

OENONE. She hoped to spare a trusting father's pride.
  She felt so sickened by your son's attempt,
  his hot eyes leering at her with contempt,
  she had no wish to live. She read out her will
  to me, then lifted up her arm to kill
  herself. I struck the sword out of her hand.
  Fainting, she babbled the secret she had planned
  to bury with her in the grave. My ears
  unwillingly interpreted her tears.

THESEUS. Oh traitor! I know why he seemed to blanch
  and toss with terror like an aspen branch
  when Phaedra saw him. Now I know why he stood
  back, then embraced me so coldly he froze my blood.
  Was Athens the first stage for his obscene
  attentions? Did he dare attack the Queen
  before our marriage?

OENONE.                    Remember her disgust
  and hate then? She already feared his lust.

THESEUS. And when I sailed, this started up again?

OENONE. I've hidden nothing. Do you want your pain
  redoubled? Phaedra calls me. Let me go,
  and save her. I have told you what I know.


### Scene 2

#### THESEUS, HIPPOLYTUS

THESEUS. My son returns! Oh God, reserved and cool,
  dressed in a casual freedom that could fool
  the sharpest. Is it right his brows should blaze
  and dazzle me with virtue's sacred rays?
  Are there not signs? Should not ADULTERER
  in looping scarlet script be branded there?

HIPPOLYTUS. What cares becloud your kingly countenance,
  Father! What is this irritated glance?
  Tell me! Are you afraid to trust your son?

THESEUS. How dare you stand here? May the great Zeus stone
  me, if I let my fondness and your birth
  protect you! Is my strength which rid the earth
  of brigands paralysed? Am I so sick
  and senile, any coward with a stick
  can strike me? Am I a schoolboy's target? Oh God,
  am I food for vultures? Some carrion you must prod
  and poke to see if it's alive or dead?
  Your hands are moist and itching for my bed,
  Coward! Wasn't begetting you enough
  dishonor to destroy me? Must I snuff
  your perjured life, my own son's life, and stain
  a thousand glories? Let the gods restrain
  my fury! Fly! live hated and alone—
  there are places where my name may be unknown.
  Go, find them, follow your disastrous star
  through filth; if I discover where you are,

I'll add another body to the hill
of vermin I've extinguished by my skill.
Fly from me, let the grieving storm-winds bear
your contagion from me. You corrupt the air.
I call upon Poseidon. Help me, Lord
of Ocean, help your servant! Once my sword
heaped crucified assassins on your shore
and let them burn like beacons. God, you swore
my first request would be fulfilled. My first!
I never made it. Even through the worst
torments of Epirus I held my peace;
no threat or torture brought me to my knees
beseeching favors; even then I knew
some greater project was reserved for you!
Poseidon, now I kneel. Avenge me, dash
my incestuous son against your rocks, and wash
his dishonor from my household; wave on wave
of roaring nothingness shall be his grave.

HIPPOLYTUS. Phaedra accuses me of lawless love!
Phaedra! My heart stops, I can hardly move
my lips and answer. I have no defense,
if you condemn me without evidence.

THESEUS. Oh coward, you were counting on the Queen
to hide your brutal insolence and screen
your outrage with her weakness! You forgot
something. You dropped your sword and spoiled your plot.
You should have kept it. Surely you had time
to kill the only witness to your crime!

HIPPOLYTUS. Why do I stand this, and forbear to clear
away these lies, and let the truth appear?
I could so easily. Where would you be,
if I spoke out? Respect my loyalty,
Father, respect your own intelligence.
Examine me. What am I? My defense
is my whole life. When have I wavered, when
have I pursued the vices of young men?
Father, you have no scaffolding to rig
your charges on. Small crimes precede the big.
Phaedra accused me of attempting rape!

Am I some Proteus, who can change his shape?
Nature despises such disparities.
Vice, like virtue, advances by degrees.
Bred by Antiope to manly arms,
I hate the fever of this lust that warms
the loins and rots the spirit. I was taught
uprightness by Theramenes. I fought
with wolves, tamed horses, gave my soul to sport,
and shunned the joys of women and the court.
I dislike praise, but those who know me best
grant me one virtue—it's that I detest
the very crimes of which I am accused.
How often you yourself have been amused
and puzzled by my love of purity,
pushed to the point of crudeness. By the sea
and in the forests, I have filled my heart
with freedom, far from women.

THESEUS.                              When this part
was dropped, could only Phaedra violate
the cold abyss of your immaculate
reptilian soul? How could this funeral urn
contain a heart, a living heart, or burn
for any woman but my wife?

HIPPOLYTUS.                              Ah no!
Father, I too have seen my passions blow
into a tempest. Why should I conceal
my true offense? I feel, Father, I feel
what other young men feel. I love, I love
Aricia. Father, I love the sister of
your worst enemies. I worship her!
I only feel and breathe and live for her!

THESEUS. You love Aricia? God! No, this is meant
to blind my eyes and throw me off the scent.

HIPPOLYTUS. Father, for six months I have done my worst
to kill this passion. You shall be the first
to know . . . You frown still. Nothing can remove
your dark obsession. Father, what will prove
my innocence? I swear by earth and sky,
and nature's solemn, shining majesty. . . .

THESEUS. Oaths and religion are the common cant
　　of all betrayers. If you wish to taunt
　　me, find a better prop than blasphemy.

HIPPOLYTUS. All's blasphemy to eyes that cannot see.
　　Could even Phaedra bear me such ill will?

THESEUS. Phaedra, Phaedra! Name her again, I'll kill
　　you! My hand's already on my sword.

HIPPOLYTUS.　　　　　　　　　　　　Explain
　　my terms of exile. What do you ordain?

THESEUS. Sail out across the ocean. Everywhere
　　on earth and under heaven is too near.

HIPPOLYTUS. Who'll take me in? Oh who will pity me,
　　and give me bread, if you abandon me?

THESEUS. You'll find fitting companions. Look for friends
　　who honor everything that most offends.
　　Pimps and jackals who praise adultery
　　and incest will protect your purity.

HIPPOLYTUS. Adultery! Is it your privilege
　　to fling this word in my teeth? I've reached the edge
　　of madness . . . No, I'll say no more. Compare
　　my breeding with Phaedra's. Think and beware . . .
　　She had a mother . . . No, I must not speak.

THESEUS. You devil, you'll attack the queen still weak
　　from your assault. How can you stand and face
　　your father? Must I drive you from this place
　　with my own hand? Run off, or I will flog
　　you with the flat of my sword like a dog!


*Scene 3*

THESEUS

THESEUS. You go to your inevitable fate,
　　Child—by the river immortals venerate.
　　Poseidon gave his word. You cannot fly;
　　death and the gods march on invisibly.

I loved you once; despite your perfidy,
my bowels writhe inside me. Must you die?
Yes; I am in too deep now to draw back.
What son has placed his father on such a rack?
What father groans for such a monstrous birth?
Oh gods, your thunder throws me to the earth.

### Scene 4

THESEUS, PHAEDRA

PHAEDRA. Theseus, I heard the deluge of your voice,
and stand here trembling. If there's time for choice,
hold back your hand, still bloodless; spare your race!
I supplicate you, here I kneel for grace.
Oh, Theseus, Theseus, will you drench the earth;
with your own blood? His virtue, youth and birth
cry out for him. Is he already slain
by you for me—spare me this incestuous pain!

THESEUS. Phaedra, my son's blood has not touched my hand;
and yet I'll be avenged. On sea and land,
spirits, the swift of foot, shall track him down.
Poseidon owes me this. Why do you frown?

PHAEDRA. Poseidon owes you this? What have you done
in anger?

THESEUS.   What! You wish to help my son?
No, stir my anger, back me to the hilt,
call for blacker colors to paint his guilt.
Lash, strike and drive me on! You cannot guess
the nerve and fury of his wickedness.
Phaedra, he slandered your sincerity,
he told me your accusation was a lie.
He swore he loved Aricia, he wants to wed
Aricia. . . .

PHAEDRA.     What, my lord?

THESEUS.                    That's what he said.
Of course, I scorn his shallow artifice.
Help me, Poseidon hear me, sacrifice
my son. I seek the altar. Come! Let us both
kneel down and beg the gods to keep their oath.


*Scene 5*

PHAEDRA

PHAEDRA. My husband's gone, still rumbling his own name
and fame. He has no inkling of the flame
his words have started. If he hadn't spoken,
I might . . . I was on my feet, I'd broken
loose from Oenone, and had just begun
to say I know not what to save his son.
Who knows how far I would have gone? Remorse,
longing and anguish shook me with such force,
I might have told the truth and suffered death,
before this revelation stopped my breath:
Hippolytus is not insensible,
only insensible to me! His dull
heart chases shadows. He is glad to rest
upon Aricia's adolescent breast!
Oh thin abstraction! When I saw his firm
repugnance spurn my passion like a worm,
I thought he had some magic to withstand
the lure of any woman in the land,
and now I see a schoolgirl leads the boy,
as simply as her puppy or a toy.
Was I about to perish for this sham,
this panting hypocrite? Perhaps I am
the only woman that he could refuse!

## Scene 6

### PHAEDRA, OENONE

PHAEDRA. Oenone, dearest, have you heard the news?

OENONE. No, I know nothing, but I am afraid.
How can I follow you? You have betrayed
your life and children. What have you revealed,
Madam?

PHAEDRA.   I have a rival in the field,
Oenone.

OENONE.   What?

PHAEDRA.          Oenone, he's in love—
this howling monster, able to disprove
my beauty, mock my passion, scorn each prayer,
and face me like a tiger in its lair—
he's tamed, the beast is harnessed to a cart;
Aricia's found an entrance to his heart.

OENONE. Aricia?

PHAEDRA.          Nurse, my last calamity
has come. This is the bottom of the sea.
All that preceded this had little force—
the flames of lust, the horrors of remorse,
the prim refusal by my grim young master,
were only feeble hints of this disaster.
They love each other! Passion blinded me.
I let them blind me, let them meet and see
each other freely! Was such bounty wrong?
Oenone, you have known this all along,
you must have seen their meetings, watched them sneak
off to their forest, playing hide-and-seek!
Alas, such rendezvous are no offence:
innocent nature smiles on innocence,
for them each natural impulse was allowed,
each day was summer and without a cloud.
Oenone, nature hated me. I fled

its light, as if a price were on my head.
I shut my eyes and hungered for my end.
Death was the only God my vows could bend.
And even while my desolation served
me gall and tears, I knew I was observed;
I never had security or leisure
for honest weeping, but must steal this pleasure.
Oh hideous pomp; a monarch only wears
the robes of majesty to hide her tears!

OENONE. How can their folly help them? They will never
enjoy its fruit.

PHAEDRA.              Ugh, they will love forever—
even while I am talking, they embrace,
they scorn me, they are laughing in my face!
In the teeth of exile, I hear them swear
they will be true forever, everywhere.
Oenone, have pity on my jealous rage;
I'll kill this happiness that jeers at age.
I'll summon Theseus; hate shall answer hate!
I'll drive my husband to annihilate
Aricia—let no trivial punishment,
her instant death, or bloodless banishment . . .
What am I saying? Have I lost my mind?
I am jealous, and call my husband! Bind
me, gag me; I am frothing with desire.
My husband is alive, and I'm on fire!
For whom? Hippolytus. When I have said
his name, blood fills my eyes, my heart stops dead.
Imposture, incest, murder! I have passed
the limits of damnation; now at last,
Aricia's lifeblood is my single food;
nothing else cools my murderous thirst for blood.
Yet I live on. I live looked down upon
by my progenitor, the sacred sun,
by Zeus, by Europa, by the universe
of gods and stars, my ancestors. They curse
their daughter. Let me die. In the great night
of Hades, I'll find shelter from their sight. /
What am I saying? I've no place to turn:

Minos, my father, holds the judge's urn.
The gods have placed damnation in his hands,
the shades in Hades follow his commands.
Will he not shake and curse his fatal star
that brings his daughter trembling to his bar?
His child by Pasiphaë forced to tell
a thousand sins unclassified in hell?
Father, when you interpret what I speak,
I fear your fortitude will be too weak
to hold the urn. I see you fumbling for
new punishments for crimes unknown before.
You'll be your own child's executioner!
You cannot kill me; look, my murderer
is Venus, who destroyed our family;
Father, she has already murdered me.
I killed myself—and what is worse I wasted
my life for pleasure I have never tasted.
My love flees me still, and my last gasp,
is for the fleeting flesh I failed to clasp.

OENONE. Madam, Madam, cast off this groundless terror!
Is love now an unprecedented error?
You love! What then? You love! Accept your fate.
You're not the first to sail into this strait.
Will chaos overturn the earth and Jove,
because a mortal woman is in love?
Such accidents are easy, all too common.
A woman must submit to being woman.
You curse a failure in the source of things.
Venus has feasted on the hearts of kings;
even the gods, man's judges, feel desire,
Zeus learned to live with his adulterous fire.

PHAEDRA. Must I still listen, and drink your poisoned breath?
My death redoubled on the edge of death—
I'd fled Hippolytus and I was free
till your entreaties stabbed and blinded me,
and dragged me howling to the pit of lust.
Oenone, I was learning to be just.
You fed my malice. Attacking the young Prince
was not enough; you clothed him with my sins.

You wished to kill him; he is dying now,
because of you, and Theseus' brutal vow.
You watch my torture; I'm the last ungorged
scrap rotting in this trap your plots have forged.
What binds you to me? Leave me, go, and die,
may your punishment be to terrify
all those who ruin princes by their lies,
hints, acquiescence, filth, and blasphemies—
panders who grease the grooves of inclination,
and lure our willing bodies from salvation.
Go die, go frighten false flatterers, the worst
friends the gods can give to kings they've cursed!

OENONE, *alone*. I have given all and left all for her service,
almighty Gods! I have been paid my price!

# ACT V

## Scene 1

### HIPPOLYTUS, ARICIA

ARICIA. Take a stand, speak the truth, if you respect
  your father's glory and your life. Protect
  yourself! I'm nothing to you. You consent
  without a struggle to your banishment.
  If you are weary of Aricia, go;
  at least do something to prevent the blow
  that dooms your honor and existence—both
  at a stroke! Your father must recall his oath;
  there is time still, but if the truth's concealed,
  you offer your accuser a free field.
  Speak to your father!

HIPPOLYTUS.                  I've already said
  what's lawful. Shall I point to his soiled bed,
  tell Athens how his marriage was foresworn,
  make Theseus curse the day that he was born?
  My aching heart recoils. I only want
  God and Aricia for my confidants.
  See how I love you; love makes me confide
  in you this horror I have tried to hide
  from my own heart. My faith must not be broken;
  forget, if possible, what I have spoken.
  Ah Princess, if even a whisper slips
  past you, it will perjure your pure lips.
  God's justice is committed to the cause
  of those who love him, and uphold his laws;
  sooner or later, heaven itself will rise
  in wrath and punish Phaedra's blasphemies.
  I must not. If I rip away her mask,

I'll kill my father. Give me what I ask.
Do this! Then throw away your chains; it's right
for you to follow me, and share my flight.
Fly from this prison; here the vices seethe
and simmer, virtue has no air to breathe.
In the confusion of my exile, none
will even notice that Aricia's gone.
Banished and broken, Princess, I am still
a force in Greece. Your guards obey my will,
powerful intercessors wish us well:
our neighbors, Argos' citadel
is armed, and in Mycenae our allies
will shelter us, if lying Phaedra tries
to harry us from our paternal throne,
and steal our sacred titles for her son.
The gods are ours, they urge us to attack.
Why do you tremble, falter and hold back?
Your interests drive me to this sacrifice.
While I'm on fire, your blood has changed to ice.
Princess, is exile more than you can face?

ARICIA. Exile with you, my lord? What sweeter place
is under heaven? Standing at your side,
I'd let the universe and heaven slide.
You're my one love, my king, but can I hope
for peace and honor, Prince, if I elope
unmarried? This . . . I wasn't questioning
the decency of flying from the king.
Is he my father? Only an abject
spirit honors tyrants with respect.
You say you love me. Prince, I am afraid.

HIPPOLYTUS. Aricia, you shall never be betrayed;
accept me! Let our love be sanctified,
then flee from your oppressor as my bride.
Bear witness, oh you gods, our love released
by danger, needs no temple or a priest.
It's faith, not ceremonial, that saves.
Here at the city gates, among these graves
the resting places of my ancient line,
there stands a sacred temple and a shrine.

Here, where no mortal ever swore in vain,
here in these shadows, where eternal pain
is ready to engulf the perjurer;
here heaven's scepter quivers to confer
its final sanction; here, my Love, we'll kneel,
and pray the gods to consecrate and seal
our love. Zeus, the father of the world will stand
here as your father and bestow your hand.
Only the pure shall be our witnesses:
Hera, the guarantor of marriages,
Demeter and the virgin Artemis.

ARICIA. The King is coming. Fly. I'll stay and meet
his anger here and cover your retreat.
Hurry. Be off, send me some friend to guide
my timid footsteps, husband, to your side.


### Scene 2

#### THESEUS, ISMENE, ARICIA

THESEUS. Oh God, illuminate my troubled mind.
Show me the answer I have failed to find.
ARICIA. Go, Ismene, be ready to escape.


### Scene 3

#### THESEUS, ARICIA

THESEUS. Princess, you are disturbed. You twist your cape
and blush. The Prince was talking to you. Why
is he running?
ARICIA.          We've said our last goodbye,
my lord.

THESEUS.    I see the beauty of your eyes
  moves even my son, and you have gained a prize
  no woman hoped for.

ARICIA.                      He hasn't taken on
  your hatred for me, though he is your son.

THESEUS. I follow. I can hear the oaths he swore.
  He knelt, he wept. He has done this before
  and worse. You are deceived.

ARICIA.                          Deceived, my lord?

THESEUS. Princess, are you so rich? Can you afford
  to hunger for this lover that my queen
  rejected? Your betrayer loves my wife.

ARICIA. How can you bear to blacken his pure life?
  Is kingship only for the blind and strong,
  unable to distinguish right from wrong?
  What insolent prerogative obscures
  a light that shines in every eye but yours?
  You have betrayed him to his enemies.
  What more, my lord? Repent your blasphemies.
  Are you not fearful lest the gods so loathe
  and hate you they will gratify your oath?
  Fear God, my lord, fear God. How many times
  he grants men's wishes to expose their crimes.

THESEUS. Love blinds you, Princess, and beclouds your reason.
  Your outburst cannot cover up his treason.
  My trust's in witnesses that cannot lie.
  I have seen Phaedra's tears. She tried to die.

ARICIA. Take care, your highness. When your killing hand
  drove all the thieves and reptiles from the land,
  you missed one monster, one was left alive,
  one. . . . No, I must not name her, sire, or strive
  to save your helpless son; he wants to spare
  your reputation. Let me go. I dare
  not stay here. If I stayed I'd be too weak
  to keep my promise. I'd be forced to speak.

### Scene 4

**THESEUS**

THESEUS. What was she saying? I must try to reach
　　the meaning of her interrupted speech.
　　Is it a pitfall? A conspiracy?
　　Are they plotting together to torture me?
　　Why did I let the rash, wild girl depart?
　　What is this whisper crying in my heart?
　　A secret pity fills my soul with pain.
　　I must question Oenone once again.
　　My guards, summon Oenone to the throne.
　　Quick, bring her. I must talk with her alone.

### Scene 5

**THESEUS, PANOPE**

PANOPE. The Queen's deranged, your highness. Some accursed
　　madness is driving her; some fury stalks
　　behind her back, possesses her, and talks
　　its evil through her, and blasphemes the world.
　　She cursed Oenone. Now Oenone's hurled
　　herself into the ocean, Sire, and drowned.
　　Why did she do it? No reason can be found.
THESEUS. Oenone's drowned?
PANOPE.　　　　　　　　　　Her death has brought no peace.
　　The cries of Phaedra's troubled soul increase.
　　Now driven by some sinister unrest,
　　she snatches up her children to her breast,
　　pets them and weeps, till something makes her scoff
　　at her affection, and she drives them off.
　　Her glance is drunken and irregular,

she looks through us and wonders who we are;
thrice she has started letters to you, Sire,
thrice tossed the shredded fragments in the fire.
Oh call her to you. Help her!

THESEUS. The nurse is drowned? Phaedra wishes to die?
Oh gods! Summon my son. Let him defend
himself, tell him I'm ready to attend.
I want him!

*Exit* PANOPE.

        Neptune, hear me, spare my son!
My vengeance was too hastily begun.
Oh why was I so eager to believe
Oenone's accusation? The gods deceive
the victims they are ready to destroy!

## Scene 6

### THESEUS, THERAMENES

THESEUS. Here is Theramenes. Where is my boy,
my first-born? He was yours to guard and keep.
Where is he? Answer me. What's this? You weep?

THERAMENES. Oh tardy, futile grief, his blood is shed.
My lord, your son, Hippolytus, is dead.

THESEUS. Oh gods have mercy!

THERAMENES.                I saw him die. The most
lovely and innocent of men is lost.

THESEUS. He's dead? The gods have hurried him away
and killed him? . . . just as I began to pray. . . .
What sudden thunderbolt has struck him down?

THERAMENES. We'd started out, and hardly left the town.
He held the reins; a few feet to his rear,
a single, silent guard held up a spear.
He followed the Mycenae highroad, deep
in thought, reins dangling, as if half asleep;

his famous horses, only he could hold,
trudged on with lowered heads, and sometimes rolled
their dull eyes slowly—they seemed to have caught
their master's melancholy, and aped his thought.
Then all at once winds struck us like a fist,
we heard a sudden roaring through the mist;
from underground a voice in agony
answered the prolonged groaning of the sea.
We shook, the horses' manes rose on their heads,
and now against a sky of blacks and reds,
we saw the flat waves hump into a mountain
of green-white water rising like a fountain,
as it reached land and crashed with a last roar
to shatter like a galley on the shore.
Out of its fragments rose a monster, half
dragon, half bull; a mouth that seemed to laugh
drooled venom on its dirty yellow scales
and python belly, forking to three tails.
The shore was shaken like a tuning fork,
ships bounced on the stung sea like bits of cork,
the earth moved, and the sun spun round and round,
a sulphur-colored venom swept the ground.
We fled; each felt his useless courage falter,
and sought asylum at a nearby altar.
Only the Prince remained; he wheeled about,
and hurled a javelin through the monster's snout.
Each kept advancing. Flung from the Prince's arm,
dart after dart struck where the blood was warm.
The monster in its death-throes felt defeat,
and bounded howling to the horses' feet.
There its stretched gullet and its armor broke,
and drenched the chariot with blood and smoke,
and then the horses, terror-struck, stampeded.
Their master's whip and shouting went unheeded,
they dragged his breathless body to the spray.
Their red mouths bit the bloody surf, men say
Poseidon stood beside them, that the god
was stabbing at their bellies with a goad.
Their terror drove them crashing on a cliff,
the chariot crashed in two, they ran as if

the Furies screamed and crackled in their manes,
their fallen hero tangled in the reins,
jounced on the rocks behind them. The sweet light
of heaven never will expunge this sight:
the horses that Hippolytus had tamed,
now dragged him headlong, and their mad hooves maimed
his face past recognition. When he tried
to call them, calling only terrified;
faster and ever faster moved their feet,
his body was a piece of bloody meat.
The cliffs and ocean trembled to our shout,
at last their panic failed, they turned about,
and stopped not far from where those hallowed graves,
the Prince's fathers, overlook the waves.
I ran on breathless, guards were at my back,
my master's blood had left a generous track.
The stones were red, each thistle in the mud
was stuck with bits of hair and skin and blood.
I came upon him, called; he stretched his right
hand to me, blinked his eyes, then closed them tight.
"I die," he whispered, "it's the gods' desire.
Friend, stand between Aricia and my sire—
some day enlightened, softened, disabused,
he will lament his son, falsely accused;
then when at last he wishes to appease
my soul, he'll treat my lover well, release
and honor Aricia. . . ." On this word, he died.
Only a broken body testified
he'd lived and loved once. On the sand now lies
something his father will not recognize.

THESEUS. My son, my son! Alas, I stand alone.
Before the gods. I never can atone.

THERAMENES. Meanwhile Aricia, rushing down the path,
approached us. She was fleeing from your wrath,
my lord, and wished to make Hippolytus
her husband in God's eyes. Then nearing us,
she saw the signs of struggle in the waste,
she saw (oh what a sight) her love defaced,
her young love lying lifeless on the sand.

At first she hardly seemed to understand;
while staring at the body in the grass,
she kept on asking where her lover was.
At last the black and fearful truth broke through
her desolation! She seemed to curse the blue
and murdering ocean, as she caught his head
up in her lap; then fainting lay half dead,
until Ismene somehow summoned back her breath,
restored the child to life—or rather death.
I come, great King, to urge my final task,
your dying son's last outcry was to ask
mercy for poor Aricia, for his bride.
Now Phaedra comes. She killed him. She has lied.

### Scene 7

PANOPE, THERAMENES, GUARDS
THESEUS, PHAEDRA, PANOPE, THERAMENES, GUARDS

THESEUS. Ah Phaedra, you have won. He's dead. A man
was killed. Were you watching? His horses ran
him down, and tore his body limb from limb.
Poseidon struck him, Theseus murdered him.
I served you! Tell me why Oenone died?
Was it to save you? Is her suicide
a proof of your truth? No, since he's dead, I must
accept your evidence, just or unjust.
I must believe my faith has been abused;
you have accused him; he shall stand accused.
He's friendless, even in the world below.
There the shades fear him! Am I forced to know
the truth? Truth cannot bring my son to life
if fathers murder, shall I kill my wife
too? Leave me, Phaedra. Far from you, exiled
from Greece, I will lament my murdered child.
I am a murdered gladiator, whirled
in black circles. I want to leave the world,
but my whole life rises to increase my guilt—

all those dazzled, dazzling eyes, my glory built
on killing killers. Less known, less magnified,
I might escape, and find a place to hide.
Stand back, Poseidon. I know the gods are hard
to please. I pleased you. This is my reward:
I killed my son. I killed him! Only a God
spares enemies, and wants his servants' blood!

PHAEDRA. No, Theseus, I must disobey your prayer.
Listen to me. I'm dying. I declare
Hippolytus was innocent.

THESEUS. Ah Phaedra, on your evidence, I sent
him to his death. Do you ask me to forgive
my son's assassin? Can I let you live?

PHAEDRA. My time's too short, your highness. It was I,
who lusted for your son with my hot eye.
The flames of Aphrodite maddened me;
I loathed myself, and yearned outrageously
like a starved wolf to fall upon the sheep.
I wished to hold him to me in my sleep
and dreamt I had him. Then Oenone's tears
troubled my mind; she played upon my fears,
until pleading forced me to declare
I loved your son. He scorned me. In despair,
I plotted with my nurse, and our conspiracy
made you believe your son assaulted me.
Oenone's punished; fleeing from my wrath,
she drowned herself, and found a too easy path
to death and hell. Perhaps you wonder why
I still survive her, and refuse to die?
Theseus, I stand before you to absolve
your noble son. Sire, only this resolve
upheld me, and made me throw down my knife.
I've chosen a slower way to end my life—
Medea's poison; chills already dart
along my boiling veins and squeeze my heart.
A cold composure I have never known
gives me a moment's poise. I stand alone
and seem to see my outraged husband fade
and waver into death's dissolving shade.

My eyes at last give up their light, and see
the day they've soiled resume its purity.

PANOPE. She's dead, my lord.

THESEUS.                          Would God, all memory
of her and me had died with her! Now I
must live. This knowledge that has come too late
must give me strength and help me expiate
my sacrilegious vow. Let's go, I'll pay
my son the honors he has earned today.
His father's tears shall mingle with his blood.
My love that did my son so little good
asks mercy from his spirit. I declare
Aricia is my daughter and my heir.

# FIGARO'S MARRIAGE

## or

## *One Mad Day*

### A COMEDY

BY

## BEAUMARCHAIS

*English Version by Jacques Barzun*

# CHARACTERS AND COSTUMING

COUNT ALMAVIVA (GOVERNOR OF ANDALUSIA) must be played with nobility of mien, but also with lightness and ease. The corruption of his heart must not diminish the perfect good form of his manners. In keeping with the morals *of those days,* the great regarded the conquest of women as a frolic. This role is an uncomfortable one in that its grandeur is invariably brought down and sacrificed to the other characters. But in the hands of a good actor, the role can bring out all the others and insure the success of the piece.

In the first and second acts the Count wears a hunting costume in the old Spanish style with half-length boots. In the remaining acts he wears a more gorgeous version of the same costume.

COUNTESS ALMAVIVA, who is moved by two opposite feelings, must show only a restrained tenderness and a moderate anger. Nothing must lower in the spectator's eyes her virtuous and lovable character. This role is one of the most difficult in the play.

The Countess's costume in the first, second, third, and fourth acts consists of a comfortable housecoat of straight and simple lines. She wears no ornament on her head. She is supposed to be indisposed and keeping to her room. In the fifth act she wears Suzanne's clothes and the high headdress that goes with them.

FIGARO (VALET TO THE COUNT AND STEWARD OF THE CASTLE). The actor who plays this role cannot be too strongly urged to study and make prevail at all times the true spirit of the character. If the actor finds in the part nothing but argumentativeness spiced with gaiety and wit; or even worse, if he allows himself any burlesquing, he will debase a role with which the greatest comedian can do himself honor by seizing upon its many nuances and sustaining the highest possibilities of its conception.

Figaro's clothes are the same as in *The Barber of Seville,* that is, the suit of a Spanish major-domo. On his hair he wears a net; his hat is white and has a colored ribbon around the crown. A silk scarf is loosely tied around his neck. His vest and breeches are of satin with buttons and buttonholes finished in silver. His silk sash is very broad, his garters tied with cord and tassels which hang down on the leg. His coat must be of a color contrasting with the vest, but the lapels match the latter. White stockings and gray shoes.

SUZANNE (CHIEF CHAMBERMAID TO THE COUNTESS). A clever girl, full of wit and laughter, but displaying nothing of the impudent frivolity of our corruptive chambermaids. In her role, though it is nearly the longest in the play, there is not a word that is not inspired by goodness and devotion to her duty. The only trickery she allows herself is in behalf of her mistress, who relies on Suzanne's attachment and who has herself none but honorable thoughts.

Suzanne's costume in the first four acts is a tight bodice with flounced skirt, elegant though modeled on the peasant style. Her hat is a high toque (later called in France *à la Suzanne*). In the festivities of Act IV, the Count places on her head a white toque adorned with a long veil, tall feathers, and ribbons. In Act V she wears the Countess's housecoat and nothing on her head.

MARCELINE (HOUSEKEEPER OF THE CASTLE) is an intelligent woman with lively instincts whose experiences and mistakes have amended her character. If the actress who plays the role can rise with a certain judicious pride to the high morality that follows the recognition scene in Act III, it will add greatly to the interest of the play.

Her costume is that of the Spanish duenna, modest in color, a black bonnet on the head.

ANTONIO (A GARDENER, UNCLE OF SUZANNE AND FATHER OF FANCHETTE) must display only a half-tipsy condition, which gradually wears off, so that by Act V it is almost unnoticeable.

His clothes are those of a Spanish peasant; the sleeves hang down behind; a hat and white shoes.

FANCHETTE (THE DAUGHTER OF ANTONIO) is a girl of twelve and very naïve. Her costume has a tight-fitting bodice, peasant style, brown with silver buttons. The skirt is of contrasting color. She wears a black toque with feathers. The other girls in the wedding party are dressed like her.

CHERUBINO (CHIEF PAGE TO THE COUNT). This role cannot be properly played except by a young and very pretty woman. There is no young man on our stage who is sufficiently educated to feel the subtleties of the part. Excessively shy before the Countess, he is elsewhere a charmingly naughty boy. A vague restless desire is at the root of his character. He is rushing headlong through adolescence, but aimlessly and without worldly knowledge; he is the plaything of each passing event. In short, he is probably what every mother would like her son to be, even when she knows she will suffer for it.

In the first and second acts, Cherubino's costume is the rich court dress of a Spanish page, white trimmed with silver lace. He wears a light blue cloak off the shoulder and a hat with large plumes. In Act IV, he wears the bodice, skirt, and toque of the peasant girls; in Act V, an officer's uniform, a sword, and a cockade.

BARTHOLO (A DOCTOR FROM SEVILLE). His character and costume are the same as in *The Barber of Seville*, that is, a short black gown, buttoned up to the neck, and a large wig. The collar and cuffs are turned back and the belt is black. Outdoors he wears a long scarlet coat. In the present play, his role is secondary.

BASIL (THE COUNTESS'S MUSIC MASTER). Also secondary, Basil's character and costume are the same as in *The Barber*, which is to say: a black hat with hanging brim, a gown like a cassock, and a long coat without turned-up collar or cuffs.

DON GUZMAN BRIDLEGOOSE (ASSOCIATE JUSTICE OF THE DISTRICT). He must have the open and easy self-assurance of an animal that has overcome its shyness. His stammer is only an additional charm, scarcely noticeable though it is. The performer would make a grave mistake to stress the ludicrous in this part, for the principle of it is the natural contrast between the solemnity of his office and the absurdity of his person. Therefore the less the actor burlesques the man, the more truly will the character appear and the actor's talent shine.

The costume is the robe of a Spanish judge, but less full than that of our state's attorneys—it is almost a cassock. He wears a great wig and a neckband Spanish style, and he carries a long white wand.

DOUBLEFIST (CLERK AND SECRETARY TO BRIDLEGOOSE). He is dressed like the justice, but carries a shorter wand.

THE BEADLE, or ALGUAZIL, wears a coat and carries at his side a sword with a leather guard, but without a leather belt. Not boots but shoes, which are black. A white curly wig and a short white wand.

SUNSTRUCK (A YOUNG SHEPHERD) wears peasant clothes, sleeves hanging down, bright colored coat, white hat.

A YOUNG SHEPHERDESS—dressed like Fanchette.

PETER (THE COUNT'S POSTILION). Short belted coat over a vest, a courier's boots, hat and whip, a net over his hair.

WALK-ON PARTS (VALETS AND PEASANTS). Some in judge's costume, others dressed as peasants, the rest in livery.

# ACT I

*The scene is a half-furnished room. An invalid chair is in the middle.* FIGARO *is measuring the floor with a yardstick.* SUZANNE, *in front of a mirror, is fixing in her hair the sprig of orange blossoms commonly called "the bride's bonnet."*

FIGARO. Nineteen feet by twenty-six.

SUZANNE. Look, Figaro—my bonnet. Do you like it better now?

FIGARO, *taking both her hands in his.* Infinitely better, my sweet. My, what that bunch of flowers—so pretty, so virginal, so suited to the head of a lovely girl—does to a lover on the morning of his wedding!

SUZANNE, *leaving.* What are you measuring there, my lad?

FIGARO. I am finding out, dear Suzy, whether the beautiful big bed that his lordship is giving us will fit into this room.

SUZANNE. *This* room?

FIGARO. He's letting us have it.

SUZANNE. But I don't want it.

FIGARO. Why not?

SUZANNE. I don't want it.

FIGARO. But tell me why.

SUZANNE. I don't like it.

FIGARO. You might give a reason.

SUZANNE. And supposing I don't?

FIGARO. Women! As soon as they have us tied down—

SUZANNE. To give a reason would imply that I might be unreasonable. Are you with me or against me?

FIGARO. You are turning down the most convenient room in the castle. It connects with both suites. At night, if my lady is unwell and wants you, she rings—and crack! there you are

in two hops. Is it something that my lord requires? A tinkle
from his side, and zing! I am at the ready in three strides.

SUZANNE. Right enough! But when he's tinkled in the morning
and given you a good long errand, zing! in three strides he
is at my door, and crack! in two hops he—

FIGARO. What do you mean by those words?

SUZANNE. You'd better listen to me carefully.

FIGARO. What the devil is going on?

SUZANNE. What is going on is that his lordship Count Almaviva
is tired of pursuing the beauties of the neighborhood and
is heading for home—not to *his* wife, you understand, but
to yours. *She* is the one he has his eye on, and he hopes
this apartment will favor his plans. And that is what the
faithful Basil, the trusted agent of the Count's pleasures, and
my noble singing master as well, tells me every day during
my lesson.

FIGARO. Basil, my boy, if ever the application of green birch
to an ailing back has helped to correct curvature of the
spine, I will—

SUZANNE. So in your innocence you thought that this dowry
the Count is giving me was for your beaux yeux and your
high merit?

FIGARO. I've done enough to hope it was.

SUZANNE. How stupid bright people are!

FIGARO. So they say.

SUZANNE. But *they* won't believe it!

FIGARO. *They* are wrong.

SUZANNE. Get it into your head that the dowry is to get from
me, privately, a certain privilege which formerly was the
right of the lord of the manor—you know what a grievous
right it was.*

FIGARO. I know it so well that if the Count had not abolished
its shameful exercise when he himself was married, I should
never have planned to marry you on his lands.

---

* This supposed right to enjoy the bride on the wedding night of
any vassal is without foundation in law or history, but was widely
believed by the anti-medieval writers.

SUZANNE. He abolished it right enough, but he has had second thoughts. And he's thinking your fiancée is the one to restore it to him.

FIGARO, *rubbing his forehead.* My head grows mushy with surprise and my sprouting forehead—*

SUZANNE. Please don't rub it.

FIGARO. What's the harm?

SUZANNE. If you brought on a little pimple, superstitious people might—

FIGARO. You're laughing at me, you slut. Now if I could think of some way to catch out this professional deceiver, turn the tables on him and pocket his money—

SUZANNE. Plotting and pocketing—you're in your element.

FIGARO. It certainly isn't shame that holds me back.

SUZANNE. Fear, then?

FIGARO. It's no great feat to start on a dangerous undertaking; the thing is to succeed and avoid trouble. Any knavish fool can go into a man's house at night, enjoy his wife, and get a beating for his pains—nothing is easier. But—

*A bell rings.*

SUZANNE. My lady is awake. She wanted me to be sure and be the first to talk to her this morning about the wedding.

FIGARO. Some more goings on?

SUZANNE. The almanac says it brings good luck to forsaken wives. Good-by, Fi-fi-garo darling; think about ways and means.

FIGARO. To prime my brains give a little kiss.

SUZANNE. To a lover, today? No, sir! What would my husband say tomorrow?

FIGARO *kisses her.*

SUZANNE. Now, now!

FIGARO. You don't know how much I love you.

SUZANNE, *adjusting her dress.* When will you learn not to bore me with it from morning till night?

---

* The play contains several allusions to the horns of the cuckold, expressed by references to his forehead.

FIGARO, *as if telling a secret*. Why, when I can prove it to you from night till morning.

*The bell rings again.*

SUZANNE, *blowing him a kiss from the door*. There's your kiss, sir, I have nothing else of yours to return.

FIGARO, *running after her*. But you didn't receive mine across the void like this.

*Exit* SUZANNE.

FIGARO, *alone*. What a ravishing girl! Always gay, laughing, full of sap, wit, love, joy—and how well behaved!

*He walks about briskly, rubbing his hands.*

Ah, my lord, my dear lord! You want to give me—something to remember? I was wondering, too, why I am first made Steward, and then supposed to become part of the embassy and serve as King's Messenger. Now I understand, Your Excellency: three promotions at one stroke—you as envoy plenipotentiary; myself as political lightning rod; and Suzy as lady in residence, as private ambassadress—and then, Sir Messenger, be off! While I gallop in one direction, you will drive my girl a long way in the other. While I wade through mud and break my neck for the glory of your family, you will collaborate in the increase of mine. What sweet reciprocity! But, my lord, there is excess in this. To carry on in London the business at once of the King your master and of your humble servant, to represent in a foreign court both him and me—that is too much by half, much too much. As for you, Basil, my pretty scoundrel, I will teach you to limp with the halt and the lame. I will—no! We must play up to both of them if we are to knock their heads together. Now, Figaro, concentrate on today. First, move ahead the time for the wedding, so as to make sure the knot is tied; then distract old Marceline, who is too fond of you; pick up whatever money and gifts there may be; mislead the Count and his little appetites; give a sound drubbing to Mister Basil, and—well, well, well, here is the fat doctor! The party is complete.

*Enter* BARTHOLO *and* MARCELINE.

Good morning, dear doctor of my heart. Is it my wedding with Suzy that brings you to the house?

BARTHOLO, *disdainful*. Not at all, my dear sir.

FIGARO. It would indeed be a generous act.

BARTHOLO. Exactly, and therefore inconceivably stupid.

FIGARO. It was my bad luck that I had to thwart your designs.*

BARTHOLO. Haven't you anything else to say?

FIGARO. Perhaps your mule hasn't been looked after?*

BARTHOLO, *furious*. Confounded babbler, leave us alone!

FIGARO. You are angry, Doctor? Yours is a cruel profession: no more kindness to animals than if they were men. Farewell, Marceline, are you still thinking of suing me at law? "Though thou love not, must thou therefore hate?"† I put it to the doctor.

BARTHOLO. What is all this about?

FIGARO, *leaving*. She will tell you.

*Exit.*

BARTHOLO, *looking at the departing* FIGARO. That fellow never improves. If someone doesn't flog him alive he will die inside the skin of the most conceited ass I know.

MARCELINE, *attracting his attention*. Well, here you are at last, Doctor Ubiquitous, you—always so grave and respectable that one could die waiting for your help, just as some time back someone got married despite your efforts.*

BARTHOLO. And you—always bitter and provoking. But why am I needed here so urgently? Has the Count met with an accident?

MARCELINE. No, Doctor.

BARTHOLO. And Rosine, his conspiring countess, could she be —God be praised—ailing?

MARCELINE. She is pining away.

BARTHOLO. What about?

MARCELINE. Her husband neglects her.

* An allusion to the events of *The Barber of Seville*, in which Figaro helped the Count to marry Rosine, the ward of Bartholo, who had himself planned to marry her. Rosine is now Countess Almaviva.

† A line from Voltaire's *Nanine*.

BARTHOLO, *with great satisfaction*. Ah, worthy husband, my avenger!

MARCELINE. It is hard to make out the Count: at once jealous and a philanderer.

BARTHOLO. A philanderer from boredom and jealous from vanity—it's clear as day.

MARCELINE. Today, for example, he is marrying off our Suzanne to Figaro, on whom he lavishes gifts in honor of this union . . .

BARTHOLO. Which His Excellency has made necessary?

MARCELINE. Not quite; but which His Excellency would like to celebrate in secret with the bride . . .

BARTHOLO. Of Mister Figaro? That's an arrangement the latter is surely willing to enter into.

MARCELINE. Basil is sure it is not so.

BARTHOLO. That other lout lives here too? It's a regular den. What does he do?

MARCELINE. All the evil he can. The worst is the hopeless passion he has so long nursed for me.

BARTHOLO. In your place I should have disposed of that for good.

MARCELINE. How?

BARTHOLO. By marrying him.

MARCELINE. Tiresome, brutish wit! Why don't you dispose of mine in the same way? You're in honor-bound: remember all your promises—and also our little Emmanuel, offspring of a forgotten love, who was to lead us to the altar.

BARTHOLO. Was it to listen to this rigmarole that you had me come from Seville? . . . What is this fit of marrying you've suddenly fallen into?

MARCELINE. We'll say no more about it. But at least help me marry someone else.

BARTHOLO. Gladly. But what mortal, bereft of heaven and women's favors, would . . .

MARCELINE. Now, who *could* it be, Doctor, but the gay, handsome, lovable Figaro!

BARTHOLO. That good-for-nothing?

MARCELINE. Never cross, always good-humored, always ready to enjoy the passing moment, worrying as little about the future as about the past—attractive, generous, oh generous! . . .

BARTHOLO. . . . as a scamp . . .

MARCELINE. . . . as a lord. Delightful, in short. But he is a monster too.

BARTHOLO. What about his Suzanne?

MARCELINE. She'd never get him, clever as she is, if you would help me, dear Doctor, and hold him to a promissory note of his that I have.

BARTHOLO. On his wedding day?

MARCELINE. Weddings have gone farther than this and been broken off. If I didn't mind giving away a feminine secret—

BARTHOLO. There aren't any secrets for a physician.

MARCELINE. You know very well I have no secrets from you. Well, our sex is ardent but shy. A certain attraction may draw us toward pleasure, yet the most adventurous woman will say to herself—"be beautiful if you can, sensible if you will, but stay respectable: you must!" Now since every woman knows what reputation is worth, we can scare off Suzanne by threatening to expose the offers that are being made to her.

BARTHOLO. What will that accomplish?

MARCELINE. Just this: ashamed and apprehensive, she will keep on refusing the Count. He, from spite, will support my opposition to her marriage, and hence mine will become a certainty.

BARTHOLO. She's right, by God! It's an excellent trick to marry off my old housekeeper to the scoundrel who pinched my young protégée . . .

MARCELINE, *quickly.* . . . the man who plans to serve his pleasure and disappoint my hopes . . .

BARTHOLO. . . . the man who once upon a time swindled me out of a hundred pounds that I haven't forgotten.

MARCELINE. Ah, what bliss!—

BARTHOLO. To punish a swindler!—

MARCELINE. To marry him, Doctor, to marry him!

*Enter* SUZANNE.

SUZANNE, *holding a bonnet with large ribbons and a woman's dress over her arm.* To marry? To marry whom? My Figaro?

MARCELINE, *sourly.* Why not? Aren't you thinking of it yourself?

BARTHOLO, *laughing.* An angry woman's typical argument! We were speaking, Suzanne my dear, of his happiness in possessing you.

MARCELINE. To say nothing of my lord besides.

SUZANNE, *with a curtsy.* Your servant, madam. There is always a touch of gall in your remarks.

MARCELINE, *curtsying.* Your servant as well, madam. Where is the gall? Isn't it justice that a freehanded nobleman should share a little in the good things he procures for his people?

SUZANNE. He procures?

MARCELINE. Yes, madam.

SUZANNE. Fortunately, your jealousy is as well known as your claims on Figaro are slight.

MARCELINE. They could have been strengthened by the same means that you chose to use.

SUZANNE. But those means, madam, are open only to learned ladies.

MARCELINE. And this poor child is all innocence—like an old judge!

BARTHOLO, *pulling* MARCELINE *away.* Good-by, little bride of Figaro!

MARCELINE, *curtsying.* Also promised to the Count.

SUZANNE, *curtsying.* She gives you best regards, madam.

MARCELINE, *curtsying.* Will she also love me a little, madam?

SUZANNE, *curtsying.* As to that, pray have no fears.

MARCELINE, *curtsying.* Madam is as kind as she is pretty.

SUZANNE, *curtsying.* Enough, perhaps, to disconcert madam.

MARCELINE, *curtsying.* And above all, respectable.

SUZANNE, *curtsying.* That's a monopoly of dowagers.

MARCELINE, *outraged.* Dowagers, dowagers!

BARTHOLO, *interrupting her.* Marceline!

MARCELINE. Let's go, Doctor, or I shan't be able to restrain myself. Good-by, madam.

*She curtsies.*

*Exeunt.*

SUZANNE. Go, madam; go, pedant. I am as little afraid of your plots as I am of your insults. Look at the old sibyl! Because she has a little learning and used it to torment my lady in her youth, she wants to rule the castle.

*Throws the dress from her arm to a chair.*

I've forgotten what I came for.

*Enter* CHERUBINO.

CHERUBINO, *running in.* Suzy, I've been waiting two hours to catch you alone. I'm miserable: you're getting married and I'm going away.

SUZANNE. How does my getting married cause the departure of his lordship's favorite page?

CHERUBINO, *piteously.* Suzanne: he's dismissed me!

SUZANNE, *mimicking him.* Cherubino: what nonsense!

CHERUBINO. He found me yesterday at your cousin's, at Fanchette's. I was rehearsing her ingénue part in tonight's show and he flew into a rage on seeing me. "Get out," he said, "you little—" I don't dare repeat the bad word he used. "Get out! Tonight is your last night in this house!" If my lady, my dear godmother, doesn't calm him down about this, it's all over with me, Suzy; I'll never lay eyes on you again.

SUZANNE. On *me?* It's my turn, is it? So you don't go sighing around my lady any more?

CHERUBINO. Oh, Suzy. She is beautiful, majestic, but so—imposing!

SUZANNE. That is to say, I am not and you can take liberties.

CHERUBINO. You're mean! You know perfectly well I never dare take anything. How lucky you are, seeing her all the time, talking to her, dressing her in the morning, undressing her at night, unpinning each pin— Oh, Suzy, I'd give anything— What's that in your hand?

SUZANNE, *mockingly*. It's the blissful bonnet and the fortunate ribbon which enclose, at night, the hair of your beautiful godmother . . .

CHERUBINO. Her ribbon—at night! Give it to me, be a dear, my love.

SUZANNE, *pulling it away*. Not so fast. "His love!" What familiarity! If you weren't just a whippersnapper—

CHERUBINO *seizes the ribbon*.

Oh, the ribbon!

CHERUBINO, *going behind and around the invalid chair*. You can say you mislaid it, ruined it, lost it. Say anything you like.

SUZANNE *chases after him around the chair*. I promise you that in three or four years you will be the biggest little miscreant on earth! Give me back that ribbon.

*She snatches at it.*

CHERUBINO, *drawing a paper from his pocket*. Let me, do let me have it, Suzy. I'll give you my song here, and while the memory of my beautiful mistress will sadden all my days, the thought of you will bring me the only ray of joy that could lighten my heart.

SUZANNE *tears the song out of his grasp*. "Lighten his heart!" The little scoundrel! Do you think you are talking to your Fanchette? My lord finds you with her; you breathe vows in secret to my lady; and on top of that you make me declarations to my face!

CHERUBINO, *excited*. It's true, on my honor! I don't know who I am or what I'm doing, but just lately, at the mere sight of a woman I've felt my breath come in gasps and my heart beat fast. The words "love" and "bliss" arouse and upset me. In short, the need to say to someone "I love you" has become so compelling that I say it to myself when I cross the park, I say it to our lady and to you, to the clouds and the wind that carries my useless words away. Yesterday I ran into Marceline—

SUZANNE, *laughing*. Ahahaha!

CHERUBINO. Why not? She's a woman! She's a maid! A maid! A woman! Oh, what sweet words are those—and how interesting!

SUZANNE. He is losing his mind.

CHERUBINO. Fanchette is very sweet: at least she listens to me and you don't.

SUZANNE. What a pity! Let us listen to the gentleman.

*She snatches again at the ribbon.*

CHERUBINO *turns and runs.* Not on your life! No one can take it, you see, except with *my* life. But if the price does not suit you, I'll increase it by a thousand kisses.

*He starts chasing her around the chair.*

SUZANNE, *turning on him as she flees.* A thousand slaps in the face if you come near me. I'll complain to my lady, and far from interceding for you I'll go to my lord and say: "Send back that petty thief to his parents. He is a good-for-nothing who puts on airs about being in love with Madam, and on the rebound tries to kiss me."

CHERUBINO *sees the* COUNT *entering and hides behind the armchair.* That's the end of me!

SUZANNE. Coward!

*Intercepts the* COUNT *and helps to conceal the* PAGE.

COUNT, *coming forward.* You are upset, Suzette, you were talking to yourself. Your little heart seems to me full of agitation—understandably enough on a day like this.

SUZANNE, *embarrassed.* My lord, what do you want with me? If someone saw us . . .

COUNT. I should hate to be surprised here. But you know the interest I take in you. Basil must have told you I love you. I have only a moment to tell you so myself. Listen—

*He sits in the armchair.*

SUZANNE. I will not listen.

COUNT, *taking her hand.* Just one word. You know the King has made me ambassador to London. I am taking Figaro with me, giving him an excellent post. Now since it is a wife's duty to follow her husband—

SUZANNE. Oh, if I had the courage to speak—

COUNT, *drawing her to him.* Don't hesitate, speak, my dear. Assume a privilege which you may use with me for life.

SUZANNE, *frightened.* I don't want to, my lord, I don't want to. Please leave me.

COUNT. But first tell me.

SUZANNE, *angrily.* I don't know what I was saying.

COUNT. Something about a wife's duty.

SUZANNE. Very well. When you, my lord, eloped with your lady from the Doctor's house and married her for love, and when in her honor you abolished that dreadful right of the lord of the manor—

COUNT. Which annoyed the girls so much, no doubt! Look, Suzette, it was a charming right and if you'll come and prattle with me about it this evening in the garden, I'll rate that little favor so high—

BASIL, *speaking from without.* My lord isn't in his room.

COUNT, *rising.* Whose voice is that?

SUZANNE. This is dreadful!

COUNT. Go out so that nobody comes in.

SUZANNE, *upset.* And leave you here?

BASIL, *from outside.* His lordship was with my lady, then he left; I'll go look for him.

COUNT. No spot where I can hide. Yes, behind that chair. It's not very good but—send him packing.

SUZANNE *bars his way; he gently pushes her; she retreats and thus comes between him and the* PAGE. *But while the* COUNT *stoops and takes* CHERUBINO'S *place, the latter throws himself kneeling on the seat and clings to the cushions.* SUZANNE *picks up the dress she formerly carried, drapes it over the* PAGE, *and takes her stand in front of the chair.*

BASIL, *entering.* Did you by any chance see the Count, miss?

SUZANNE, *brusquely.* How could I? Please go.

BASIL, *coming nearer.* If you only think a little you will see there was nothing surprising about my question. Figaro is looking for him.

SUZANNE. So he's looking for the man who is his worst enemy after yourself.

COUNT, *aside.* Let's see how he takes my part.

BASIL. Is it being a man's enemy to wish his wife well?

SUZANNE. Not in your book of rules, you vile corrupter.

BASIL. What does anyone ask of you that you aren't going to bestow on another? Thanks to a lovely ceremony, the things that were forbidden yesterday will be required tomorrow.

SUZANNE. Disgusting wretch!

BASIL. Marriage being the most comic of all serious things, I had thought—

SUZANNE, *outraged.* Contemptible thought! Who gave you leave to come in here!

BASIL. There, there, naughty girl. God grant you peace! You'll do just as you like. But don't go thinking that I regard Mister Figaro as an impediment to my lord—and if it weren't for the little page . . .

SUZANNE, *shyly.* Don Cherubino?

BASIL, *mimicking her. Cherubino di amore,* yes. He's always buzzing about you and this morning again was at this door when I left you: say it isn't true.

SUZANNE. What lies! Slanderer! Go away!

BASIL. A slanderer because I see things as they are. Isn't it also for you the page has a song he carries mysteriously about him?

SUZANNE, *angrily.* For me indeed!

BASIL. Unless he made it up for her ladyship. Truth to tell, when he serves at table, they say that he cannot take his eyes off her. But let him look out: my lord is a brute upon that point.

SUZANNE, *outraged.* And you are a scoundrel, going about spreading gossip and ruining a wretched child who is already in disgrace with his master.

BASIL. Did I make it up? I say these things because everybody says them.

COUNT, *rising.* Who, everybody?

SUZANNE. Heavens!

BASIL. Ha ha!

COUNT. Run along, Basil, and see that the boy is sent away.

BASIL. I am truly sorry that I came in here.

SUZANNE, *upset*. Oh dear, oh dear!

COUNT. She is faint, help her into the chair.

SUZANNE, *fending him off energetically*. I don't want to sit. To walk in here without leave is an outrage.

COUNT. But there are two of us with you, my dear. There's not the slightest danger.

BASIL. For my part, I deeply regret having made light of the page—since you overheard me. I was using it to ascertain her feelings, because essentially—

COUNT. Fifty pounds, a horse, and back to his parents.

BASIL. My lord, it was frivolous gossip.

COUNT. A young libertine whom I found only yesterday with the gardener's daughter.

BASIL. With Fanchette?

COUNT. In her room.

SUZANNE, *outraged*. Where my lord had business also?

COUNT, *cheerfully*. That's an idea!

BASIL. It is of good omen.

COUNT, *still cheerful*. Of course not. I was looking for your uncle Antonio, my drunken gardener, to give him some instructions. I knock. No one opens for quite a while. Your little cousin looks embarrassed. I grow suspicious while I talk to her and as I do so I cast an eye about. Behind the door there was a curtain of sorts, a wardrobe, something for old clothes. Without seeming to, I gently, slowly lift the curtain . . .

*He illustrates by lifting the dress off the armchair.*

And I see . . .

*He catches sight of* CHERUBINO.

. . . I say!

BASIL. Ha ha!

COUNT. This is as good as before.

BASIL. It's better.

COUNT, *to* SUZANNE. Congratulations, dear lady: hardly engaged to be married and yet able to manage such tricks!
Was it to entertain my page that you wished to be alone?
As for you, sir, whose behavior never varies, the only lack of
respect for your godmother you had so far overlooked was
to pay your addresses to her maid, who is the bride of your
friend. But I will not allow Figaro, a man I love and esteem,
to be the victim of this deception. Was he with you, Basil?

SUZANNE, *indignant.* There is no deception and no victim.

*Pointing.*

He was here while you were talking to me.

COUNT, *carried away.* I hope you lie when you say so. His
worst enemy could wish him nothing worse.

SUZANNE. He was asking me to beseech my lady to obtain his
pardon from you. Your coming in upset him so much that
he hid in the chair.

COUNT, *angrily.* Infernal cleverness! But I sat in that chair the
moment I arrived.

CHERUBINO. Alas, my lord, I was shaking in my shoes behind it.

COUNT. Another trick! I stood there myself just now.

CHERUBINO. Forgive me, but that is when I came around and
crouched inside.

COUNT. This young snake in the grass must be a—poisonous
adder: he heard what we said?

CHERUBINO. On the contrary, my lord, I did my best to hear
nothing at all.

COUNT. O treachery!

*To* SUZANNE.

You shan't marry Figaro!

BASIL. Moderation, if you please: someone's coming.

COUNT, *pulling* CHERUBINO *out of the armchair and setting him
on his feet.* He would stay there in front of the whole world!

*Enter* FIGARO, *the* COUNTESS, FANCHETTE, *with several footmen and country people dressed in white.*

FIGARO, *holding a woman's hat covered with white feathers
and ribbons and speaking to the* COUNTESS. Only you, my
lady, can obtain this favor for us.

COUNTESS. You hear him, Count? They imagine that I wield an influence I do not in fact possess. Still, as their request is not unreasonable—

COUNT, *embarrassed*. It would indeed have to be very much so—

FIGARO, *speaking low to* SUZANNE. Back up my attempt—

SUZANNE, *the same to* FIGARO. Which won't help any.

FIGARO, *in low voice*. Never mind, do it.

COUNT, *to* FIGARO. What is it you want?

FIGARO. My lord, your vassals, who are deeply touched by the abolition of a certain regrettable right that you gave up out of love for my lady—

COUNT. Well, the right *is* abolished; what are you getting at?

FIGARO. Only that it is high time the virtue of so good a master should be manifest. I myself stand to gain so much from it today that I want to be the first to glorify it at our wedding.

COUNT, *still more embarrassed*. You can't be serious. The abolition of a shameful right is only the payment of a debt to decency. A Spaniard may want to conquer beauty by devotion, but to be the first to exact the sweetest of rewards as if it were a servile due—why, that's the tyrannical violence of a Vandal, not the acknowledged right of a Castilian nobleman!

FIGARO, *holding* SUZANNE's *hand*. Then deign that this young creature, whose honor has been preserved by your noble reason, receive from your hand the virgin's coif of white feathers and ribbons as a symbol of the purity of your intentions. Have this ceremony become a custom at all weddings and let an appropriate chorus be sung each time to commemorate the event.

COUNT, *embarrassed*. If I did not know that to be a lover, a poet, and a musician excused every kind of folly—

FIGARO. Join with me, my friends.

ALL, *together*. My lord! My lord!

SUZANNE, *to the* COUNT. Why brush aside an honor you so much deserve?

COUNT, *aside*. Deceitful wench!

FIGARO. Look at her, my lord: no prettier face will ever signalize the extent of your sacrifice.

SUZANNE. Leave my face out of it and let us only praise his virtue.

COUNT, *aside*. The whole thing is a plot.

COUNTESS. I too join with them, Count, knowing as I do that this ceremony, ever to be cherished, owes its being to the gracious love you used to have for me.

COUNT. Which I still have, madam, and because of which I now yield.

ALL, *together*. Bravo!

COUNT, *aside*. I've been had.

*Aloud.*

In order to give the ceremony yet more splendor, I should like to see it postponed till somewhat later.

*Aside.*

Quick, let us get hold of Marceline!

FIGARO, *to* CHERUBINO. What about you, my lad, you don't applaud?

SUZANNE. He is in despair; his lordship is sending him home.

COUNTESS. Ah, my lord, I ask for his pardon.

COUNT. He doesn't deserve it.

COUNTESS. The poor boy is so young.

COUNT. Not so young as you think.

CHERUBINO, *trembling*. Clemency is not the lordly right you gave up when you married my lady.

COUNTESS. He only gave up the one that afflicted you all.

SUZANNE. If my lord had abandoned the right to pardon, it would surely be the first right he would want to restore in secret.

COUNT, *embarrassed*. Oh, quite.

COUNTESS. So what need to restore it?

CHERUBINO, *to the* COUNT. I was giddy in my actions, my lord, that is true. But there never was the least impropriety in my words.

COUNT, *embarrassed*. All right, that's enough.

FIGARO. What does he mean?

COUNT, *sharply*. Enough, enough! Everybody wants him pardoned: I so order it. I'll do more: I'll give him a company in my regiment.

ALL, *together*. Bravo!

COUNT. But on one condition—that he leave at once to join up in Catalonia.

FIGARO. Oh, my lord, make it tomorrow.

COUNT. I have given an order.

CHERUBINO. And I obey.

COUNT. Salute your godmother and entreat her protection.

CHERUBINO *kneels on one knee before the* COUNTESS, *unable to utter a word.*

COUNTESS, *much moved*. Since you cannot stay even for today, young man, go. New duties call you: fulfill them worthily. Honor your benefactor. Remember this house where your youth was so leniently treated. Be upright, obedient, and brave. We shall all share in the pleasure of your success.

CHERUBINO *gets up and goes back to where he stood before.*

COUNT. You seem deeply moved, madam.

COUNTESS. I do not apologize for it. Who knows what fate is in store for a child thrown into such a dangerous career? He is related to my family, as well as being my godson.

COUNT, *aside*. Basil was evidently right.

*Aloud.*

Young man, give a kiss to Suzanne, for the last time.

FIGARO. Why the last, my lord? He'll come and spend the winters with us. Give me a kiss too, captain.

*They embrace.*

Good-by, Cherubino. You are going to lead a very different life, my child. Thus: no more hanging about the women's quarters the livelong day, no more sweet drinks and pastries, no more blindman's buff and spinning the bottle. Just veteran soldiers, by God, weather-beaten and dressed in rags, a huge musket that weighs a ton—Right . . . turn!

Left . . . turn! Forward! march! To glory—and don't you go stumbling on the way—unless a well-placed shot—

SUZANNE. Horror! Be quiet!

COUNTESS. What a send-off!

COUNT. Where can Marceline be? Isn't it odd that she isn't with the rest of you?

FANCHETTE. My lord, she went walking to town, by the lane along the farm.

COUNT. And she is coming back?

BASIL. When it may please God.

FIGARO. May it please Him never to please . . .

FANCHETTE. The gentleman doctor was giving her his arm.

COUNT, *quickly*. The doctor is here?

BASIL. She fastened upon him at once . . .

COUNT, *aside*. He could not come at a better time.

FANCHETTE. She was all excited. She spoke very loud and paced back and forth and stopped and did like this with her arms. And the gentleman doctor, he did like this with his hand, to calm her down. She mentioned my cousin Figaro.

COUNT, *taking her chin in his hand*. Cousin . . . yet to be.

FANCHETTE, *pointing to* CHERUBINO. My lord, have you forgiven us for yesterday?

COUNT, *interrupting*. Good day, good day, my dear.

FIGARO. It's her confounded love that keeps her obsessed.* She would have spoiled our party.

COUNT, *aside*. She will spoil it yet, I promise you.

   *Aloud.*

Come, madam, let us go in. Basil, please stop in to see me.

SUZANNE, *to* FIGARO. You'll be joining me, sonny?

FIGARO, *in low voice to* SUZANNE. Wasn't he properly stuck?

SUZANNE, *low*. Delightful character!†

   *Exeunt all but* FIGARO, CHERUBINO, *and* BASIL.

---

\* This remark refers to Marceline, not to Fanchette.
† She means Figaro.

FIGARO. By the way, you fellows: the new ceremony having been adopted, the show tonight becomes a sequel to it and we mustn't forget our lines. Let's not be like those players who never act so poorly as on the night when the critics are wide awake. We haven't any tomorrow to recoup ourselves, so let's learn our parts today.

BASIL, *maliciously.* Mine is more difficult than you think.

FIGARO, *in pantomime, unseen by* BASIL, *pretends to give him a beating.* But you don't suspect the ovation you will get.

CHERUBINO. Dear friend, you forget that I am leaving—

FIGARO. —when you would like to stay.

CHERUBINO. Oh, if I only could!

FIGARO. Then we must have a scheme. Not a murmur against your leaving. Traveling cloak on your shoulders. Make a show of packing, your horse at the gates, a brief gallop as far as the farm and come back on foot by the back way. My lord will think you gone: just keep out of his sight. I undertake to calm him down after the wedding party.

CHERUBINO. But Fanchette does not know her part.

BASIL. What the dickens were you teaching her this last week when you've hardly been away from her?

FIGARO. You have nothing to do today—for heaven's sake coach her in her lines.

BASIL. Be careful, young man, be careful! Her father is suspicious; the girl has been slapped and hasn't learned her lines—Cherubino, Cherubino, she will be sorry—the pot that goes once too often to the well . . .

FIGARO. Ah, there's our curmudgeon with his old proverbs. Tell us, you old pedant, what the wisdom of nations has to say about the pot that goes to the well.

BASIL. It gets filled.

FIGARO, *leaving.* Not so dumb as I thought.

## ACT II

*A magnificent bedroom with a large bed in an alcove and a platform in front. The main door is upstage to the right, the dressing-room door downstage to the left. A third door, at the back, leads to the women's quarters. The window is on the opposite side.* SUZANNE *and the* COUNTESS *enter, right.*

COUNTESS, *throws herself into a wing chair.* Shut the door, Suzanne, and tell me everything in detail.

SUZANNE. I do not mean to hold anything back, my lady.

COUNTESS. And so he wanted to seduce you?

SUZANNE. Certainly not! My lord does not take that much trouble with servants: he wanted to buy me.

COUNTESS. And the little page was there all the while?

SUZANNE. Yes, that is to say, he was hidden behind the big armchair. He had come to ask me to intercede with you for his pardon.

COUNTESS. Why not come to me direct? Do you suppose I would have refused him, Suzy?

SUZANNE. That's what I told him, but his sadness at leaving, especially at leaving you— "Ah, Suzy," he said, "how noble and beautiful she is, but how imposing!"

COUNTESS. Do I really look that way, Suzy, I who have always stood up for him?

SUZANNE. Then he saw the ribbon of your nightdress which I had in my hand and he jumped and grabbed it.

COUNTESS, *smiling.* My ribbon? What a child!

SUZANNE. I tried to take it from him, madam, but he was like a wild beast, his eyes shone: "You'll get it only with my life," he said, and his voice cracked.

COUNTESS, *dreamily.* And then, Suzy?

SUZANNE. Well, madam, how can one put a stop to it? The little devil! "My godmother," he says, and "I wish I could," says he. And just because he wouldn't even dare kiss the hem of your gown, my lady, he always wants to be kissing me in earnest.

COUNTESS, *still dreaming.* Enough . . . enough nonsense. At last, then, my husband came to the point and told you . . .

SUZANNE. . . . that if I refused to listen to him, he would use his influence in behalf of Marceline.

COUNTESS, *rising, pacing, and fanning herself vigorously.* He does not love me at all any more.

SUZANNE. Why then is he so jealous?

COUNTESS. Like every husband, my dear—it is pride. Ah, I loved him too much. I wearied him with my caresses, bored him with my love. That is my chief wrong in relation to him. But I do not intend that his charming thoughts should bring you harm; you shall marry Figaro. He alone can help us: is he going to join us?

SUZANNE. As soon as the hunt is on its way.

COUNTESS, *using her fan again.* Open the window on the garden a bit. It's exceedingly warm in here.

SUZANNE. That is because my lady has been talking and walking so actively.

*She opens the window at the back.*

COUNTESS, *absent-mindedly.* In avoiding me of set purpose . . . men are creatures full of guilt.

SUZANNE, *shouting from the window.* There is my lord riding through the big field. Peter is with him and one, two, three, four—setters.

COUNTESS. That gives us plenty of time.

*She sits.*

Someone is knocking, Suzy.

SUZANNE *runs singing to the door.* Why, it's my Figaro, it's my Figaro!

*Enter* FIGARO.

SUZANNE. Dear friend, come in. My lady can hardly wait.

FIGARO. And what about you, little Sue? Her ladyship must not take on so. After all, what is all the fuss about? —A trifle. My lord Count finds our young lady charming and would like to make her his mistress—perfectly natural.

SUZANNE. Natural?

FIGARO. Then he appointed me King's Messenger and my Suzy —er—attachée to the embassy. No mental confusion there.

SUZANNE. Are you through?

FIGARO. And because Suzanne, my bride, declines the post and privileges, he wants to promote the plans of Marceline. Could anything be more simple? To seek revenge on those who thwart our purpose by interfering with theirs is what everybody does, it's what we ourselves are about to do. And that, so to speak, is that.

COUNTESS. Figaro, how can you joke about a project that will rob us all of happiness?

FIGARO. Who says it will, my lady?

SUZANNE. Instead of sharing our grief, you—

FIGARO. Isn't it enough that I am busy about it? No, no, let us be as methodical as he, and cool his desire for our belongings by arousing in him an apprehension for his own.

COUNTESS. A good idea, but how?

FIGARO. It is all done, madam. A piece of false information about you—

COUNTESS. About me! You are out of your mind!

FIGARO. No: it is he who must be driven out of his.

COUNTESS. A man as jealous as he—

FIGARO. So much the better. To make the most out of people like him, all you have to do is to whip up their blood—a device all women use. As soon as a man of his type is red-hot with passion, the most trifling subterfuge enables one to lead him by the nose into the nearest fishpond. I have used Basil to deliver an anonymous note which informs his lordship that tonight a gallant will try to approach you during the ball.

COUNTESS. You play fast and loose with the truth about a woman of honor?

FIGARO. There are but few I would have dared to risk it with, madam, for fear of stating no more than the facts.

COUNTESS. So now you'll expect me to thank you!

FIGARO. Honestly, isn't it delightful to have cut out his work for him so that he will be prowling around his lady and swearing under his breath during the time that he counted on for dallying with mine? Already he is bewildered: will he gallop over this one, shall he mount guard over that one?

*At the window.*

In his disturbed state of mind—look, look, how he races across the meadow after a poor hare who can't help himself! The hour of the wedding hastens on, but he won't be able to decide against it: he will never dare oppose it to my lady's face.

SUZANNE. No, but Marceline, that *grande dame,* will not hesitate to dare.

FIGARO. Ah! That doesn't worry me. Just let my lord know that you will meet him at dusk in the garden.

SUZANNE. So that's your great device—to rely on him?

FIGARO. See here: people who don't want to do anything about anything never achieve anything and aren't good for anything. That's my last word.

SUZANNE. A pleasant one!

COUNTESS. And so is her question: you really would let her meet him in the garden?

FIGARO. Not at all. I'll arrange for someone to put on one of Suzy's dresses. Taken in the act, how can he get out of it?

SUZANNE. Who will wear my dress?

FIGARO. Cherubino.

COUNTESS. He's gone.

FIGARO. Not as far as I'm concerned. Will the ladies allow me?

SUZANNE. One can always trust this fellow to hatch a scheme.

FIGARO. A scheme! Two, three, or four at once, well scrambled and working from both ends against the middle: I was born to be a courtier.

SUZANNE. They say it's a difficult profession.

FIGARO. Accept, take, and ask—that's the secret in three words.

COUNTESS. He has so much self-confidence it rubs off on me!

FIGARO. That was my idea.

SUZANNE. You were saying?

FIGARO. That during the Count's absence I will send you Cherubino. Dress him up and do his hair and I'll conceal and indoctrinate him. After which, my lord, how you will dance! *Exit.*

COUNTESS, *holding her box of patches.* Heavens, Suzy, I look a sight, and this young man is coming in!

SUZANNE. Don't you want him to get over it?

COUNTESS, *gazing in the mirror.* I? You'll see how I'm going to scold him!

SUZANNE. Let's get him to sing his romance.

*She lays it on the* COUNTESS's *lap.*

COUNTESS. But really my hair is in a state—

SUZANNE. I'll just roll up these two curls; they will help your ladyship to scold him.

COUNTESS, *returning to reality.* What are you saying, missy?

SUZANNE. Come in, officer. We are visible.

*Enter* CHERUBINO.

CHERUBINO, *trembling.* Oh how that title distresses me, madam. It tells me I must leave a place . . . a godmother . . . so good to me.

SUZANNE. And so beautiful.

CHERUBINO, *with a sigh.* Oh, yes.

SUZANNE, *mimicking him.* "Oh, yes." The nice young man, with his long, hypocritical lashes. Come, bluebird, sing us a song for my lady.

COUNTESS, *unfolding the paper.* Whose is it?

SUZANNE. See the guilty blush: it's a foot deep on his face.

CHERUBINO. Is it forbidden to—cherish?

SUZANNE, *shaking her fist in his face.* I am going to tell on you, ne'er-do-well!

COUNTESS. Enough. Does he sing?

CHERUBINO. Please, madam, I am shaking all over.

SUZANNE, *laughing and mimicking.* Nya, nya, nya, nya, nya, nya, nya. As soon as madam wishes. These modest authors! I'll accompany him.

COUNTESS. Take my guitar.

*Seated, she holds the paper to follow the words.* SUZANNE, *behind her armchair, begins the introduction, reading the notes over her mistress's head. The* PAGE *stands in front, his eyes lowered. The scene duplicates the beautiful print made from Vanloo's painting entitled "Conversation in Spain."*

(To the tune of "Malbrouck") \*

> *My weary steed astride*
> *(Oh my heart, oh my heart, it is breaking)*
> *Uncaring where, I ride*
> *The solitary plain.*

> *Uncaring where I ride,*
> *No squire is at my side,*
> *(Oh my heart, oh my heart, it is breaking)*
> *For my godmother I pine,*
> *And weep for her in vain.*

> *For her I weep in vain,*
> *And as the fates decree,*
> *I carve upon a tree*
> *(Oh my heart, oh my heart, it is breaking)*
> *The letters of her name—*
> *The King that moment came.*

> *The King that moment came,*
> *His bishops and his peers.*
> *"Sweet page," spoke up the Queen,*
> *(Oh my heart, oh my heart, it is breaking)*
> *"'Tis sore distress, I ween,*
> *"That draws from you these tears:*

\* As in Beaumarchais, the verses do not everywhere fit the tune accurately. But his ballad, being an early (though feeble) attempt to imitate folk poetry, deserves to be translated as closely as possible.

"What draws from you these tears,
"Declare to us, poor lad."
"My lady Queen, my lord,"
(Oh my heart, oh my heart, it is breaking)
"A godmother I had,
"Whom always I adored—

"Whom always I adored
"And I'll die dreaming of."
"Sweet page," the Queen implored,
(Oh my heart, oh my heart, it is breaking)
"That godmother you love,
"Pray let me take her place.

"Yes, let me take her place,
"And give you, page of mine,
"A maiden fair of face
(Oh my heart, oh my heart, it is breaking)
"A captain's daughter true,
"To whom I'll marry you."

" 'To whom I'll marry you!'
"Those words I must deny
"And for one favor sue:
(Oh my heart, oh my heart, it is breaking)
"To let me live in grief,
"And from my grieving die."

COUNTESS. It is full of naïve simplicity, and even of true sentiment.

SUZANNE, *laying the guitar on a chair.* Oh, as far as sentiment goes, this young man is— But say, officer, have you been told that to enliven this evening's party we need to know whether one of my gowns will more or less fit you?

COUNTESS. I'm afraid it won't.

SUZANNE, *comparing their statures.* He's about my size. Let's take off the coat.

*She takes it off him.*

COUNTESS. What if someone comes in?

SUZANNE. We're not doing anything wrong. I'll shut the door.

*She runs.*

But it's the hair I want to see.

COUNTESS. In my dressing room, one of my wrappers.

*SUZANNE goes into the dressing room.*

COUNTESS. Until the ball opens, the Count will not know that you are still in the castle. We shall tell him afterward that the time required to prepare your commission gave us the idea of—

CHERUBINO, *showing her the paper.* Unfortunately, madam, my commission is here, signed. Basil gave it to me from my lord.

COUNTESS. Already! Not a minute lost.

*She reads.*

In such a hurry that he forgot to affix the seal.

*She hands it back.*

SUZANNE, *carrying also a wide-brimmed hat.* The seal to what?

COUNTESS. His commission.

SUZANNE. Already?

COUNTESS. That's what I was saying. Is that the wrapper?

SUZANNE, *seated near the* COUNTESS. The handsomest of all.

*She sings with pins in her mouth.*

> *Turn your head, oh Johnny my dear,*
> *Turn, my handsome cavalier.*

CHERUBINO *kneels beside her to have his hair dressed.*

Madam, he is sweet!

COUNTESS. Pull his collar more like a woman.

SUZANNE. There—look at that ragamuffin, what a pretty girl he makes. I'm jealous.

*She takes his chin in her hand.*

Will you please not be so pretty as you are?

COUNTESS. Silly girl! You must turn back the cuff so that the undersleeve shows up better.

*She lifts the sleeve.*

What has he put on his arm? —A ribbon!

SUZANNE. *Your* ribbon. I am glad madam saw it. I warned him I would tell on him. I swear, if my lord had not come in, I would have got the ribbon back. I'm almost as strong as he is.

COUNTESS. I see blood.

*She takes off the ribbon.*

CHERUBINO, *shamefaced.* This morning, when I knew I had to leave, I was adjusting the snaffle on my horse. He tossed his head and the boss on the bit scratched my arm.

COUNTESS. But why put a ribbon—

SUZANNE. A *stolen* ribbon at that! Just imagine what the baffle —the snaffle—the raffle—I can't keep these things straight— look at that white skin! It's a woman's arm, whiter than mine, see?

*She compares.*

COUNTESS, *freezingly.* Kindly get me some court plaster from my dressing table.

SUZANNE *gives* CHERUBINO *a shove; he falls forward on his hands. She goes into the dressing room. The* COUNTESS *remains silent a moment, her eyes on the ribbon.* CHERUBINO *gazes at her intently.*

As to my ribbon, sir—it's the color I find most becoming to me—I was very much annoyed to be without it.

SUZANNE, *returning.* The bandage for his arm.

*She gives the* COUNTESS *the plaster and a pair of scissors.*

COUNTESS. When you go for your dress, bring back the ribbon from some other bonnet.

SUZANNE *leaves by the center door, taking the* PAGE'S *coat with her.*

CHERUBINO, *eyes lowered.* The ribbon you're taking from me would have cured me in no time.

COUNTESS. Owing to what specific virtue?

*Pointing to the plaster.*

That is so much better.

CHERUBINO, *hesitating.* When a ribbon . . . has bound the head . . . or touched the skin . . . of a person . . .

COUNTESS, *breaking in.*  . . . of a stranger, it cures wounds? That is news to me. I will test it by keeping the one you put around your arm. At the first scratch—on one of my maids—I shall try it out.

CHERUBINO, *deeply moved.* You are keeping it—but I'm leaving!

COUNTESS. But not forever.

CHERUBINO. I'm so unhappy!

COUNTESS, *moved.* Now he is weeping. It's Figaro's fault for prophesying—

CHERUBINO. Oh, how I wish the time had come that he spoke about! If I were sure of dying at once, perhaps my lips would dare—

COUNTESS *interrupts by wiping his eyes with her handkerchief.* Be quiet, child, be quiet. There isn't a grain of sense in what you're saying.

*A knock at the door; she raises her voice.*

Who is it?

COUNT, *outside.* Why are you locked in?

COUNTESS, *upset.* It's my husband. Heavens!  . . .

*To* CHERUBINO, *who has also got up.*

You, without your coat, your collar open and your arms bare—alone with me—the general disarray—the anonymous letter he received, his jealousy—

COUNT, *outside.* You won't open?

COUNTESS. The fact is . . . I am alone.

COUNT. Alone? With whom are you talking, then?

COUNTESS, *fumbling.* With you, I should think.

CHERUBINO, *aside.* After those scenes of yesterday and this morning he would kill me on the spot.

*He runs into the dressing room and shuts the door.*

COUNTESS *removes the key and opens the other door to admit the* COUNT. What a dreadful mistake!

COUNT, *somewhat severe.* You are not in the habit of shutting yourself up.

COUNTESS, *upset.* I was trying on—yes—odds and ends—with Suzanne. She went for a minute to her room.

COUNT. You look and sound quite strange.

COUNTESS. It's not surprising, not surprising at all, I assure you. We were speaking about you. She just left, as I said—

COUNT. You were speaking about me? Well, here I am. I've come back much disturbed. On setting out, I was handed a note—though I take no stock in it—it upset me.

COUNTESS. How so, what note, sir?

COUNT. You must admit, madam, that you or I must be surrounded by people who are—uncommonly wicked. Someone informs me that a person, whom I falsely suppose to be absent, will attempt to approach you.

COUNTESS. Whoever this rash being may be, he will have to make his way to this very spot, for I do not intend to stir for the rest of the day.

COUNT. What about tonight, for Suzanne's wedding?

COUNTESS. Not on any account; I am quite indisposed.

COUNT. Fortunately the doctor is here.

*The* PAGE *overturns a chair in the dressing room.*

What noise was that?

COUNTESS, *distraught.* Noise?

COUNT. Someone in there upset a piece of furniture.

COUNTESS. I—I heard nothing.

COUNT. You must be powerfully preoccupied.

COUNTESS. Preoccupied? What about?

COUNT. Madam: there is someone in that dressing room!

COUNTESS. Indeed, who could there be, sir?

COUNT. It is for me to ask that question: I have just arrived.

COUNTESS. It must be Suzanne putting things away.

COUNT. You told me she had gone to her room.

COUNTESS. Gone there—or here—I don't know which.

COUNT. If it is Suzanne, why your evident distress?

COUNTESS. Distress—over my maid?

COUNT. Over your maid it may be, but distress without a doubt.

COUNTESS. Without a doubt, sir, that girl concerns and occupies your mind much more than I.

COUNT. She concerns me so much that I want to see her at once.

COUNTESS. I readily believe that this is what you often want. But your ill-founded suspicions—

SUZANNE *enters at the back, unseen, with clothes in her arms.*

COUNT. If so, they will be easily dispelled.

*He speaks through the dressing-room door.*

Come out, Suzanne, I order you to.

SUZANNE *stops near the alcove at the back.*

COUNTESS. She is almost naked, sir. How can you intrude in this way on women in their apartments? She was trying on some old things I am giving her on the occasion of her wedding. She fled when she heard you.

COUNT. If she is afraid to show herself, she can at least speak.

*He turns again to the closed door.*

Answer me, Suzanne: are you in the dressing room?

SUZANNE, *still at the back of the alcove, hides behind the bed.*

COUNTESS, *quickly, to the closed door.* Suzy, I forbid you to answer.

*To the* COUNT.

No one has ever carried tyranny so far!

COUNT, *turning again.* If she won't speak, dressed or undressed I shall see her.

COUNTESS, *intercepting him.* Anywhere else I can't prevent you, but I trust that in my own room—

COUNT. And I trust that in one minute I shall know who this mysterious Suzanne is. I can see it is useless to ask you for the key, but it is not hard to break down this trumpery door. Ho, there, anybody!

COUNTESS. You would bring in your people, create a public scandal—all on the strength of a vague suspicion! We'll be the talk of the castle.

COUNT. An excellent point, madam, I can do without help. This instant I go to my rooms and return with what I need.

*He starts to go and turns back.*

But in order that everything shall remain as it is, will you kindly accompany me, quietly and decently—since scandal displeases you so? My simple request will surely not be denied?

COUNTESS, *upset.* Sir, who would dream of crossing you?

COUNT. Oh, I was forgetting: the door which leads to your maids' quarters. I must also shut it so that you may be fully vindicated.

*He shuts the center door and takes the key.*

COUNTESS, *aside.* Oh, what a fateful whim!

COUNT, *returning.* Now that this chamber is sealed, I beg you to accept my arm.

*He raises his voice.*

As for the Suzanne in the dressing room, she will have the goodness to await my return. The least of the evils that may befall her then is—

COUNTESS. Really, sir, this is the most odious performance—

*The* COUNT *leads her out and locks the door.*

SUZANNE *runs from the alcove to the dressing-room door and speaks through the keyhole.* Open up, Cherubino, open, quick, it's Suzanne, open and hurry out.

CHERUBINO, *coming out.* Oh, Suzy, what a dreadful mess!

SUZANNE. Go, go, you haven't a minute to lose.

CHERUBINO, *frightened.* How can I get out?

SUZANNE. Don't ask me, just go.

CHERUBINO. But I can't if I'm locked in.

SUZANNE. After this afternoon's encounter he would break you, and she and I would be doomed. Go tell Figaro—

CHERUBINO. Maybe the window over the garden isn't too high up.

*He runs to see.*

SUZANNE, *frightened.* A whole story—you can't do it! Oh, my poor lady! And my marriage, dear God!

CHERUBINO, *coming back.* It overlooks the melon patch. All it would spoil is a couple of beds.

SUZANNE, *holding him back and crying out.* You will kill your-self!

CHERUBINO, *excited.* I'd throw myself into an open furnace—I would, Suzy—rather than cause her harm. And a kiss from you will bring me luck.

*Kisses her, runs toward the window, and leaps out.*

SUZANNE *again cries out; then, overcome, falls into a chair, finally drags herself to the window and comes back.* He's off and away, the young devil! As light on his feet as he's pretty to look at. He'll have all the women he wants, I bet. Now to take his place, quick!

*Goes into the dressing room.*

From here on, my lord, you can tear down the wall if it gives you pleasure, you don't get a word out of me.

*Shuts the door.*

*The* COUNT *and* COUNTESS *return. He holds a pair of pliers which he soon throws upon a chair.*

COUNT. Everything is as I left it. Madam, if you compel me to break down that door you must think of the consequences: once again, will you open it yourself?

COUNTESS. But sir, what singular ill-temper can so destroy con-siderateness between husband and wife? If it were love that possessed you to the point of causing this fury, I could ex-cuse it, however demented. The motive could make me for-get the offense. But how can mere vanity move a well-bred man to such excesses?

COUNT. Love or vanity, you open that door or I do it on the spot.

COUNTESS, *before the door.* My lord, please desist! Can you think me capable of forgetting what I owe to my self-respect?

COUNT. Put it any way you like, madam, I mean to see who is in that dressing room.

COUNTESS, *frightened.* Very well, you shall see. But first listen to me quietly.

COUNT. So it isn't Suzanne?

COUNTESS, *embarrassed.* At least it isn't a person . . . about whom you should have any . . . we were bent on a practical joke . . . quite harmless, really, for this evening . . . and I swear to you . . .

COUNT. You swear to me—what?

COUNTESS. That neither he nor I meant to offend you.

COUNT. He—it is a man, then?

COUNTESS. A child, dear sir.

COUNT. And who, pray tell?

COUNTESS. I hardly dare give his name.

COUNT, *furious.* I'll kill him!

COUNTESS. Merciful powers!

COUNT. Speak up!

COUNTESS. The young . . . Cherubino.

COUNT. That impudent whelp! That explains my suspicions—and the anonymous note.

COUNTESS, *her hands joined in prayer.* Oh, sir, do not allow yourself to suppose—

COUNT, *stamping his foot and speaking aside.* That accursèd page turns up wherever I go.
*Aloud.*

Come, madam, now that I know everything, open up. You would not have been so moved saying good-by to him this morning, you would not have used such elaborate lies in your tale of Suzanne, and he would not have hidden so quickly and so long, unless misconduct and guilt were the reason.

COUNTESS. He was afraid of irritating you by showing himself.

COUNT, *beside himself, shouting at the dressing-room door.* Come out of there, you little scrub!

COUNTESS, *seizing the* COUNT *with both arms and thrusting him aside.* My dear sir, my dear sir, your anger makes me afraid for him. Don't, I beg, trust your own suspicions, which are unjust, and don't let his disheveled state—

COUNT. Disheveled!

COUNTESS. Alas, you will see—one of my bonnets on his head, without his coat, his neckband open and arms bare, ready to dress up as a woman. He was going to try to—

COUNT. And you wanted to stay all day in your room! Worthless woman! You shall keep to your room—I shall see to it—and for a long time! But first I must kick out that insolent stripling that I may never come upon him again.

COUNTESS, *on her knees, arms uplifted.* Count, you must spare a mere child. I shall never forgive myself for being the cause of—

COUNT. Your fears deepen his guilt.

COUNTESS. He is not guilty—he was leaving. It is I who had him fetched.

COUNT, *in anger.* Get up. Remove yourself—shameless woman, to dare entreat me in behalf of another.

COUNTESS. Very well. I will remove myself, I will get up and give you the key to the door, but in the name of your love—

COUNT. My love, hypocrite!

COUNTESS *gets up and gives him the key.* Promise that you will let the child go harmless—and may you vent your fury on me later if I do not convince you that—

COUNT, *taking the key.* I'm no longer listening.

COUNTESS *throws herself into an armchair, her handkerchief over her face.* God, oh God, he will be killed!

COUNT *opens the door.* You!

SUZANNE *comes out laughing.* "I will kill him—I will kill him!" Why *don't* you kill him, your villainous page?

COUNT, *aside.* Lord! What a lesson!

*Looking at the* COUNTESS, *who is stupefied.*

And you pretend to be surprised, too? But perhaps Suzanne wasn't alone.

*He goes in.*

SUZANNE, *going to* COUNTESS. Recover yourself, madam, he's nowhere near—he jumped (*gesture*).

COUNTESS. Oh, Suzy, I am all in.

COUNT *emerges, vexed and silent.* There's no one else and this time I was wrong. Madam, you are a good actress—

SUZANNE. What about me, my lord?

    COUNTESS *holds her handkerchief to her mouth and says nothing, to regain her composure.*

COUNT, *approaching.* And so, madam, you were joking?

COUNTESS, *recovering.* And why not, sir?

COUNT. An absurd practical joke, and for what reason, tell me?

COUNTESS. Does your outrageous behavior deserve consideration?

COUNT. Do you call outrageous what relates to honor?

COUNTESS, *gradually herself again.* Did I join my life to yours only to be a perpetual victim of your neglect and your jealousy, two things which only you can reconcile?

COUNT. Ah, madam, you spare me nothing—

SUZANNE. She did! My lady had only to let you call the servants—

COUNT. You are right and I abase myself. Forgive me. I am discomfited.

SUZANNE. And deserve to be, you must admit.

COUNT. But why wouldn't you come out when I called to you?

SUZANNE. I was putting on some clothes as well as I could, with a multitude of pins: my lady's forbidding me to stir was for a good reason.

COUNT. Instead of reminding me of my error, help me to soothe her.

COUNTESS. No, my lord, an offense such as this is not to be palliated. I am about to retire to a convent. It is high time I did.

COUNT. Shall you be without regrets?

SUZANNE. For my part, I am sure the day you leave will be the beginning of endless grief.

COUNTESS. Even if it is, Suzy, I'd rather miss him than basely forgive him. He has wounded me too deeply.

COUNT. Rosine!

COUNTESS. I am Rosine no longer, the Rosine you so tenaciously pursued. I am the poor Countess Almaviva, the sad forsaken wife you no longer love.

SUZANNE. Oh, madam!

COUNT, *suppliant*. For charity's sake!

COUNTESS. When have you ever shown me any?

COUNT. But that anonymous letter—it curdled my blood.

COUNTESS. I did not agree to its being written.

COUNT. You knew about it?

COUNTESS. It was that harebrained Figaro—

COUNT. He was party to it?

COUNTESS. —who gave it to Basil—

COUNT. —who told me he had it from a peasant. Oh, sinister singing-master, two-faced underling: you shall pay for everybody's crimes!

COUNTESS. How like a man! You beg for yourself a forgiveness you deny to others. Let me tell you: if ever I consent to pardon you for the error you committed on the strength of that note, I shall demand that the amnesty be general.

COUNT. With all my heart, Countess. But how can I ever make up for so humiliating a blunder?

COUNTESS, *rising*. It humiliated us both.

COUNT. No, no, only myself, believe me. But I am still amazed at the ease with which you women take on the proper look and tone of each circumstance. You were flushed, crying, your face was working—I assure you, you still look undone.

COUNTESS, *trying to smile*. I was flushing with resentment against your suspiciousness. But men are not delicate enough creatures to distinguish between the indignation of an honorable person suffering outrage and the confusion produced by a justified accusation.

COUNT, *smiling*. What about the disheveled page, coatless and half naked?

COUNTESS, *pointing to* SUZANNE. There he is. Aren't you glad to have caught this one instead of the other? Generally speaking, you do not hate to catch this one.

COUNT, *laughing*. And your entreaties and simulated tears?

COUNTESS. You make me laugh and I do not feel like it.

COUNT. We men think we are practiced in the art of politics, but we are children. It is you, you madam, whom the King should appoint ambassador to London! Your sex must have made a deep study of the art of controlling the countenance to succeed as you did today.

COUNTESS. We are forced into it—and always by men.

SUZANNE. But put us on parole and you will see what honorable beings we are.

COUNTESS. Enough for the moment, Count. Possibly I went too far, but my leniency in so grave a case must be matched by yours.

COUNT. Do say again that you forgive me.

COUNTESS. Have I said it at all, Suzy?

SUZANNE. I did not hear it, madam.

COUNT. Well then, let the words slip out.

COUNTESS. You think you deserve it, you ungrateful man?

COUNT. I do, I do—because I repent.

SUZANNE. To suspect a man in my lady's dressing room!

COUNT. She has already punished me so severely!

SUZANNE. Not to believe her when she says it is her chambermaid!

COUNT. Rosine, are you unrelenting?

COUNTESS. Oh, Suzy, how weak I am! What a poor example I give you!

*Holding out her hand to the* COUNT.

No one will ever believe again in a woman's anger.

SUZANNE. It's all right, madam. One always comes to this with men.

*The* COUNT *ardently kisses his wife's hand.*

FIGARO *enters, breathless.* I heard that madam was seriously unwell. I've been running. I see there is no truth in the report.

COUNT, *dryly.* You are most attentive.

FIGARO. It is my duty. But since there is nothing in it, my lord, let me say that all your younger vassals of either sex are downstairs with their violins and pipes, awaiting the mo-

ment when you will allow me to bring my bride, so that they
may accompany—

COUNT. And who will look after the Countess indoors?

FIGARO. Look after her—but she's not ill?

COUNT. No, but there is a mysterious stranger who will try to
approach her.

FIGARO. What stranger?

COUNT. The man in the note that you gave to Basil.

FIGARO. Who said I gave him a note?

COUNT. Even if I hadn't been told, rascal, I could read it in
your lying face.

FIGARO. Then it's my face deceiving you, not I.

SUZANNE. Figaro, my poor darling, don't waste your eloquence
in defeat: we told his lordship everything.

FIGARO. Told what? You treat me as if I were Basil!

SUZANNE. Told him you had written a note to make my lord
believe that when he came in here he would find the young
page in the dressing room where I shut myself up.

COUNT. What have you to say to that?

COUNTESS. There's no further need to conceal anything, Figaro,
the joke is over.

FIGARO, *trying to guess*. The joke is over?

COUNT. Yes, over, consummated: what do you say to that?

FIGARO. Consummated? I say that—that I wish I could say the
same about my marriage. You have only to give the word—

COUNT. You admit the anonymous note?

FIGARO. Since my lady wants it so, and Suzanne wants it so,
and you want it so, I can't help wanting it too. But if I
were you, my lord, really, I wouldn't believe a word of
anything we are telling you.

COUNT. You're always telling lies and always in the teeth of
evidence; it's beginning to get on my nerves.

COUNTESS, *laughing*. The poor fellow! Why should you expect,
sir, that he would tell the truth even once?

FIGARO, *low, to* SUZANNE. I've warned him of the danger ahead
—that's all a gentleman can do.

SUZANNE, *low*. Did you see the page?

FIGARO, *low*. Yes, all rumpled.

SUZANNE, *low*. Oh, wretched!

COUNTESS. Look, my dear Count, they long to be united. Their impatience is understandable: let us go and celebrate the wedding.

COUNT, *aside*. But Marceline . . . where is Marceline? *Aloud.*

I'd like a moment to dress.

COUNTESS. To be with our own people? You see what I have on.

ANTONIO, *half tipsy, holding a pot of partly crushed flowers.* My lord, my lord!

COUNT. What do you want with me, Antonio?

ANTONIO. I wish you'd have the windows over my beds fitted with bars. They throw every kind of thing out of those windows, a while back they threw out a man.

COUNT. Out of these windows?

ANTONIO. Just look at my gillyflowers!

SUZANNE, *low, to* FIGARO. Look out, Figaro, on your toes!

FIGARO. My lord, he gets drunk every day from the crack of dawn.

ANTONIO. You're wrong—with me there's always a little left over from the day before. But that's how people judge you —in the dark.

COUNT, *breathing fire*. The man, the man, where is he?

ANTONIO. Where he is?

COUNT. Yes, where?

ANTONIO. That's what *I* say. I want to have him found. I'm your servant. There's only me takes real care of your garden. Man falls on it—you can't help . . . appreciating . . . my reputation is . . . uprooted.

SUZANNE, *low, to* FIGARO. Change the subject, quick!

FIGARO. Won't you ever give up drinking?

ANTONIO. If I didn't drink I'd go out of my mind.

COUNTESS. But to drink as you do, without thirst . . .

ANTONIO. To drink without thirst and make love at any time, my lady, 'swhat distinguishes us from the other animals.

COUNT, *fiercely*. Answer me or I'll have you thrown on the parish.

ANTONIO. I wouldn't go.

COUNT. What's that?

ANTONIO, *touching his forehead*. If *that* isn't enough to make you keep a good servant, on my side I'm not so dumb as to get rid of a good master.

COUNT, *shaking him violently*. You say they threw a man out the window.

ANTONIO. Yes, excellency, just a while back, in a white vest, and he picked himself up and ran away.

COUNT, *impatient*. And then?

ANTONIO. I tried to run after him, but I bumped into the fence so hard my finger . . .

*He shows which.*

. . . is still numb. It can't move hand or foot of itself.

COUNT. But you'd recognize the man?

ANTONIO. That I could if I had seen him, as you might say.

SUZANNE, *low, to* FIGARO. He never saw him.

FIGARO. What a pother about a pot! How long do you mean to carry on about your bluebells, you old watering jug? No use asking, my lord, it was I who jumped down.

COUNT. You? Why?

ANTONIO. "How long I carry on," eh? Why, you must have grown since I saw you jump, 'cause you were smaller and thinner at the time.

FIGARO. Naturally: when one jumps one gathers oneself together.

ANTONIO. Methought 'twas rather the whippersnapper I saw—the page.

COUNT. Cherubino, you mean?

FIGARO. Of course, having come back—he and his horse—from the gates of Seville, where he probably is now.

ANTONIO. I didn't say that, I didn't say that! I didn't see a horse jump, or I'd say so.

COUNT. Oh, to be patient!

FIGARO. I was in the women's quarters in my white vest—terribly hot day. I was waiting there for Suzanette, when suddenly I heard your voice, my lord, and a great noise going on. I don't know why, I was seized with fear—perhaps about the anonymous note. . . . To make a clean breast of it, I lost my head and jumped down on the flowers, spraining my ankle for my pains.

*He rubs his foot.*

ANTONIO. As it's you, then I've got to give you back this bit of paper that fell out of your vest when you landed.

COUNT, *snatching it.* Give it to me.

*He unfolds the paper and folds it again.*

FIGARO, *aside.* This is the end.

COUNT, *to* FIGARO. Your great fright has surely not made you forget the contents of this paper, nor how it got into your pocket?

FIGARO, *embarrassed, looks into all his pockets, bringing out letters and papers.* Oh, certainly not—but I carry so many about me—every one has to be answered.

*He looks at a paper.*

This, for instance, what's—? Ah, yes, a letter from Marceline, four pages, a beautiful letter. Could that other one be the petition from that poacher who is in prison? No—here it is. I also had a list of the furniture in the pavilion, in my other pocket—

*The* COUNT *reopens the paper in his hand.*

COUNTESS, *low, to* SUZANNE. Heavens, Suzy, it's the officer's commission.

SUZANNE, *low, to* FIGARO. We're undone: it's the commission!

COUNT, *folding the paper.* Well, resourceful sir, you can't guess?

ANTONIO, *going toward* FIGARO. My lord says as how can't you guess?

FIGARO, *pushing him away.* Hence, varlet, and don't speak into my nose!

COUNT. You cannot recall for me what the paper might be?

FIGARO. Ah, ah, ah! I have it! The poor boy! It must be Cherubino's commission, which the dear child showed me and I forgot to give back. What a scatterbrain I am! But how can he manage without his commission? We must go after him—

COUNT. Why should he have given it to you?

FIGARO, *embarrassed*. He wanted—something done to it.

COUNT *looks at paper*. There's nothing needs doing.

COUNTESS, *low, to* SUZANNE. The seal.

SUZANNE, *low, to* FIGARO. The seal's not on it.

COUNT, *to* FIGARO. You have nothing to say?

FIGARO. Yes, the fact is . . . something *is* missing. He says it is customary.

COUNT. Customary? What is customary?

FIGARO. To affix the seal showing your coat of arms. But perhaps it isn't worth the trouble.

COUNT *reopens the paper and crumples it up angrily*. Confound it! My fate decrees that I'm to be kept in the dark.

*Aside.*

This—this Figaro is the mastermind, and I—I should keep from striking back!

*He starts to stalk out.*

FIGARO, *stopping him*. You're not going without giving the word about my wedding?

*Enter* BASIL, BARTHOLO, MARCELINE, *and* SUNSTRUCK.

MARCELINE, *to the* COUNT. Don't give the word, my lord. Before you do him a favor, you must do me justice. He has obligations toward me.

COUNT, *aside*. My revenge at last!

FIGARO. Obligations? Of what sort? Please explain.

MARCELINE. Of course I shall explain, false knave!

COUNTESS *sits in an armchair,* SUZANNE *behind her.*

COUNT. What is it you are referring to, Marceline?

MARCELINE. A promise of marriage.

FIGARO. A promissory note for money I borrowed, nothing more.

MARCELINE, *to* COUNT. But with the forfeit of marrying me.
You are a great lord, the highest judge in the province . . .

COUNT. Come to the assizes. I will give everybody justice.

BASIL, *pointing to* MARCELINE. In that case, your worship will
permit me to put in evidence my claims on Marceline?

COUNT, *aside.* This is the scoundrel of the anonymous note.

FIGARO. As mad as she is—birds of a feather!

COUNT, *to* BASIL, *angrily.* Your claims, your claims! What right
have you to speak up in my presence, master fool?

ANTONIO, *striking his fist into the palm of his other hand.* Got
him the first time: it sure is his right name!

COUNT. Marceline, everything is recessed until the public hearing of your plea, which shall take place in the large reception room. You, wise Basil, as my faithful and reliable agent,
shall go into town and summon the bench.

BASIL. For her case?

COUNT. And bring along the peasant who gave you the note.

BASIL. How should I know him?

COUNT. You object?

BASIL. I did not enter your service to run errands.

COUNT. What's that?

BASIL. A talented performer on the parish organ, I teach my
lady the keyboard, coach her women in singing and your
pages on the mandolin. But my chief employment is to entertain your company on the guitar, when it pleases you to
command me.

SUNSTRUCK, *coming forward.* I'll go, your lordsy, if they's what
you want.

COUNT. What is your name and your employment?

SUNSTRUCK. My name is Sunstruck, good lordsy. I watch the
goats, and bin asked in for the fireworks. It's holiday today
for all us herds. But I know where's the roaring big trial-
shop in town.

COUNT. Your gumption pleases me, go do my errand. As for
you . . .

*To* BASIL

. . . go along with this gentleman, singing and playing the guitar to entertain him on the way, for he is of my company.

SUNSTRUCK, *elated.* I—I'm of the—

SUZANNE *calms him down by pointing to the* COUNTESS.

BASIL, *taken aback.* Go along with Sunstruck while playing the guitar?

COUNT. It is your profession: off you go, or you're dismissed. *Exit.*

BASIL, *to himself.* I'm certainly not going to fight the iron pot, I who am—

FIGARO. —already cracked.

BASIL, *aside.* Instead of furthering their wedding, I am going to insure Marceline's and mine.

*To* FIGARO.

Don't sign anything, I warn you, until I come back.

*He picks up his guitar from a chair at the back.*

FIGARO, *following him.* Sign anything? Don't worry! I shan't, even if you never come back. But you don't seem in the mood for song. Would you like me to begin? Come on, a smile, and the high *la-mi-la* for my bride.

*He walks backward and dances the following* seguidilla. BASIL *accompanies him and everyone joins in.*

ALL, *together.*

> Better than riches, I love
>     The goodness of
>     My Suzanne,
> Zann, zann, zann,
> Zann, zann, zann,
> Zann, zann, zann
>
> Always on her I'll depend
>     And madly end
>     As I began
> Gan, gan, gan,
> Gan, gan, gan,
> Gan, gan, gan.

*Exeunt singing and dancing.*

COUNTESS, *in the wing chair.* You see, Suzanne, the ordeal I had to go through, thanks to your wild friend's anonymous note?

SUZANNE. Oh, madam, if you could have seen your face when I came out of the dressing room—you lost all your color, but only for an instant, then you grew red—oh so red!

COUNTESS. And he jumped out of the window?

SUZANNE. Without a moment's hesitation, the dear child—light as a bird.

COUNTESS. That deplorable gardener! The whole thing made me so dizzy I couldn't keep two ideas together in my mind.

SUZANNE. Not at all, my lady, on the contrary. I saw at once what facility the habit of high society confers on respectable ladies who have to tell lies.

COUNTESS. Do you think the Count was taken in? What if he finds the poor child in the castle?

SUZANNE. I'm going to make sure he is well hidden.

COUNTESS. He must go away. After what happened, you can imagine I'm not tempted to send him into the garden dressed like you.

SUZANNE. And I shan't go either, so once again my wedding is—

COUNTESS. Wait! What if in your place, or another's—why shouldn't *I* go?

SUZANNE. You, madam?

COUNTESS. No one could be reprimanded—and the Count couldn't explain the facts away. First to have punished his jealousy, and then to demonstrate his infidelity—it would be . . . ! Come, our luck in the first adventure encourages me to try a second. Let him know quickly that you will go into the garden. But be sure no one knows—

SUZANNE. Not Figaro?

COUNTESS. No, no. He would want to contribute ideas . . . Fetch me my stick and my velvet mask. I'll go out on the terrace and daydream.

SUZANNE *goes into the dressing room.*

COUNTESS. My scheme is surely brash enough.

*She turns around.*

Ah, my ribbon, my pretty ribbon, I had forgotten you.

*She takes it, sits, and rolls it up.*

Henceforth you will be with me always, you will remind me of the scene in which that poor boy . . . Oh, Count, what have you done! And what am *I* doing right now?

*SUZANNE re-enters; the COUNTESS furtively slips the ribbon into her bosom.*

SUZANNE. Here is the stick and your mask.

COUNTESS. Remember, I forbid you to say one word to Figaro.

SUZANNE, *joyful.* Your plan is delightful, my lady. I've been thinking about it. It brings everything together, concludes everything, embraces everything. Whatever comes of it, my marriage is now assured.

*She kisses the COUNTESS's hand. Exeunt.*

*During the intermission, the courtroom is prepared. Two settees are brought in for counsel, one on each side of the stage, but allowing free passage behind. In the center, toward the back, a raised platform with two steps, on which is put the COUNT's chair of state. The CLERK's table and his stool are to one side downstage; seats for BRIDLEGOOSE and the other judges are placed alongside the COUNT's platform.*

# ACT III

*A room in the castle, known as the throne room and used as a reception room. To one side a canopy over a monumental chair, and on the wall, a portrait of the King. The* COUNT *with* PETER, *who is wearing coat and boots and is holding a sealed package.*

COUNT, *speaking fast.* It's clearly understood?

PETER. Yes, Your Excellency.

*Exit.*

COUNT, *shouting.* Peter!

PETER, *returning.* Excellency?

COUNT. No one saw you?

PETER. Not a soul.

COUNT. Take the arab.

PETER. He's at the garden gate saddled and ready.

COUNT. Straight to Seville without a stop.

PETER. It's only ten miles and a fair road.

COUNT. As soon as you arrive, find out if the page is there.

PETER. At the house?

COUNT. Yes, and how long he's been there.

PETER. I understand.

COUNT. Give him his commission and come back as fast as you can.

PETER. What if he isn't there?

COUNT. Come back even faster. Tell me at once. Quick, be off! (*Exit* PETER.)

COUNT, *pacing and meditating.* It was clumsy of me to send Basil away . . . Anger is a bad counselor . . . That note he gave me telling of an attempt to approach the Countess . . . The chambermaid locked in that room when I came back

. . . Her mistress making believe she was a prey to terror, or really terrified . . . A man jumps out of the window and the other, later, owns up to it, or pretends it was he. There is a link missing. Something devious is going on. A certain license among my vassals—what can it matter? But the Countess, if some upstart dared! . . . My mind wanders. Truly, when anger rules, the most controlled imagination runs wild, as in a dream. She was laughing—I heard her smothered giggles, their ill-concealed amusement. But she has self-respect . . . and my honor—in whose keeping is it? As to the other affair, where do I stand? Did that rascally Suzanne give me away? . . . seeing it isn't *her* secret yet. Why am I so bent on having her? A dozen times, I've thought of giving her up. The results of indecision are certainly strange: if I wanted her without hesitation, I shouldn't feel nearly so much desire. Figaro is behind time as usual: I must deftly plumb his thoughts.

FIGARO *enters upstage and stops.*

At any rate I must find out from his replies to what I shall put to him casually whether or not he knows I'm in love with Suzanne.

FIGARO, *aside.* Here it comes.

COUNT. That is, if she has dropped a hint.

FIGARO, *aside.* I guessed it, I guess.

COUNT. Next, I marry him off to the old girl . . .

FIGARO, *aside.* Mister Basil's belovèd?

COUNT. And then see what I can do with the young one.

FIGARO, *aside.* With my wife, if you please.

COUNT, *turning around.* Eh, what? Who is it?

FIGARO. Me, at your service.

COUNT. What were you saying?

FIGARO. I haven't breathed a word.

COUNT. "My wife, if you please."

FIGARO. Oh, that! —That is the conclusion of a reply I was making: "Go and tell my wife, if you please."

COUNT, *pacing.* His wife! I am curious to know what business can detain your lordship when I have you called.

FIGARO, *pretending to adjust his clothing.* I'd got dirty falling on that flower bed, so I changed.

COUNT. Does it take an hour?

FIGARO. It takes the time it takes.

COUNT. The servants here need longer to dress than the masters.

FIGARO. That's because they have no valets to help them.

COUNT. I didn't quite understand what compelled you a moment ago to risk your life for nothing by jumping—

FIGARO. Risk my life! One would suppose I had leaped into a bottomless pit!

COUNT. Don't try to put me off the point by pretending you missed it yourself, you devious lackey. You understand very well that it isn't the danger to your life that concerns me, but your motive.

FIGARO. On the strength of a false alarm you come rushing in furiously, overturning everything like a mountain torrent. You're looking for a man: you have to find one or you will break down the doors and splinter the walls! I happen to be in your way—how am I to know that in your wrath—

COUNT. You could have escaped by the stairs—

FIGARO. And you'd catch me in the hall.

COUNT, *angry.* In the hall!

*Aside.*

I'm getting the worst of it and no nearer finding out what I am after.

FIGARO, *aside.* Let us see his game and match him trick for trick.

COUNT, *softening his tone.* That isn't what I wanted to tell you. Let's drop the subject. I thought—as a matter of fact, I did think of taking you with me to London, as King's Messenger, but on second thoughts—

FIGARO. Your lordship has changed his mind?

COUNT. In the first place you don't know English.

FIGARO. I know "God damn!"

COUNT. I don't follow you.

FIGARO. I say that I know "God damn!"

COUNT. What about it?

FIGARO. I mean, English is a wonderful language—it takes but a few words to cover a lot of ground. With "God damn," in English, a man need lack for nothing. Do you want to sink your teeth into a nice juicy fowl? Go into a tavern and make this gesture (*Turning a spit.*) and say "God damn!" The waiter brings you a joint of salt beef with no bread —it's marvelous! Do you want a good glass of burgundy or claret—just do this (*Drawing a cork.*) "God damn!" and they bring you a foaming tankard of beer—it's perfectly wonderful! Should you meet one of those attractive ladies who go trotting about with their elbows pulled back and their hips swinging a bit, just put your four fingers delicately on your lips—"God damn!"—and you get slapped as by a stevedore. That proves they get your meaning. The English people, it is true, use a word or two more, here and there in conversation, but it is clear that "God damn" is the core of the language—so if your only reason for leaving me behind in Spain is—

COUNT, *aside.* He wants to go to London: she hasn't told him.

FIGARO, *aside.* He thinks I know nothing. Let's encourage his delusion.

COUNT. What motive did the Countess have for playing that trick on me?

FIGARO. Really, my lord, you know the reason better than I.

COUNT. I anticipate all her wishes and smother her with gifts.

FIGARO. You give but you aren't faithful: would anyone be grateful for luxuries who is starved of necessities?

COUNT. You used to tell me everything.

FIGARO. And now I keep nothing from you.

COUNT. How much did the Countess give you for being in league with her?

FIGARO. How much did you give me to extricate her from Bartholo's hands?* Look here, my lord, it's best not to humiliate a man who serves you well, for fear he may turn into a nasty underling.

* The implied answer is: "Nothing." The allusion is to the plot for freeing Rosine in *The Barber of Seville*.

COUNT. Why is there something shady about everything you do?

FIGARO. Things always look bad when someone is bent on finding fault.

COUNT. You have a hateful reputation!

FIGARO. Maybe it's undeserved: how many noblemen can say as much?

COUNT. Time and again I've seen you on the path to fame and fortune—you always go astray.

FIGARO. What do you expect? The mob is all around, pushing, struggling, crowding, using their elbows, knocking you down. Survives who can; the rest are crushed. And so my mind's made up: I'm through.

COUNT. Through with success?

*Aside.*

That's news.

FIGARO, *aside*. My turn now.

*Aloud.*

Your Excellency favored me with the stewardship of the castle: my lot is a happy one. True, I shan't be King's Messenger and be the first to hear interesting news; but by way of compensation, I'll enjoy wedded bliss here in the heart of Andalusia.

COUNT. Why not take your wife to London?

FIGARO. I'd have to leave her so often I'd soon find marriage a bore.

COUNT. With your brains and character, you could make your way in the administration.

FIGARO. Make your way with brains? You must think mine are addled: be dull and obsequious if you want to succeed.

COUNT. All you'd have to do is to learn statecraft under me.

FIGARO. I know all about it.

COUNT. As you do English—the basic tongue?

FIGARO. Yes—and it's nothing to boast about. Only pretend not to know what you do know and vice versa; understand what's unintelligible and fail to take in what is clear; above all, put forth more strength than you possess; make a secret, often, of what no one is hiding; shut yourself up and trim goose quills so as to seem deep when you are only, as they say, a stuffed shirt; play a part well or ill, send out spies and hire informers, tamper with seals and intercept letters, and try to make ignoble tricks look noble in the light of important ends—that's all of statecraft or God strike me dead!

COUNT. But that's mere intrigue you're describing.

FIGARO. Statecraft, intrigue—as you like. To me, they're kith and kin, and the world is welcome to them. "I'd rather have my own best girl," as the man told the king in the ballad.*

COUNT, *aside*. He wants to stay. I see. . . . Suzanne gave me away.

FIGARO, *aside*. I've scored and paid him back in his own coin.

COUNT. And so you hope to win your case against Marceline?

FIGARO. Do you impute it to me as a crime that I refuse an old maid when Your Excellency feels free to snatch all the young ones?

COUNT, *bantering*. On the bench the judge will put self aside and heed nothing but the law.

FIGARO. The law! Lenient to the great, harsh to the humble.

COUNT. Do you think I am joking?

FIGARO. Who knows, my lord? But *"Tempo è galant 'uomo,"* as the Italian proverb says. Time always tells the truth— that's how I'll learn what good or ill is to befall me.

COUNT, *aside*. I can see she's told him everything; he's got to marry the duenna.

FIGARO, *aside*. He thinks he has me fooled. Actually, what has he found out?

FOOTMAN, *announcing*. Don Guzman Bridlegoose.†

COUNT. Bridlegoose?

---

* *J'aime mieux ma mie, o gué*, a song of the time of Henry IV which is quoted in Molière's *Misanthrope*.
† The don's first name is an allusion to the judge whom Beaumarchais fought and satirized in the course of his protracted lawsuit. Bridlegoose is from Rabelais, though Beaumarchais modestly changed the name to "Bridlegosling" to suggest his descent.

FIGARO. Of course, the associate justice, your understudy and right-hand man.

COUNT. Let him wait.

*Exit* FOOTMAN.

FIGARO, *waiting a moment longer while the* COUNT *is abstracted*. What else did your lordship require?

COUNT, *wide awake*. I? I was saying this room should be prepared for the public hearing.

FIGARO. It's all set: the big chair for you, pretty good chairs for the justices, the clerk's stool, benches for the lawyers, the foreground for the quality and the rest of the floor for the groundlings. I shall dismiss the cleaning women.
*Exit.*

COUNT, *to himself*. That upstart is becoming a nuisance. When he argues he gets the best of me. He presses in and corners you. Oh, fox and vixen! You have combined to take me in. Well, be friends, be lovers, be what you will—I don't care. But when it comes to marrying—

SUZANNE, *breathless*. My lord, forgive me, my lord.

COUNT, *crossly*. What is it, miss?

SUZANNE. You are angry?

COUNT. I take it there is something you want?

SUZANNE, *shyly*. It's because my lady has the vapors. I ran to ask you to lend us your bottle of ether. I'll bring it back immediately.

COUNT, *giving it to her*. Never mind. Keep it for yourself: you'll soon need it.

SUZANNE. Do women of my sort have vapors too? Isn't it a class disease, which is caught only in boudoirs?

COUNT. Well, a girl who is in love and engaged and who loses her intended—

SUZANNE. But if he pays Marceline out of the dowry you promised me—

COUNT. *I* promised you?

SUZANNE, *lowering her eyes*. Sir, I believe I heard you say so.

COUNT. You did, but only if on your side you were willing to listen to me.

SUZANNE, *eyes still lowered.* Isn't it my duty to listen to you?

COUNT. Then, cruel girl, why didn't you tell me sooner?

SUZANNE. It's never too late to tell the truth.

COUNT. You'll come into the garden tonight?

SUZANNE. As if I didn't go walking there every evening.

COUNT. This morning you behaved very harshly to me.

SUZANNE. This morning, yes, with the page behind the armchair.

COUNT. You are right. I forgot. But why your stubbornness before, when Basil spoke to you on my behalf?

SUZANNE. Why should someone like Basil—

COUNT. You are *always* right. Still, there is a certain Figaro to whom I think you have told everything.

SUZANNE. To be sure: I tell him everything . . . except what need never be told.

COUNT, *laughing.* You darling! You promise, then? If you break your word—let's be clear about it, sweetheart—no dowry, no marriage.

SUZANNE, *curtsying.* By the same token, my lord, no marriage, no right of the lord of the manor.

COUNT. Where does she learn this repartee? I swear, I'm crazy about her—but your mistress is waiting for the ether.

SUZANNE, *laughing and giving back the bottle.* How could I have talked to you without a pretext?

COUNT, *trying to kiss her.* Lovely creature!

SUZANNE, *starts to run off.* People are coming.

COUNT, *aside.* She is mine!

*He runs off.*

SUZANNE. Quick, now, to report to my lady.

FIGARO, *entering from upstage right.* Suzanne, Suzanne, where are you off to in such a hurry after leaving my lord?

SUZANNE. You can go to court now, you've just won your suit.

*Running offstage.*

FIGARO, *following.* See here—

*Exit.*

COUNT, *returning.* "You've just won your suit!" So I was pitching headlong into a trap! O my dear damnable schemers, you will rue the day! . . . a sound, solid decision from the bench . . . of course, he might pay off the duenna . . . but what with? If he should pay. . . . Ah, ah, I have the proud Antonio, whose worthy ambition looks down on Figaro as rootless and unworthy of his niece. By nursing this *idée fixe*—and why not? In the field of intrigue one must cultivate everything, even the vanity of fools.

*He starts to call.*

Anto—

*He sees* MARCELINE *and* OTHERS, *exit.*

*Enter* MARCELINE, BARTHOLO, *and* BRIDLEGOOSE.

MARCELINE, *to* BRIDLEGOOSE. Sir, pray listen to my case.

BRIDLEGOOSE, *gowned and stammering slightly.* Very well, let us s-s-speak of it verbally.

BARTHOLO. It's a promise of marriage—

MARCELINE. Linked with a loan of money.

BRIDLEGOOSE. I und-derstand, et cetera and the rest.

MARCELINE. No, sir, no et cetera.

BRIDLEGOOSE. I und-derstand: you have the money?

MARCELINE. No, sir, it was I who lent it.

BRIDLEGOOSE. I quite und-derstand: you want the money back.

MARCELINE. No, sir, I want him to marry me.

BRIDLEGOOSE. I told you I und-derstood. But he—does he want to m-marry you?

MARCELINE. No, sir, that is the point of the case.

BRIDLEGOOSE. Do you mean to imply that I do not und-derstand the case?

MARCELINE. No, sir.

*To* BARTHOLO.

What a spot we're in!

*To* BRIDLEGOOSE.

You say you are going to decide the case?

BRIDLEGOOSE. Why else would I have bought my j-judge-
ship?

MARCELINE, *sighing*. It seems to me a great wrong to sell
them.

BRIDLEGOOSE. True, it would be better to g-give them to us
for n-nothing. Whom are you suing?

*Enter* FIGARO, *rubbing his hands.*

MARCELINE, *pointing*. That unscrupulous man!

FIGARO, *cheerfully, to* MARCELINE. Perhaps I'm in your way?
My lord will be back in a moment, Your Worship.

BRIDLEGOOSE. I've seen that fellow somewhere.

FIGARO. In the house of your lady wife, at Seville, and in her
service, counselor.

BRIDLEGOOSE. In what year?

FIGARO. A little less than a year before the birth of your
younger son, who is a very pretty child if I do say so myself.

BRIDLEGOOSE. Yes, he is the b-best-looking of them all. They
tell me here that you are up to your old tricks.

FIGARO. You flatter me, sir. It's only a trifle.

BRIDLEGOOSE. A promise of marriage! What a booby it is!

FIGARO. Sir!

BRIDLEGOOSE. Have you seen my secretary, a very nice chap?

FIGARO. You mean Doublefist, the clerk?

BRIDLEGOOSE. Yes, I do. He feeds in two places, too.

FIGARO. Feeds! I'll swear he wolfs. Yes indeed, I saw him
about the writ, and then again about the supplement to the
writ, as is customary.

BRIDLEGOOSE. Forms must be observed.

FIGARO. Unquestionably. Just as the cause of the suit belongs
to the parties, so the forms are the property of the court.

BRIDLEGOOSE. The lad is not so stupid as I thought at first.
Well, friend, since you know so much, we'll t-take care of
you in court.

FIGARO. Sir, I rely on your sense of equity even though you
are one of our justices.

BRIDLEGOOSE. What? . . . It's true I am a j-justice. But what if you owe and don't pay?

FIGARO. Surely you can see it comes out exactly as if I didn't owe.

BRIDLEGOOSE. No d-doubt . . . what? What? What did he say?

*Enter the* COUNT *and a* BEADLE, *who walks ahead of him shouting for silence.*

COUNT. Gown and bands in this place, Master Bridlegoose? For a hearing in camera, ordinary clothes are good enough.

BRIDLEGOOSE. 'Tis you are good enough, my lord. But I never go out ung-gowned, don't you see, it is a matter of f-form. A man will laugh at a judge in a short coat but tremble at the sight of an attorney in a g-gown, thanks to the f-form, the f-form.

COUNT. Let the court convene.

BEADLE, *croaking as he opens the doors.* The court! the court!

*Enter* ANTONIO, *the* COUNT'S *servants and his tenants, men and women, who are dressed for the wedding. The* COUNT *sits in the big chair,* BRIDLEGOOSE *to one side, the clerk* DOUBLEFIST *on his stool. The justices and counsel on the benches,* MARCELINE *next to* BARTHOLO, FIGARO *on another bench, the servants and tenants behind them.*

BRIDLEGOOSE, *to* DOUBLEFIST. Doublefist, call up the cases.

DOUBLEFIST, *reading from a paper.* The noble, high, and puissant Don Pedro George, Hidalgo and Baron de los Altos y Montes Fieros y otros montes v. Alonzo Calderón, a young playwright, in the matter of a stillborn play, which each disowns and attributes to the other.

COUNT. They are both right. With a view to insuring public attention if they write another work together, it is ordered that the nobleman shall contribute his name and the poet his talent. Case dismissed.

DOUBLEFIST, *from another paper.* Andrea Petrucchio, farmer, v. the tax collector, in the matter of an arbitrary foreclosure.

COUNT. Not within my jurisdiction. I shall serve my vassals best by sponsoring them at the King's court. Next.

DOUBLEFIST, *reading a third paper.* BARTHOLO *and* FIGARO *rise.* Barbara Hagar Rahab Magdelene Nicola Marceline Greenleaf, spinster of age . . .

MARCELINE *rises and bows.*

. . . *v.* Figaro, first name missing—

FIGARO. Anonymous.

BRIDLEGOOSE. Anonymous? What patron s-saint is that?

FIGARO. Mine.

DOUBLEFIST, *writing.* . . . *versus* "Anonymous Figaro." Profession?

FIGARO. Gentleman.

COUNT. You, a gentleman?

DOUBLEFIST *is still writing.*

FIGARO. God willing, I should have been the son of a prince.

COUNT, *to* DOUBLEFIST. Go on.

BEADLE, *croaking.* Silence in court!

DOUBLEFIST, *reading.* . . . in the matter of a dispute about the marriage of the said Figaro to the said Greenleaf, the learned Dr. Bartholo appearing for the plaintiff and the said Figaro for himself—provided the court allows it against the tenor of custom and the rules of the bench.

FIGARO. Custom, Mister Doublefist, is often mere corruption. A party to a suit always knows his case better than some barrister who sweats without conviction and shouts his head off about everything he knows, except the facts, and who does not mind ruining the suitor, boring the court, and putting the jury to sleep. And afterward he is as puffed up as if he had written Cicero's orations. I can put my case in two words. Gentlemen—

DOUBLEFIST. Those you've uttered so far are wasted, for you are not the plaintiff. You can only defend. Come forward, Doctor, and read into the evidence the promise of marriage.

FIGARO. Yes, the promise.

BARTHOLO, *putting on his glasses.* It is explicit.

BRIDLEGOOSE. We have to see.

DOUBLEFIST. Gentlemen, please be quiet.

BEADLE, *croaking*. Silence in court!

BARTHOLO. "I, the undersigned, acknowledge having received from the Damozel, et cetera, Marceline Greenleaf, of the manor of Aguas-Frescas, the sum of two thousand piastres, which sum I shall repay on her demand and in the said manor,—er—and shall marry her as a token of gratitude, et cetera, signed: Figaro—er—just Figaro." My client asks for the payment of the note and the execution of the promise, with costs.

*Pleading.*

Gentlemen! Never was a more moving request brought to the bar of a court. Since the case of Alexander the Great, who promised marriage to the beautiful Thalestris—

COUNT, *interrupting*. Before you go farther, counsel, is the genuineness of the document stipulated?

BRIDLEGOOSE, *to* FIGARO. What do you say to the f-f-facts just read into the evidence?

FIGARO. I say there is malice, error, or inadvertence in the manner in which the document was read. For the statement does not say: "Which sum I shall repay *and* I shall marry her"; it says: "Which sum I shall repay *or* I shall marry her," which is very different.

COUNT. Does the document say *and* or does it say *or?*

BARTHOLO. It says *and.*

FIGARO. It says *or.*

BRIDLEGOOSE. Doublefist, you read it.

DOUBLEFIST, *taking the paper*. That's always wise, because the parties twist things as they read. Er—er—er— "Damozel—er —Greenleaf—er— Ha! Which sum I shall repay on her demand, and in the said manor,—er—shall marry—and . . . or . . ." there's *and* after demand and *o r* at the end of man*or*, but after that it's hard to make out—there is a blot.

BRIDLEGOOSE. A b-blot? Ah, I und-derstand!

BARTHOLO, *pleading again*. I submit, my lord and gentlemen, that the decisive word is the copulative conjunction *and* which links the correlative members of the sentence: "I shall pay the Damozel, et cetera, *and* I shall marry her."

FIGARO, *in the same tone*. And I maintain that it is the alternative conjunction *or*, which separates the said members: "I shall pay the damsel *or* I shall marry her." To his pedantry I oppose my superpedantry: if he drops into Latin, I come up with Greek and exterminate him.

COUNT. How am I to adjudicate such a question?

BARTHOLO. To settle it and no longer quibble over a syllable, we stipulate the absence of the second *and* after *manor*.

FIGARO. I ask for an affidavit to that effect.

BARTHOLO. We stand by our stipulation. But it affords no escape for the guilty, for let us examine the document with the stipulation in mind: "Which sum I shall repay on demand and in the said manor shall marry her . . ." It is as if one said: "I shall have myself bled in this room—and in this bed will remain until I feel better." Or again: "He will take a dose of calomel tonight—and in the morning will experience the good effect." Thus, my lord and gentlemen, "he will repay on demand—and in the said manor will marry. . . ."

FIGARO. Nothing of the kind! There is a word under the blot and it is *or*, as thus: "Either illness carries you off, OR your physician will see to it." That is irrefutable. Another example: "Either you write wretched stuff, OR all the fools will mark you down." Does Dr. Bartholo think that I have forgotten my grammar? "I shall repay, on her demand and in the said manor COMMA or I shall marry her."

BARTHOLO, *quickly*. There's no comma.

FIGARO, *just as quickly*. There is. It goes: "COMMA, or I shall marry her."

BARTHOLO, *glancing at the paper*. It's without a comma.

FIGARO. It was there, my lord and gentlemen, before the blot. Besides, does a man who marries have to pay the debt as well?

BARTHOLO, *instantly*. Yes, because we marry under a separate property agreement.

FIGARO, *just as fast*. If marriage does not cancel the debt, we insist on the separation of persons *and* property!

*The judges rise and confer.*

BARTHOLO. A rewarding cancellation!

DOUBLEFIST. Silence, gentlemen!

BEADLE, *croaking.* Silence in court!

BARTHOLO. Scoundrels of this stripe call it paying their debts!

FIGARO. Are you speaking now on your own behalf?

BARTHOLO. I am defending this lady.

FIGARO. You may go on raving, but please stop casting aspersions. When the law, fearing the passions of the interested parties, allowed the intervention of counsel, it did not mean to permit these temperate defenders to become privileged slanderers. That would have been to degrade the noblest of institutions.

*The judges are still conferring.*

ANTONIO, *to* MARCELINE, *and pointing to the judges.* Why must they palaverate so long?

MARCELINE. They got at the chief justice, he is getting around the other one, and I am about to lose the case.

BARTHOLO, *somberly.* I am afraid so.

FIGARO, *gaily.* Cheer up, Marceline!

DOUBLEFIST, *jumping up and addressing* MARCELINE. That's too much! I denounce you, and for the honor of the court I ask that before the other case is settled you be tried for contempt!

COUNT, *sitting down.* No, master clerk. I shall not judge in my own case for an insult to my person. No Spanish judge will have to blush for such an abuse of power, worthy only of an oriental despot. We commit enough wrongs as it is. I am now going to correct one of these by stating the reasons for my decision. Any judge who rules and gives no reason is an enemy of the law. What does the plaintiff ask? Marriage failing payment. Both together would be contradictory.

DOUBLEFIST. Silence, gentlemen!

BEADLE, *croaking.* Silence in court!

COUNT. What does the defendant rejoin? That he wants to retain possession of his person. Permission is granted.

FIGARO. I've won!

COUNT. But since the text says: Which sum I shall repay on the first demand *or* I shall marry, etc., the court orders the defendant to pay the plaintiff two thousand piastres *or* to marry her within the day.

*Rises.*

FIGARO, *petrified.* I've lost!

ANTONIO, *delighted.* A magnificent decision!

FIGARO. How, magnificent?

ANTONIO. On account of how you aren't no longer my nephew-in-law, thank the Lord!

BEADLE, *croaking.* Move along, gem'mun.

*Exeunt.*

ANTONIO. I'm off to tell all about it to my niece.

MARCELINE, *sitting down.* Now I can breathe freely.

FIGARO. But I am suffocating.

COUNT, *aside.* And I am avenged; it's very soothing.

FIGARO, *aside.* Where's Basil, who was supposed to prevent Marceline's marriage—he's back in good time, I don't think!

*To the* COUNT, *on his way out.*

Leaving us, my lord?

COUNT. There's nothing more to judge.

FIGARO, *looking at* BRIDLEGOOSE. If it weren't for that fathead—

BRIDLEGOOSE. Me, a fathead?

FIGARO. Who can doubt it? And I shan't marry her: I am a gentleman after all.

*The* COUNT *stops.*

BARTHOLO. You will marry her.

FIGARO. Without my noble progenitors' consent?

BARTHOLO. Give us their name, exhibit them.

FIGARO. Give me a little time. I must be close to finding them, I've been looking for fifteen years.

BARTHOLO. Conceited ass! A foundling!

FIGARO. Not found, Doctor, lost, or rather, stolen.

COUNT, *returning.* Stolen, lost—where's the proof? Otherwise he'll cry out that he's being cheated.

FIGARO. My lord, even if the lace on my baby clothes, and the embroidered coverlet, and the gold and jewels I wore when the brigands snatched me, did not suffice to prove my high birth, the care that had been taken to put distinctive marks on me would show that I was a valuable offspring. I have hieroglyphics on my arm . . .

*He starts to roll up his right sleeve.*

MARCELINE, *rising quickly.* You have a mark like a spatula on your right arm?

FIGARO. How do you know I have?

MARCELINE. Good God, it's he!

FIGARO. Of course it's me.

BARTHOLO, *to* MARCELINE. Who?

MARCELINE, *quickly.* It's Emmanuel!

BARTHOLO, *to* FIGARO. You were kidnaped by gypsies?

FIGARO, *excited.* Near a castle, yes. My good Doctor, if you restore me to my noble family, set a high price on your services. Gold and treasure are trifles to my illustrious parents.

BARTHOLO, *pointing to* MARCELINE. There is your mother.

FIGARO. Foster mother?

BARTHOLO. Your own mother.

COUNT. His mother?

FIGARO. Explain.

MARCELINE, *pointing to* BARTHOLO. There is your father.

FIGARO, *in distress.* Ah, oh, woe is me!

MARCELINE. Didn't the voice of nature tell you so again and again?

FIGARO. Not once.

COUNT, *aside.* His mother!

BRIDLEGOOSE. One thing is c-c-clear: he won't marry her.*

COUNT. Stupid turn of events—most annoying!

---

* At this point occurs a declamatory passage of about two pages on society's unjust treatment of women. It was omitted in the original production and has not been played since, though Beaumarchais printed it in his Preface.

BRIDLEGOOSE, *to* FIGARO. And your nobility? Your castle? You would hoodwink the law with false pretenses?

FIGARO. The law! It nearly made me commit a prize blunder, the law did—on top of the fact that for those accursèd hundred pounds,° many is the time I almost beat up this gentleman who turns out to be my father. But since heaven has saved my virtue from these temptations, Father of mine, please accept my apologies . . . And you, Mother mine, fold me in your arms—as maternally as you can.

MARCELINE *clasps him about the neck.*

SUZANNE, *running with a purse in her hand.* My lord, stop everything! Do not marry them: I've come to pay this lady with the dowry madam has given me.

COUNT, *aside.* The devil take the Countess! It is as if everything conspired . . .

*Exit.*

ANTONIO, *seeing* FIGARO *embracing his mother, addresses* SUZANNE. Payment, eh? I see, I see.

SUZANNE, *turning her back.* I've seen enough; let's go, Uncle.

FIGARO. Please don't! What is it you've seen enough?

SUZANNE. My weakness of mind and your lack of integrity—

FIGARO. Neither of them a fact.

SUZANNE, *angrily.*   . . . and your willingness to marry her and caress her.

FIGARO, *gaily.* I caress but don't marry.

SUZANNE *tries to leave;* FIGARO *prevents her;* SUZANNE *slaps him.*

SUZANNE. You are impertinent and rude, let me go!

FIGARO, *to the company.* That's love for you! Before you go, though, I beg you take a good look at the dear woman in front of you.

SUZANNE. I'm looking.

FIGARO. How does she strike you?

SUZANNE. Horrible!

---

° An allusion to Figaro's successful swindle of Bartholo in *The Barber of Seville.*

FIGARO. Long live jealousy! No half measures about it.

MARCELINE, *arms open to* SUZANNE. Come kiss your mother, my pretty Suzanette. The naughty boy who is tormenting you is my son.

SUZANNE, *running to her.* You—his mother!

*They stay clasped in each other's arms.*

ANTONIO. It must have just happened.

FIGARO. No, only just disclosed.

MARCELINE, *with fervor.* My heart was right to be so strongly drawn to him, though mistaking its reason. Blood was speaking to me.

FIGARO. And good sense to me, which worked like instinct to make me refuse you. For I was far from hating you, witness the money . . .

MARCELINE, *handing him a paper.* The money is yours: take back your note. It is your dowry.

SUZANNE, *throwing the purse to him.* And take this too!

FIGARO. Many thanks!

MARCELINE, *excited.* I was unfortunate as a girl, and, just now was about to become the most wretched of wives; I am now the happiest of mothers. Come kiss me, children: all my feelings of love are centered upon you. I am as happy as anyone can be and—oh, children, how I am going to love you!

FIGARO, *moved and speaking with vehemence.* Please stop, dearest Mother, or you will see my eyes dissolve away in the first tears I have ever shed. They are tears of joy—but what a fool I am: I nearly felt ashamed of myself as I felt the drops on my hands.

*He shows his hands, fingers outspread.*

I stupidly tried to hold them back. Away, false shame! I want to laugh and cry all at once. What I now feel does not come to a man twice in a lifetime.

*He kisses his mother to one side of him,* SUZANNE *on the other.*

MARCELINE. Oh, my dear!

SUZANNE. My very dear!

BRIDLEGOOSE, *wiping his eyes*. It seems I am a f-fool also!

FIGARO, *excited*. Grief! I can now defy you: afflict me if you can, between these two women I love.

ANTONIO, *to* FIGARO. Not so many pretty speeches, if you please. Apropos of marriage, in good families, that of the parents is supposed to precede. Do your parents ask each other's hand?

BARTHOLO. May my hand rot and fall off if I ever offer it to the mother of such a character!

ANTONIO, *to* BARTHOLO. In other words you're nothing but an unnatural father?

*To* FIGARO.

In that case, Lothario, the bargain's off.

SUZANNE. Oh, Uncle!

ANTONIO. D'you think I'll give my sister's child to this here who's no one's child?

BRIDLEGOOSE. How do you make that out, idiot? Everyone is somebody's child!

ANTONIO. Yah, yah: he shan't have her nohow.

*Exit.*

BARTHOLO, *to* FIGARO. Better look for somebody to adopt you. *He tries to go, but* MARCELINE *seizes him around the middle and pulls him back.*

MARCELINE. One moment, Doctor, don't go.

FIGARO, *aside*. It's incredible but all the fools in Andalusia are rabid against my poor desire to get married.

SUZANNE, *to* BARTHOLO. Dear little Father, he is your son.

MARCELINE. He has wit, talent, and presence.

FIGARO. And he never cost you a penny.

BARTHOLO. What about the hundred pounds he robbed me of?

MARCELINE, *cuddling him*. We'll take such good care of you, Papa!*

SUZANNE, *cuddling*. We'll love you so much, dear little Papa!

BARTHOLO, *yielding*. "Papa, Papa, dear Papa—" Now I'm going to be as big a fool as this gentleman . . .

* Accent on the second syllable, as in Mamma later.

*Pointing to* BRIDLEGOOSE.

I'm being led like a child.

MARCELINE *and* SUZANNE *kiss him.*

Now, now, I haven't said yes.

*Turning around.*

What's become of his lordship?

FIGARO. Let's join him, quick, and force a decision from him. If he were to think up some new scheme, we'd have to start all over again.

ALL, *together.* Let's go, let's go!

*They drag* BARTHOLO *outside.*

BRIDLEGOOSE, *left alone.* "As big a fool as this gentleman." A man can say that sort of thing about himself, but . . . they're not at all p-polite in this p-place.

*Exit.*

## ACT IV

*A large room with candelabra all lighted, floral decorations, and other ornaments indicative of preparations for a party. Downstage right stands a table and on it a writing case. Behind the table is an armchair.*

FIGARO, *hugging* SUZANNE. Well, love, are you happy? She got round the doctor, didn't she, my silver-tongued mother? Despite his distaste he is marrying her, and your curmudgeon of an uncle can't help himself. That leaves only my lord in a rage; for after all, our marriage is the upshot of theirs. What a happy ending! Aren't you inclined to laugh?

SUZANNE. I never knew anything so odd.

FIGARO. Say rather so jolly. All we wanted was a dowry, squeezed out of His Excellency. Now we have two which owe nothing to him. A relentless rival was hounding you and I was bedeviled by a fury. That trouble has for us both taken the form of a loving mother. Yesterday I was, so to speak, alone in the world; today I have all my relatives complete about me. True, they're not so resplendent as if I had designed them myself, but good enough for us who haven't the ambition to be rich.

SUZANNE. And yet none of the things that you had planned and expected came through.

FIGARO. Chance did a better job, my sweet. That's the way of the world. You toil, you scheme, you make projects, all in your own corner; Fortune works in another. From the insatiable conqueror who would like to swallow the globe to the peaceable blind man led by his dog, all human beings are the playthings of fate. Indeed, the blind man is often better served by his dog, less deceived in his opinions, than some other self-blinded man with his retinue. As for that delightful blind fellow called Love . . .

*He again embraces her tenderly.*

SUZANNE. He's the only one I care about.

FIGARO. Well then, let me be the serviceable dog in folly's employ, who makes it his job to lead him to your charming little door. And there we'll be cozy for the rest of our lives.

SUZANNE, *laughing.* Love and you?

FIGARO. I and Love.

SUZANNE. And you won't look for other lodgings?

FIGARO. If you catch me at it, I'm willing to have a hundred million philanderers—

SUZANNE. You're going to say more than you mean: tell me the honest truth.

FIGARO. My truest truth?

SUZANNE. Shame on you, rascal! Is there more than one?

FIGARO. I should say so! Ever since it has been observed that with the passage of time old follies turn into wisdom, and that early little lies, even though poorly planted, bloom into great big truths—ever since then, there have been endless species of truths. There are those one dare not utter, for not every truth is fit to say; there are those one flaunts without putting faith in them, for not every truth is fit to believe. And then there are the passionate promises, the parental threats, the resolutions of drinkers, the assurances of office holders, the "positively final offers" of businessmen—there's no end to them. Only my love for my Suzy is true coin.

SUZANNE. I love your gaiety because it is wild. It shows you are happy. But let's talk about meeting the Count in the garden.

FIGARO. Far better never speak of that again. It nearly cost me my Sue.

SUZANNE. You don't want me to go through with it?

FIGARO. If you love me, Suzy, give me your word on this. Let him eat his heart out—it'll be his punishment.

SUZANNE. I found it harder at first to agree to it than now to give it up—I'll never mention it again.

FIGARO. That's your truest truth?

SUZANNE. I'm not like you learned people. I have only one truth.

FIGARO. And you'll love me a little?

SUZANNE. Much.

FIGARO. That isn't much.

SUZANNE. What do you mean?

FIGARO. Why, in love, don't you see, too much is barely enough.

SUZANNE. Your subtleties are beyond me, but I intend to love only my husband.

FIGARO. Stick to it and you will represent a remarkable exception to the rule.

*Starts to kiss her. Enter* COUNTESS.

COUNTESS. I was just saying: wherever they happen to be, you may be sure they're together. I really think, Figaro, that each time you indulge in a tête-à-tête you are living off the future, drawing on wedded bliss, and robbing yourself. People look for you and get impatient.

FIGARO. You are right, madam. I was forgetting myself. I will show them my excuse.

*He tries to take* SUZANNE *with him.*

COUNTESS, *holding her back.* She'll follow later.

*Exit* FIGARO.

*To* SUZANNE.

Have you what's needed to change clothes with me?

SUZANNE. Nothing is needed, madam. The assignation is off.

COUNTESS. You have changed your mind?

SUZANNE. It's Figaro—

COUNTESS. You are deceiving me.

SUZANNE. God is my witness!

COUNTESS. Figaro is not a man to let a dowry slip from his grasp.

SUZANNE. Oh, madam, what can you be thinking?

COUNTESS. Why, that in concert with the Count, you are now sorry you made me privy to his plans. I can read you like a book. Leave me to myself.

*She starts to leave.*

SUZANNE, *on her knees.* In the name of heaven which is our hope, you cannot know the wrong you do me. When you have been so endlessly good to me, after the dowry you've given me, how could I—

COUNTESS, *lifting her up.* But—of course! I must have been out of my mind. Since you are changing places with me, dear heart, you won't be going into the garden. You'll be keeping your word to your husband and helping me recapture mine.

SUZANNE. Oh, how you upset me!

COUNTESS. I've been terribly scatterbrained.

*Kisses* SUZANNE *on the forehead.*

Where is the meeting place?

SUZANNE *kisses the* COUNTESS's *hand.* All I heard was "garden."

COUNTESS, *motioning* SUZANNE *to the table.* Take that pen and we will name a spot.

SUZANNE. I, write to him?

COUNTESS. You must.

SUZANNE. But at least, madam, you—

COUNTESS. I'll take the responsibility for everything.

*SUZANNE sits at the table.*

COUNTESS, *dictating.* "A new song to the tune of: 'How lovely under the elms at night, How lovely . . .'"

SUZANNE, *writing.* "'. . . under the elms.'" Yes, nothing else?

COUNTESS. Have you the slightest fear that he won't understand?

SUZANNE. You're right.

*She folds the note.*

What sort of seal?

COUNTESS. A pin, quick—it will serve to reply with. Write on the back: "Please return the seal."

SUZANNE, *laughing.* Ho! the seal! This seal, my lady, is a funnier joke than the one on the officer's commission.

COUNTESS, *in painful recollection.* Oh!

SUZANNE, *looking on her person.* I haven't a pin on me.

COUNTESS, *unpinning her coat collar.* Take this.

*The* PAGE's *ribbon falls from her bosom.*

Oh, my ribbon!

SUZANNE, *picking it up.* Ah, the little thief's property . . . and you were cruel enough to—

COUNTESS. Could I let him wear it on his arm? A fine spectacle! Give it back to me.

SUZANNE. Your ladyship cannot wear it: it is spotted with the young man's blood.

COUNTESS. It will be just right for Fanchette . . . when she next brings me flowers.

*Enter a young shepherdess,* CHERUBINO *dressed as a girl,* FANCHETTE *and other girls dressed like her and carrying bouquets.*

FANCHETTE. My lady, these girls from the village bring you flowers.

COUNTESS *quickly hides the ribbon again.* They are delightful. It grieves me, dears, not to know you all by name.

*Pointing to* CHERUBINO.

But who is this lovely child who seems so shy?

SHEPHERDESS. A cousin of mine, ma'am, come to visit for the wedding.

COUNTESS. So pretty! Since I can't wear all twenty of your posies, I'll honor the stranger.

*She takes* CHERUBINO's *bouquet and kisses him on the forehead.*

She's blushing. Suzy, don't you think she looks like someone we know?

SUZANNE. So much so I can hardly tell them apart.

CHERUBINO, *aside, both hands on his heart.* Oh, that kiss went right through me!

ANTONIO, *entering with the* COUNT. And I tell you he's here somewhere. They dressed him at my daughter's, all the clothes are still around, and here's his regulation hat, which I picked out of the lot.

*Steps forward, scans the girls' faces, and recognizes* CHERU-
BINO, *whose female bonnet he pulls off. As* CHERUBINO's *long
hair falls in ringlets,* ANTONIO *tosses the military hat on top.*

By gum, there's your officer!

COUNTESS, *stepping back.* Heavens!

SUZANNE. The rapscallion!

ANTONIO. I was telling you upstairs it was him.

COUNT, *angry.* Well, madam?

COUNTESS. Well, sir, you find me as surprised as you and
equally angry.

COUNT. It may be, but what about this morning?

COUNTESS. I should be guilty indeed if I kept up the deception
any longer. He had dropped in to see me, and it was then
we undertook the practical joke which these children have
completed. You discovered Suzanne and me dressing him
up. You are so quick to anger that he ran away, I lost my
good judgment, and general dismay did the rest.

COUNT, *disgruntled.* Why haven't you left?

CHERUBINO, *flinging off the hat.* My lord—

COUNT. I shall punish you for disobeying.

FANCHETTE, *thoughtlessly.* Oh, my lord, please listen to me:
every time you come by and kiss me you always say: "Fanchette, dear, if you will love me, I'll give you anything you
want."

COUNT, *flushing.* I have said that?

FANCHETTE. Yes, my lord. Well, instead of punishing Cherubino, give him to me for a husband, and then I'll love you
madly.

COUNT, *aside.* Diddled by a page!

COUNTESS. Count, it is your turn now. This child's naïve confession, as innocent as mine, bears witness to a double truth,
which is that when I cause you anguish it is always unin-
tentionally, whereas you do your utmost to increase and
justify my own.

ANTONIO. You too, my lord? By gum, I'm going to get after
that chit as I did after her mother, now gathered. . . . Not

that it's of consequence, but as my lady knows, these little girls when they grow up. . . .

COUNT, *discomfited, aside.* There is an evil genius in this place who turns everything against me.

FIGARO, *entering.* My lord, if you detain the young ladies, the party can't begin, or the dance either.

COUNT. You want to dance? Have you forgotten how you fell this morning and sprained your right foot?

FIGARO, *swinging his leg.* It's still a trifle sore, but it's nothing.
*To the girls.*
Come along, darlings, come.

COUNT, *turning* FIGARO *about.* You were lucky the flower bed was soft earth.

FIGARO. Very lucky—otherwise . . .

ANTONIO *twists him the other way.* Besides he "gathered himself together" as he fell all the way to the bottom.

FIGARO. A really clever man would have stopped halfway down.
*To the girls.*
Are you coming, ladies?

ANTONIO, *twisting* FIGARO *again.* All the while the little page was galloping on his horse toward Seville.

FIGARO. Galloping, or maybe sauntering . . .

COUNT *twists* FIGARO *the other way.* And his commission was in your pocket.

FIGARO, *somewhat surprised.* Undoubtedly, but why this examination?
*To the girls.*
Now come on, girls!

ANTONIO, *pulling* CHERUBINO *by the arm.* Here's one who says my future nephew is a liar.

FIGARO, *taken aback.* Cherubino!
*Aside.*
Blast the little braggart!

ANTONIO. Have you got it now?

FIGARO. Got it, got it! . . . By the by, what's his story?

COUNT, *dryly*. Hardly a story; he says it was he who jumped into the gillyflowers.

FIGARO, *abstracted*. Hm, if he says so . . . it may well be. I don't argue about what I don't know.

COUNT. So both you and he . . .

FIGARO. Why not? The jumping fever is catching—just think of sheep over a fence.* And when my lord is angry, anyone would prefer to risk his neck—

COUNT. Now really, two by two?

FIGARO. We'd have done it by the dozen—and why should you care, my lord, seeing no one was hurt?

*To the girls.*

I say, are you coming in or aren't you?

COUNT, *outraged*. Is it a farce we're playing together, you and I?

*Music begins off stage.*

FIGARO. There's the opening march. Fall in, my beauties, fall in. Here, Suzanne, give me your arm.

*Exeunt except* CHERUBINO, *who stays behind, his head hung down.*

COUNT, *gazing at* FIGARO'S *back*. Did you ever see greater nerve?

*To* CHERUBINO.

As for you, sly boots who now pretend to be ashamed, go dress yourself properly and let me not see your face for the rest of the evening.

COUNTESS. He will be terribly bored.

CHERUBINO, *thoughtlessly*. Bored? I carry on my brow enough happiness to outweigh a hundred years in jail!

*He puts on his hat and leaves. The* COUNTESS *fans herself violently.*

COUNT. What is so happy about his brow?

* In the original Beaumarchais refers to the sheep in Rabelais which Panurge induced to jump overboard by throwing over the first one.

COUNTESS, *embarrassed*. His first military hat, I suppose. With children any novelty is like a toy.

*She starts to leave.*

COUNT. You won't stay, Countess?

COUNTESS. I told you I did not feel well.

COUNT. One moment more for the sake of your protégée—or I'll think you are cross.

COUNTESS. Here come the two wedding processions. Let us sit and receive them.

COUNT, *aside*. The wedding! . . . Well, what can't be cured must be endured.

COUNT *and* COUNTESS *sit to one side of the room. Enter the processions to a march based on the* Folies d'Espagne:*

*A Gamekeeper, a musket on his shoulder.*

*The mayor, the aldermen,* BRIDLEGOOSE.

*Peasants and their women in party dress.*

*Two young girls carrying the virgin's bonnet.*

*Two others in white veils.*

*Two others, wearing gloves and a corsage at the waist.*

ANTONIO *holding* SUZANNE'S *hand to give her away to* FIGARO.

*Other girls with other types of bonnets and veils.*

MARCELINE *wearing a white veil and bonnet similar to the first.*

FIGARO *holding* MARCELINE'S *hand to give her away to:*

*The doctor, who brings up the rear of the procession, wearing a large boutonniere.*

*The girls, as they pass in front of the* COUNT, *deliver to his footmen the paraphernalia for* SUZANNE *and* MARCELINE.

*The peasants, men and women, in two lines, dance the fandango to an accompaniment of castanets. Then the orchestra plays the introduction of the duet, during which* ANTONIO

---

* Presumed to be an old Spanish dance, but known to us only through a theme in ¾ time called Follia in Corelli's Solos, op. 5, and used also by Vivaldi and others. *Folies* here does not imply folly but foliage, as in *Folies Bergère*.

*takes* SUZANNE *to the* COUNT. *She kneels before him, he puts the virgin's bonnet on her head, and gives her a bouquet. During this ceremony the girls sing the following duet:*

> Sing, young bride, the grateful benefaction!
> Your master has his selfish lust displaced:
> He gives up pleasure for a noble action,
> And to your husband hands you pure and chaste.

*As the duet concludes,* SUZANNE, *still kneeling, tugs at the* COUNT's *cloak and shows him the note she has for him. She then puts her hand to her hair and he takes the note while seeming to adjust her bonnet. He puts the note inside his coat, the duet ends,* SUZANNE *rises and makes a low curtsy.*

FIGARO *receives* SUZANNE *from the hand of the* COUNT *and steps back with her to the other end of the room, near* MARCELINE.

*There is meanwhile a reprise of the fandango. The* COUNT, *being in a hurry to read his note, comes downstage and pulls the paper from his pocket. The pin evidently pricks him, for he shakes his finger, squeezes it, and licks it. He looks at the folded paper and speaks.*

COUNT. The devil take all women! They stick pins into everything.

*He throws the pin on the ground, reads the note, and kisses it. While he and* FIGARO *speak, the orchestra plays pianissimo.* FIGARO, *who has seen the byplay, speaks to* SUZANNE *and his mother.*

FIGARO. It must be a billet-doux some little wench slipped into his hand as she walked by. It was sealed with a pin which impudently pricked him.

*The dance resumes. The* COUNT *turns the note over and sees the request to return the pin. He looks for it on the ground, finds it, and sticks it in his sleeve.*

FIGARO, *to* SUZANNE *and* MARCELINE. From the beloved any object is dear, so he's retrieved the pin. What a harlequin he is!

*Meanwhile,* SUZANNE *and the* COUNTESS *have been exchanging signals. The dance concludes and the introduction of the duet is played again.* FIGARO *takes* MARCELINE *to the* COUNT, *and the ceremony repeats. But just as the* COUNT *lifts the bonnet and as the duet strikes up, the proceedings are interrupted by a great noise at the door.*

FOOTMAN. Keep back, keep back, gentlemen, you can't all get in together. Help here! The guards!

*Guards step quickly toward the door.*

COUNT, *rising.* What is the matter there?

FOOTMAN. My lord, it is Mister Basil, who is followed by the whole township because he sings as he walks.

COUNT. Admit him alone.

COUNTESS. Please command me to withdraw.

COUNT. I shan't forget your obliging me.

COUNTESS. Suzanne! . . .

*To the* COUNT.

She will be back at once.

*Aside, to* SUZANNE.

Let's go change our clothes.

*Exeunt.*

MARCELINE. He never shows up but to do harm.

FIGARO. You see if I don't change his tune.

*Enter* BASIL, *guitar in hand, followed by* SUNSTRUCK.

BASIL *sings to the music of the final song of the play.*

> Faithful, tender, loving hearts
> Who condemn love's wanderings
> Do not launch your angry darts:
> It is not a crime to change,
> For if Cupid carries wings
> It must be to flit and range!
> It must be to flit and range!

FIGARO, *going toward* BASIL. Yes, that's the reason precisely why Love has wings on his back. Friend, what do you mean by your song?

BASIL, *pointing to* SUNSTRUCK. I mean that after showing submissiveness to my lord and entertaining this gentleman, who is of my lord's company, I want to claim my lord's justice.

SUNSTRUCK. Pah, your lordsy, he didn't entertain me at all—he just had fits of yodeling!

COUNT. What is it you want, Basil?

BASIL. That which already belongs to me, my lord—the hand of Marceline.

FIGARO, *drawing near*. How long has it been since you saw the face of a lunatic?

BASIL. My good sir, I see one right now.

FIGARO. Since you use my eyes as a mirror, study the effect therein of the prophecy I am about to make: if you so much as seem to gravitate toward madame—

BARTHOLO, *laughing*. But why? Let him speak.

BRIDLEGOOSE, *coming forward*. Is it n-necessary for two old f-friends . . .

FIGARO. He and I friends?

BASIL. Absurd!

FIGARO, *setting a rapid pace for the ensuing dialogue*. Friends because he writes the dullest church music?

BASIL. While he writes newspaper verse?

FIGARO. A tavern musician!

BASIL. A penny-a-liner!

FIGARO. An oratorio-monger!

BASIL. A diplomatic nag!

COUNT, *seated*. Vulgarians both!

BASIL. He's failed me at every turn.

FIGARO. That's an idea I wish were true.

BASIL. He goes round calling me an ass.

FIGARO. Don't mistake me for public opinion.

BASIL. Whereas there's hardly a talented singer I haven't trained.

FIGARO. Strained!

BASIL. He persists!

FIGARO. And why shouldn't I, if I speak the truth? Are you a prince that you should be flattered? Learn to live with the truth, faker! It's certain no liar could make much of you.

Perhaps you're afraid the truth will come out of our mouths? If so, why did you interrupt our nuptials?

BASIL, *to* MARCELINE. Did you or did you not promise me that if you weren't provided for within four years, you would give me your hand?

MARCELINE. Under what condition did I promise this?

BASIL. That if you found your lost child, I would adopt him out of kindness to you.

ALL, *together*. He's been found!

BASIL. All right, I'm ready.

ALL, *together, pointing to* FIGARO. There he is!

BASIL, *shrinking back*. Get thee behind me!

BRIDLEGOOSE. That means you g-give up his d-dear mother?

BASIL. What could be worse than to be thought the father of such a fellow?

FIGARO. Why, to be thought your son! You're pulling my leg!

BASIL, *pointing to* FIGARO. The moment this character is somebody in this house, I want everyone to know that I am nobody.

*Exit.*

BARTHOLO, *laughing*. Hahahaha!

FIGARO, *leaping with joy*. At last, at last, I'll have my bride!

COUNT, *aside*. And I my mistress.

*He rises.*

BRIDLEGOOSE, *to* MARCELINE. With everybody s-satisfied.

COUNT. Let the two marriage contracts be drawn up. I shall sign them.

ALL, *together*. Bravo!

COUNT. I need time to myself.

*He starts to leave with the others.*

SUNSTRUCK, *to* FIGARO. Now I'm going to set up the fireworks under the elms as I was told.

COUNT, *coming back*. What idiot gave you that order?

FIGARO. What's wrong with it?

COUNT. Why, the Countess is indisposed. How can she see the

display from indoors unless it's on the terrace, below her room?

FIGARO. You heard him, Sunstruck? On the terrace.

COUNT. Under the elms, the idea!

*Leaving, aside.*

They were going to set fire to my tête-à-tête.

FIGARO. What considerateness for his wife!

*Starts to leave.*

MARCELINE, *stopping him.* A word with you, my son. I owe you an apology. Mistaken feeling for you made me unjust to your wife: I thought her in league with the Count, even though Basil had told me she always rejected his advances.

FIGARO. You don't know your son if you think that female whims and wiles can shake him. I challenge the cleverest to upset me.

MARCELINE. It's nice to feel that way, at any rate, because jealousy—

FIGARO. Is but a stupid child of pride, or else it's a madman's disease. I assure you, Mother, on this point I'm a philosopher —unshakable. So if Suzanne ever deceives me, I forgive her in advance, for she will have worked hard and long to do it.

*He turns and sees* FANCHETTE, *who is looking everywhere for someone.*

FIGARO. So-o, little cousin! Getting an earful?

FANCHETTE. Oh, no! I was brought up to think it's not nice.

FIGARO. True enough, but since it's useful, it's often considered worth the trouble.

FANCHETTE. I was finding out if somebody was here.

FIGARO. So young and so full of guile! You know perfectly well he can't be here.

FANCHETTE. Who's that?

FIGARO. Cherubino.

FANCHETTE. It isn't he I'm after. I know where *he* is. It's cousin Sue.

FIGARO. And what do you want with her?

FANCHETTE. I can tell *you*, because you're my cousin now. It's about a pin I'm supposed to give her.

FIGARO, *startled*. A pin? A pin did you say? And from whom, you little hussy? At your age you're already in the business of—

*He catches himself and goes on gently.*

You're already pretty good at whatever you do, Fanchette; and my pretty cousin is so obliging that—

FANCHETTE. What did I do to make you cross with me? I'm going . . .

FIGARO. Don't. I was only teasing. I'll tell you: that pin of yours is one that my lord told you to give to Suzanne. It's the one that fastened the paper he had in his hand: you see I know what I'm talking about.

FANCHETTE. Why ask me if you know?

FIGARO, *fumbling*. Oh . . . because it's fun to know how his lordship went about sending you on your errand.

FANCHETTE, *with naïveté*. Well, he did it almost as you say: "Here, Fanchette," he said, "give back this pin to your beautiful cousin; just tell her it's the seal for the big elms."

FIGARO. "The big—?

FANCHETTE. "—elms." Oh, yes, and he added: "Be sure no one sees you."

FIGARO. Well, cousin, you must do as you're told and it's lucky no one *has* seen you. Run your pretty errand and don't tell Suzanne a word more than his lordship told you.

FANCHETTE. Why should I say more, cousin? He takes me for a child.

*She goes out, skipping.*

FIGARO. Well, Mother?

MARCELINE. Well, my son?

FIGARO, *choking*. That cursèd clown! Really some things are too much!

MARCELINE. Some things? What things?

FIGARO, *hands on his breast*. What I've just learned, Mother, weighs on me like lead—here.

MARCELINE, *laughing*. It would seem that your assured countenance of a while ago was only an inflated bag of wind—
a pin has made it collapse.

FIGARO, *furious*. But that pin, Mother, that pin was the one he
picked up!

MARCELINE, *recalling his words*. "As for jealousy, I am a philosopher—unshakable: if Suzanne deceives me, I forgive
her . . ."

FIGARO. Oh, Mother, a man speaks as he feels at the time. Let
the coolest judge on the bench plead his own case and see
how he explains the law. I understand now why he was so
annoyed about the fireworks. As for my darling and her
subtlety with pins, she hasn't got where she thinks she is,
elms or no elms. It's true my marriage is enough to warrant
my anger, but it isn't enough to keep me from dropping one
wife and wedding another.

MARCELINE. A splendid conclusion! Let's wreck everything
on a mere suspicion. How do you know it's you she's deceiving and not the Count? Have you studied her thoroughly
that you condemn her without appeal? Do you know for a
fact that she is going under those trees, or what her intentions are, or what she will say and do if she goes there? I
thought you had more judgment!

FIGARO, *kissing her hand*. A mother is always right, Mother,
and you are right, entirely right! But make allowance, dear
Mamma, for natural impulse. One feels better after giving
way to it. Now let us weigh before accusing and acting. I
know where the assignation is to be. Farewell, Mother.
*Exit.*

MARCELINE. Farewell. And I too know where it is. Now that
I've stopped him, I'd better look after Suzanne—or rather,
give her warning. She is such a pretty creature! I must say,
when our own interest does not divide us, we women are
all inclined to make common cause in defense of our down-
trodden sex against this proud, terrifying (*laughing*) and
somewhat slow-witted masculine sex.
*Exit.*

# ACT V

*A stand of elms in the park. Two pavilions, kiosks, or garden temples occupy respectively the right and left middle ground. Behind is a clearing hung with decorations; in front a lawn with seats. The scene is dark.*

FANCHETTE, *alone and carrying in one hand two small cakes and an orange; in the other, a lighted paper lantern.* He said the pavilion on the left. It must be this one. But what if my fine fellow doesn't show up? They wouldn't even give me an orange and two cookies, those kitchen people. "But for whom, miss?" "Why, sir, it's for somebody." "We thought as much, miss." Supposing the worst—just because my lord doesn't want to set eyes on him, that's no reason he should starve. All the same, it cost me a big kiss on the cheek. Who knows, maybe he'll pay me back for it in kind.

*She catches sight of* FIGARO, *who comes forward to identify her. She cries out.*

Ah! . . .

*Runs away and enters pavilion at left.*

FIGARO, *in a large cloak, alone at first.* It's Fanchette!

*He scans the others as they arrive and speaks roughly to them.*

Good day, gentlemen, good evening. Are you all here?

BASIL. All those you asked to come.

FIGARO. What time is it, about?

ANTONIO, *nose in the air.* The moon should be up.

BARTHOLO. What black arts are you getting ready for? He looks like a conspirator.

FIGARO. Isn't it for a wedding that you're gathered at the castle?

BRIDLEGOOSE. C-certainly.

ANTONIO. We were going over yonder, in the park, and wait for the signal to start the festivities.

FIGARO. You shan't go a step farther. It's here, under the elms, that we're going to celebrate the faithful bride I am marrying and the faithful lord who has reassigned her to himself.

BASIL, *recalling the day's events.* Ah, yes. I know all about it. Let's remove ourselves, if you please. It's a matter of a rendezvous. I'll tell you about it later.

BRIDLEGOOSE, *to* FIGARO. We'll c-come back.

FIGARO. When you hear me call, don't fail to appear. You can curse me if I don't provide you with a fine spectacle.

BARTHOLO. Remember that a wise man does not start a quarrel with the great and powerful.

FIGARO. I'll remember.

BARTHOLO. They begin with a score of forty-love against us, thanks to their rank.

FIGARO. To say nothing of their capacity for hard work, which you're forgetting. But remember also that once a man is known to be scared, he's at the mercy of every scoundrel.

BARTHOLO. Well said.

FIGARO. And among my names is Greenleaf, from my mother's side.

BARTHOLO. He is full of the devil.

BRIDLEGOOSE. He y-y-is.

BASIL, *aside.* The Count and Suzanne planned this without me—I'm rather glad of this ambush.

FIGARO, *to the footmen.* You fellows do as I told you—light up all around here, or in the name of Death, which I'd like to throttle, when I grab the arm of one of you—

*He grabs* SUNSTRUCK.

SUNSTRUCK *goes off crying.* Ah, oh, ah, perish the brute!

BASIL, *leaving.* God give you joy, young newlywed!

FIGARO, *pacing up and down alone in the dark and speaking in somber tones.* Oh, woman, woman, woman! weak and deceitful creature! No animal on earth can go against in-

stinct; is it yours to deceive? After refusing me stubbornly
when I begged her in front of her mistress—in the very instant of plighting her troth to me, in the middle of the ceremony— He was laughing as he read, the traitor! And I,
like a poor booby . . . No, my lord Count, you shan't have
her, you shan't! Because you are a great lord you think you
are a great genius. Nobility, wealth, honors, emoluments—
it all makes a man so proud! What have you done to earn
so many advantages? You took the trouble to be born, nothing more. Apart from that, you're a rather common type.
Whereas I—by God!—lost in the nameless crowd, I had to
exert more strategy and skill merely to survive than has
been spent for a hundred years in governing the Spanish
Empire. . . . And you want to tangle with me!

Someone's coming—it is she—no, it's nobody. The night is
dark as pitch and here am I plying the silly trade of husband, even though I'm only half of one.

*He sits on a bench.*

Can anything be stranger than my career? The son of God
knows whom, stolen by bandits and reared in their ways, I
become disgusted and try to lead an honest life. Everywhere
I am repulsed. I learn chemistry, pharmacy, surgery, yet
the whole influence of a great lord hardly succeeds in secur-
ing me the practice of a veterinary. Tired of pestering sick
animals, hoping in fact to do just the opposite, I go headlong
for the stage. Far better have hung a millstone around my
neck! I write a play satirizing life in the harem: being a
Spanish author I thought I could make fun of Mohammed
without fear. At once, an emissary from God knows where
complains that my verses offend the Sublime Porte, Persia,
part of the Indian peninsula, all of Egypt, the kingdoms of
Barca, Tripoli, Tunis, Algiers, and Morocco—and there goes
my play up the spout, to please the Mohammedan princes,
not one of whom (I believe) can read, and all of whom
brand us on the shoulder and call us Christian dogs. Whoever fails to degrade the mind avenges himself by insulting
it. My cheeks were growing hollow, my lodging was unpaid,
I could see from afar the threatening bailiff with a pen
stuck in his wig, so I shudder and exert myself afresh. A

public debate starts up about the nature of wealth, and since
one needn't own something in order to argue about it, being
in fact penniless, I write on the value of money and interest.
Immediately, I find myself inside a coach looking at the
drawbridge of a prison and leaving hope and freedom
behind.

*He gets up.*

How I should like to hold in the hollow of my hand one of
these potentates who last four days in office and are so ready
to ordain punishments! When a healthy fall from grace had
sobered his pride, I'd let him know that printed nonsense
is dangerous only in countries where its free circulation is
hampered; that without the right to criticize, praise and
approval are worthless, and that only petty men fear petty
writings.

*Sits down.*

One day, tired of feeding an obscure guest, they threw me
out into the street, and since a man must eat even when
out of jail, I sharpen my quill once more and ask people
what is in the news. I am told that during my retreat at
public expense, free trade and a free press have been established in Madrid, so that, provided I do not write about the
government, or about religion, or politics, or morals, or those
in power, or public bodies, or the Opera, or the other state
theatres, or about anybody who is active in anything, I can
print whatever I want with perfect freedom under the super-
vision of two or three censors. To take advantage of such
sweet liberty, I let it be known that I am starting a periodi-
cal, and to make sure that I am not treading on anybody's
heels, I call it *The Useless Journal*. Mercy! No sooner done
than I see a thousand poor devils of subsidized hacks in arms
against me. I am put down and once again unemployed.
Despair nearly had me by the throat when someone thought
of me for a vacant place. Unfortunately I was qualified for
it. They needed an accountant and put in a dancer. The
only way out was to turn thief. I set up as croupier of a
gambling den. Ah, then, my dears, I was in the swim! I dine
out and people known as respectable courteously open their
houses to me, keeping for themselves only three quarters of

the take. I could have recouped all my losses—I had even begun to understand that to grow rich, know-how is better than knowledge, but since everyone around me was robbing the till while requiring that I stay honest, I went under for the third time.

I'd had enough and meant to break with the world—five fathoms of water would suffice, and nearly did, when my guardian angel recalled me to my original trade. I take up my razors and lancet and leave glory to the fools who feed on its aroma. With it also, I leave behind dishonor, which is too heavy a load for a pedestrian. Hiking from town to town, shaving as I go, I live at last a life without care. But a great lord passing through Seville recognizes me. I get him married off, and as a reward for my helping him secure a wife, he now wants to intercept mine. Thereupon, storms and intrigues. I am on the edge of an abyss, nearly wedded to my own mother, when lo! my relatives materialize, Indian file.

*He gets up and grows vehement.*

Follows a regular scrimmage— "It's he, it's you, it's I. No, it isn't, not I." Well, who then?

*He falls back into the seat.*

What an incredible series of events! How did it happen to me? Why these things and not others? Who drew them down on my head? Forcibly set on the road of life, not knowing where it leads, and bound to leave it against my will, I've tried to keep it as rosy as my natural cheerfulness permits. Here again I say *my* cheerfulness without knowing if it belongs to me any more than those other things; nor do I know who this *I* may be with which I am so concerned— it's first a shapeless collection of unknown parts, then a help-less puny thing, then a lively little animal, then a young man thirsting for pleasure, with a full capacity to enjoy and ready to use any shifts to live—master here and valet there, at the whim of fortune; ambitious from vanity, industrious from need—and lazy . . . with delight! An orator in tight spots, a poet for relaxation, a musician from time to time, a lover in hot fits: I have seen everything, done everything, worn out

everything. At last my illusion is shattered and I'm now
wholly disabused . . . blasé. . . . Oh, Suzy! Suzy! my
Suzy, what torments you are putting me through! I hear
footsteps . . . some one's coming . . . This is the crisis.

*He retires into the downstage wing on his right. Enter the*
COUNTESS *dressed as* SUZANNE, SUZANNE *dressed as the*
COUNTESS, *and* MARCELINE.

SUZANNE, *speaking low to the* COUNTESS. Yes, Marceline said
Figaro would be here.

MARCELINE. And so he is; be quiet.

SUZANNE. I see; the one's eavesdropping, the other's coming
to fetch me—let the show begin.

MARCELINE. I don't want to miss a word; I'm going to hide in
the pavilion.

*Enters the same pavilion as* FANCHETTE.

SUZANNE, *aloud.* You're trembling, madam: are you cold?

COUNTESS, *aloud.* The evening is damp, I am going in.

SUZANNE, *aloud.* If my lady does not need me, I should like
to take the air a little while under the trees.

COUNTESS, *aloud.* Take the air! Catch your death, you mean.

SUZANNE. I'm used to it.

FIGARO, *aside.* Her death, my eye!

SUZANNE *retreats to a spot near the wings, on the opposite
side from* FIGARO.

CHERUBINO, *dressed as an officer, comes on singing the words
of his song.* "Tra-la-la-la-la,/A godmother I had,/Whom always I adored!"

COUNTESS, *aside.* The little page!

CHERUBINO. People are walking about. I must take to my refuge, where Fanchette is—oh, it's a woman!

COUNTESS. Oh, mercy!

CHERUBINO, *stooping and peering.* Am I mistaken? That hat I
see with feathers outlined against the sky looks to me like
Suzy.

COUNTESS. Oh, if the Count were to appear!

*The* COUNT *enters from the back.*

CHERUBINO *goes up to* COUNTESS *and takes her hand; she pulls away.* I'm right, it's that adorable girl named Sue! How could I mistake this soft hand, or that slight trembling . . . or the beating of my own heart!

*He tries to put the* COUNTESS's *hand against his heart.*

COUNTESS, *whispering.* Go away!

CHERUBINO. Could it be that you took pity on my lot and came here where I have been hiding since afternoon?

COUNTESS. Figaro is coming.

COUNT, *stepping forward, aside.* Isn't that Suzanne I see?

CHERUBINO, *to* COUNTESS. I'm not afraid of Figaro and it's not him you're waiting for.

COUNTESS. Who then?

COUNT, *aside.* Somebody is with her.

CHERUBINO. It's my lord, hussy, who asked you out here this morning when I hid behind the chair.

COUNT, *aside, furious.* It's that infernal page again!

FIGARO, *aside.* And they say it isn't nice to eavesdrop!

SUZANNE, *aside.* The little chatterbox!

COUNTESS, *to* CHERUBINO. Do me the kindness to go away.

CHERUBINO. Not without a reward for my compliance.

COUNTESS, *frightened.* You claim—?

CHERUBINO, *with heat.* Twenty kisses on your account first; then a hundred for your fair mistress.

COUNTESS. You would not dare!

CHERUBINO. Yes, I would! You're taking her place with my lord, I take his with you. The one who gets left is Figaro.

FIGARO, *aside.* The rapscallion!

SUZANNE, *aside.* Brash as a little page!

CHERUBINO *tries to kiss the* COUNTESS; *the* COUNT *comes between them and receives the kiss.*

COUNTESS, *retreating.* Dear God!

FIGARO, *aside, hearing the sound of the kiss.* It's a pretty baggage I'm marrying!

*Listens intently.*

CHERUBINO, *feeling the* COUNT's *clothes; aside.* It's my lord!
*He flees into the pavilion where* FANCHETTE *and* MARCELINE
*are hiding.*

FIGARO, *approaching.* I'm going to—

COUNT, *thinking the* PAGE *still there.* Since you don't repeat
the kiss . . .
*Lashes out with his hand.*

FIGARO, *coming within range, gets the slap.* Ow!

COUNT. That's one paid off, anyhow.

FIGARO, *retreating and rubbing his cheek.* This eavesdropping
business isn't all pure gain.

SUZANNE, *laughing.* Hahahaha!

COUNT, *to* COUNTESS, *whom he mistakes for* SUZANNE. That
page is beyond belief—he gets slapped full in the face and
goes off laughing.

FIGARO, *aside.* He should be grieving for me!

COUNT. And he's intolerable: I can't take a step— But let's
forget the puzzle or it will spoil the delight I feel in finding
you here.

COUNTESS, *imitating* SUZANNE's *voice.* Were you expecting me?

COUNT. What do you think, after your clever note?
*He takes her hand.*
You're trembling.

COUNTESS. I've been frightened.

COUNT. It wasn't to deprive you of a kiss that I took his.
*Kisses her on the forehead.*

COUNTESS. Such liberties!

FIGARO, *aside.* The trollop!

SUZANNE, *aside.* The darling!

COUNT *takes* COUNTESS's *hand.* How fine and soft your skin is!
Your hand is more lovely than the Countess's.

COUNTESS, *aside.* What preconception will do!

COUNT. And this little arm, how firm and round . . . these
pretty fingers full of grace and mischief!

COUNTESS, *speaking like* SUZANNE. And what of love . . . ?

COUNT. Love . . . is the fiction of the heart. Its history is pleasure, and hence you find me at your feet.

COUNTESS. You do not love her any more?

COUNT. I love her very much, but three years make marriage so respectable.

COUNTESS. What did you want from her?

COUNT, *caressing her*. What I find in you, my sweet.

COUNTESS. But tell me what . . .

COUNT. I don't know . . . less sameness, perhaps; more spice in your manner—something, I don't know what, which makes for charm, it's because you deny me sometimes, I don't know. Our wives think they can't do better than to love us. They take this for granted and love us and love us —if they love us—and they are so compliant and constant, always and without stint, that suddenly one day one finds satiety where one looked for happiness.

COUNTESS, *aside*. What a lesson to me!

COUNT. To tell the truth, Suzy, I have often thought that when we seek elsewhere the pleasure we miss in them, it is because they make no effort to sustain our interest, to renew their attractions in love, to resurrect (so to speak) the delight of possession by affording that of variety.

COUNTESS, *vexed*. And so theirs is the whole responsibility?

COUNT, *laughing*. And the man has none, you mean? Well, can we change nature? Our task is to obtain . . .

COUNTESS. Yes, and theirs—?

COUNT. Is to . . . retain . . . That's generally overlooked.

COUNTESS. Not by me.

COUNT. Nor me.

FIGARO, *aside*. Nor me.

SUZANNE, *aside*. Nor me.

COUNT, *taking* COUNTESS's *hand again*. There's an echo hereabouts; let's lower our voices. You for one needn't worry about holding a man! Love has fashioned you so fair and sprightly. Add a touch of caprice and you would be the most titillating mistress.

*Kisses her forehead.*

My Suzy, a Castilian has nothing but his word of honor. I give you the ransom I promised, to redeem that old claim I no longer have upon the sweet concession you are about to make me.

COUNTESS, *curtsying.* Your Suzanne accepts everything.

FIGARO, *aside.* They don't exist more wanton than that.

SUZANNE, *aside.* It means good money in our pockets.

COUNT, *aside.* She's mercenary—all the better!

COUNTESS, *turning toward the back.* I see torches.

COUNT. That's for your wedding. Let's go into the pavilion until they're by.

COUNTESS. Without a light?

COUNT, *pulling her gently.* Why a light? We don't intend to read.

FIGARO, *aside.* She's going in, the drab! I thought so.

*He steps forward.*

COUNT, *turning around, in a voice of command.* Who's wandering around there?

FIGARO, *angry.* Nobody's wandering; I'm coming on purpose!

COUNT, *to* COUNTESS. It's Figaro.

*He runs away.*

COUNTESS. I'll follow you.

*She enters the pavilion on the right while the* COUNT *hides in the wood at the back.*

FIGARO, *trying to find them both.* I don't hear anything. They must have gone in. So here we are.

*In a changed voice.*

Oh, you clumsy husbands who hire spies and toy with suspicion for months without confirming it, why not take your cue from me? I shadow my wife from the beginning, the first day. I listen secretly, and in a twinkling I know everything: it's enchanting—no doubts left, all is known.

*Pacing briskly.*

Lucky that it doesn't bother me and that I'm no longer upset by her treachery. I've got them at last.

SUZANNE, *creeping up behind him; aside.* You're going to pay for those fine suspicions!

*Imitating the* COUNTESS.

Who goes there?

FIGARO, *wildly.* "Who goes there?" A man who thinks the plague should have taken—

SUZANNE. Why, it's Figaro!

FIGARO, *quickly.* My lady Countess!

SUZANNE. Speak low!

FIGARO, *quickly.* Ah, madam, how fortunate that you should have come. Where do you think my lord may be?

SUZANNE. What does an ungrateful husband matter to me? Tell me rather—

FIGARO, *speaking still more rapidly.* And Suzanne, my bride, where do you imagine she might be?

SUZANNE. *Please* lower your voice!

FIGARO. Suzanne, my Suzy whom everybody thought so virtuous, who acted so modest! Well, they're locked up in there. I'm going to call out.

SUZANNE, *putting her hand on his mouth and forgetting to disguise her voice. Don't* call out!

FIGARO, *aside. This* is Suzy! Damn!

SUZANNE, *imitating the* COUNTESS. You seem upset.

FIGARO, *aside.* The minx! Trying to catch me!

SUZANNE. We must avenge ourselves, Figaro.

FIGARO. Do you feel a pressing need of it?

SUZANNE. Am I not a woman? Men, though, have better means.

FIGARO, *confiding.* Madam, your presence is as necessary as mine. And women's means . . . are the best.

SUZANNE, *aside.* I'd like to slap the lout!

FIGARO, *aside.* Wouldn't it be fun if even before we're married . . .

SUZANNE. But what kind of revenge is it that lacks the spice of love?

FIGARO. If you see no signs of love, you may be sure I am only restrained by deference.

SUZANNE, *nettled.* I can't tell whether you mean that honestly, but you certainly don't say it gracefully.

FIGARO, *with comical fervor, kneeling.* Oh, madam, I worship you. But consider the time, the place, the circumstance, and let your anger supply the fire which my entreaty lacks.

SUZANNE, *aside.* My hand is itching.

FIGARO, *aside.* My heart is beating.

SUZANNE. But sir, have you reflected?

FIGARO. Oh, yes, madam, yes indeed, I have reflected.

SUZANNE. In anger and in love—

FIGARO. Delay is fatal, I know. Your hand, madam.

SUZANNE, *in her own voice and slapping him.* Here it is.

FIGARO. Lucifer, what a fist!

SUZANNE. What fist—is this the one?
*Slaps him again.*

FIGARO. Now, what the devil? Are you playing windmill?

SUZANNE, *slapping him with each phrase.* "Ah, Lucifer, Suzanne!" Take *that* for your suspicion, and *that* for your revenge, and *that* for your schemes, and your insults, and your double-dealing. Then you can say as you did this morning! "That's love for you!"

FIGARO, *laughing as he gets up.* By all the saints, it is!—pure love! What happiness, what bliss! Thrice-blessed Figaro. Hit me, belovèd, again and again. Only, when you're through painting me black and blue, Suzy, look kindly upon the luckiest man ever beaten by a woman.

SUZANNE. The luckiest, you scoundrel? As if you weren't busy seducing the Countess with your pretty turns of phrase, to the point where I was forgetting myself and yielding in her place!

FIGARO. As if I had mistaken the sound of your lovely voice!

SUZANNE, *laughing.* You recognized me, did you? I'll take my toll for that too.

FIGARO. Just like a woman to beat a body and bear a grudge besides. But tell me by what good fortune I find you here when I thought you there. And these clothes, which fooled me at first, and now prove you innocent . . .

SUZANNE. *You* are the innocent, to walk into a trap laid for someone else. Is it our fault if in trying to catch a fox we catch two?

FIGARO. Who's catching the other?

SUZANNE. His wife.

FIGARO. His wife?

SUZANNE. His wife.

FIGARO, *wildly*. Ah, Figaro, go hang yourself on the nearest tree. You never guessed! His wife! Oh, clever, clever, clever women. So all those resounding kisses . . .

SUZANNE. Fell on my lady.

FIGARO. And the one from the page?

SUZANNE. On my lord.

FIGARO. And this morning, behind the chair?

SUZANNE. On nobody.

FIGARO. Are you sure?

SUZANNE, *laughing*. Figaro! You know how fists fly about at dusk!

FIGARO *seizes her hand and kisses it*. Yours are jewels to me. But the Count's in my face was fair enough.

SUZANNE. Come, proud one, abase yourself.

FIGARO, *acting as he speaks*. Fair enough: on my knees, bowed low, prone and flat on the ground.

SUZANNE, *laughing*. The poor Count! What trouble he's gone to . . .

FIGARO, *rising and kneeling*. . . . to seduce his wife.

COUNT, *entering from the back and going straight to the pavilion on the right; aside*. I can't find her in the wood; perhaps she's stepped in here.

SUZANNE, *whispering to* FIGARO. There he goes.

COUNT, *at the open door of the pavilion*. Suzanne, are you there?

FIGARO, *low*. He's looking for her. I thought . . .

SUZANNE, *low*. He never recognized her.

FIGARO. Let's finish him off, shall we?

*Kisses her hand noisily.*

COUNT, *turning round.* A man kneeling before the Countess
. . . And I'm unarmed.

*He comes forward.*

FIGARO, *rising and disguising his voice.* Forgive me, madam, if
I did not realize that this meeting place would be in the
path of the festivities.

COUNT, *aside.* That's the man of this morning in the dressing
room.

*He strikes his forehead.*

FIGARO. But such a silly interference shan't postpone our
pleasure.

COUNT, *aside.* Death and damnation!

FIGARO, *leading* SUZANNE *to the pavilion; aside.* He's cursing.
*Aloud.*

Let us hasten, madam, and repair the misfortune we suffered
earlier when I jumped out of the window.

COUNT, *aside.* Now I see it all!

SUZANNE, *near the pavilion on the left.* Before we go in, make
sure nobody is following.

*He kisses her forehead.*

COUNT, *shouting.* Revenge!

SUZANNE *flees into the pavilion where* MARCELINE, FAN-
CHETTE, *and* CHERUBINO *already are. The* COUNT *seizes* FIG-
ARO *by the arm.*

FIGARO, *pretending great fright.* It's the master!

COUNT. Ah, villain, it's you! Ho, somebody, come at once!

*Enter* PETER, *booted and spurred.*

PETER. So there you are, my lord, at last.

COUNT. Good! Are you alone, Peter?

PETER. Back from Seville, hell for leather.

COUNT. Come close to me and shout very loud.

PETER, *at the top of his lungs.* No more page in Seville than
on the back of my hand—and that's a fact!

COUNT, *pushing him away.* Stupid oaf!

PETER. Your lordship said I must shout aloud.

COUNT, *holding* FIGARO. It was to call for help. Ho, there, somebody! Whoever hears me, come quick!

PETER. Figaro's here with me: what are you afraid of?

*Enter* BRIDLEGOOSE, BARTHOLO, BASIL, ANTONIO, *and* SUN-STRUCK, *followed by the wedding party carrying torches.*

BARTHOLO, *to* FIGARO. You see: we came as soon as we heard you.

COUNT, *pointing to the pavilion on the left.* Peter, guard that door.

PETER *goes.*

BASIL, *low, to* FIGARO. You caught him with Suzanne?

COUNT, *pointing to* FIGARO. You, vassals, surround this man and answer for him with your lives.

BASIL. Oh, oh!

COUNT, *angry.* Be quiet.

*To* FIGARO, *freezingly.*

Sir Knight, will you answer a few questions?

FIGARO, *coolly.* Who indeed could give me leave not to? You have command of everybody here except yourself.

COUNT, *mastering his fury.* Except myself?

ANTONIO. That's the way to talk!

COUNT, *giving way to his anger.* If anything could make me angrier, it's the air of calmness he puts on.

FIGARO. Are we like soldiers, killing and being killed for reasons they know nothing of? For my part, I always like to know what I'm angry about.

COUNT, *beside himself.* Murder!

*Controlling himself.*

Man of gentle birth who pretend not to know my reasons, would you at least do us the favor of telling us what lady you have brought into this pavilion?

FIGARO, *mischievously pointing to the other.* Into that one?

COUNT, *quickly.* Into this.

FIGARO, *coldly.* That's different. It's a young lady who honors me with her favors.

BASIL, *surprised.* Oh?

COUNT, *quickly.* You heard him, gentlemen?

BARTHOLO, *surprised.* We heard him.

COUNT. And this young person is otherwise unattached?

FIGARO, *coldly.* I know that a great lord paid her some attentions for a while. But whether it be that he neglected her or that she likes me better, I am the one preferred.

COUNT, *quickly.* The one pref—

*Restraining himself.*

At least he is candid. What he has just admitted, I myself have seen and heard, gentlemen, from the mouth of his accomplice. I give you my word on it.

BRIDLEGOOSE, *petrified.* His ac-complice!

COUNT, *in a fury.* Now, when dishonor is public, so must be the revenge!

*He goes into the pavilion.*

ANTONIO. He's right.

BRIDLEGOOSE, *to* FIGARO. Who took who-o-o's wife?

FIGARO, *laughing.* No one had that special satisfaction.

COUNT, *speaking from inside the pavilion and tugging at someone not yet identifiable.* It is no use, madam, the hour has struck and you are doomed.

*He comes out and turns to the rest without looking.*

How fortunate that there lives no pledge of our hateful union—!

FIGARO, *calling out.* Cherubino!

COUNT. The page!

BASIL. Haha!

COUNT. Always the damned page! What were you doing in that room?

CHERUBINO, *shyly.* I was hiding, as you ordered me to do.

PETER. What use was it to nearly kill a horse!

COUNT. Go in there, Antonio, and bring before her judge the criminal who has dishonored me.

BRIDLEGOOSE. Is it my lady that you are l-looking for?

ANTONIO. 'Tis Providence, by gum, for your carryings-on all over the countryside.

COUNT, *furious.* Get in there!

ANTONIO *goes in.*

COUNT. You shall see, gentlemen, that the page was not alone.

CHERUBINO, *shyly.* It would have been hard on me if a gentle soul had not sweetened the bitter pill.

ANTONIO, *pulling out someone not recognizable at first.* Come, my lady, don't make me coax you, everybody knows you went in.

FIGARO, *calling out.* My little cousin!

BASIL. Haha!

COUNT. Fanchette!

ANTONIO turns around. By jiminy 'twas right smart, my lord, to pick on me to show the company it's my daughter caused all the randan, now wasn't it?

COUNT, *indignant.* Who could suppose she was in there?

*He tries to go in.*

BARTHOLO, *interposing.* Allow me, my lord. All this is far too upsetting for you; but perhaps I can deal with it in cold blood.

*He goes in.*

BRIDLEGOOSE. It's certainly too confusing for me.

BARTHOLO, *speaking from inside and coming out.* Do not be afraid, madam, no one will hurt you, I promise you.

*He turns around and cries out.*

Marceline!

BASIL. Haha!

FIGARO, *laughing.* A madhouse! My mother in it too!

ANTONIO. The jades are playing who can be the worst.

COUNT, *outraged.* What is that to me? It's the Countess . . .

SUZANNE *comes out, her face behind a fan.*

Ah, there she is at last, gentlemen.

*He takes her violently by the arm.*

What does such an odious woman deserve, gentlemen—?

SUZANNE *falls on her knees, bowing her head.*

COUNT. Never, never!

FIGARO *kneels next to her.*

COUNT, *louder.* Never!

MARCELINE *kneels beside the others.*

COUNT, *still louder.* Never, never!

*They all kneel.*

COUNT, *beside himself.* Never, not if there were a hundred of you!

COUNTESS, *coming out of the other pavilion.* At least, I can make one more.

*She kneels.*

COUNT, *looking alternately at* SUZANNE *and the* COUNTESS. What do I see?

BRIDLEGOOSE, *laughing.* What d'you kn-n-know, it's my lady!

COUNT, *trying to lift her up.* It was you, Countess?

*In a supplicating tone.*

Only the most generous forgiveness . . .

COUNTESS, *laughing.* In my place, you would say "Never, never!" whereas I, for the third time today, forgive you unconditionally.

*She gets up.*

SUZANNE, *getting up.* And so do I.

MARCELINE, *getting up.* And I.

FIGARO, *getting up.* And I. There's an echo hereabouts.

*All get up.*

COUNT. An echo! I tried to outsmart them and they fooled me like a child.

COUNTESS, *laughing.* Don't act as if you were sorry, my lord.

FIGARO, *brushing off his knees with his hat.* A day like today is ideal training for an ambassador.

COUNT, *to* SUZANNE. That note sealed with a pin? . . .

SUZANNE. Madam dictated it.

COUNT. The answer is overdue.

*He kisses the* COUNTESS's *hand.*

COUNTESS. Each will regain his own.

*She gives the purse to* FIGARO *and the diamond to* SUZANNE.

SUZANNE, *to* FIGARO. Still another dowry!

FIGARO, *striking the purse*. That makes three. But this one took some contriving.

SUZANNE. Like our marriage.

SUNSTRUCK. What about the bride's garter? Can I have it?

COUNTESS, *taking out the ribbon from her bosom*. The garter? It was in her clothes. Here you are.

*She throws the ribbon; the boys try to scramble for it.*

CHERUBINO, *swiftly picking it up*. Try and get it!

COUNT, *laughing*. Since you're so touchy a gentleman, what made you laugh so hard when I boxed your ear?

CHERUBINO, *taking a step backward and half drawing his sword*. My ear, colonel?

FIGARO, *comically angry*. He got it on *my* cheek, as always happens when lords mete out justice.

COUNT, *laughing*. On your cheek, ha, ha, ha, isn't that good, what do you say, dear Countess?

COUNTESS, *abstracted and returning to reality*. Indeed, dear Count, I do—for life, unswervingly: I swear it.

COUNT, *slapping* BRIDLEGOOSE *on the shoulder*. And you, Bridlegoose, let us have your opinion.

BRIDLEGOOSE. On what has taken p-place, my lord? Well, my opinion is that I d-don't know what to think, and that's my op-pinion.

ALL, *together*. A very sound judgment!

FIGARO. I was poor and despised. When I showed a little cleverness, hatred dogged me. Now with a pretty girl and some money . . .

BARTHOLO, *laughing*. Everybody will crowd around you!

FIGARO. Do you think so?

BARTHOLO. I know my kind.

FIGARO, *bowing to the spectators*. Aside from my wife and my goods, you are welcome to all I have.

*The orchestra plays the introduction to the entertainment.*

BASIL.
*Triple dowry, handsome wife—*
*To a husband, what largesse!*

*'Gainst a lord or beardless page*
*Only fools feel jealous rage.*
*Let the Latin proverb bless*
*Man's incalculable life:*

FIGARO. Don't I know that proverb!

*Sings.*

"Happy those of noble birth!"

BASIL. No you *don't* know it!

*Sings.*

"Happy those who own the earth!"

SUZANNE.

*Let a man his wife betray*
*He is boastful, all are gay;*
*Let his wife indulge her whim*
*She is punished, unlike him.*
*If you ask why this is so,*
*'Tis the stronger's wicked law.*

MARCELINE.

*Every man his mother knows,*
*Her who gives sweet life to him.*
*But beyond this all is dim—*
*How explain love's secret lure?*

FIGARO, *breaking in.*

*Secret, though the end disclose*
*That the offspring of a boor*
*May turn out a gentleman.*

FIGARO.

*By the accident of birth,*
*One is shepherd, t'other king.*
*Chance made lord and underling,*
*Only genius threads the maze:*
*Twenty kings are fed on praise*
*Who in death are common earth,*
*While Voltaire immortal stays.*

CHERUBINO.

*Flighty sex we all adore,*
*You who torment all our days,*

*Everyone complains of you;*
*In the end we kneel and sue.*
*To the pit thus players do:*
*Such a one professes scorn*
*Who would crawl to earn your bays.*

### FIGARO.

*Jack McJohn, the jealous lout,*
*Hoped to have both wife and peace;*
*Hired a dog to roam about*
*In the garden, fierce and free;*
*Barks as claimed in guaranty:*
*All are bitten by the beast,*
*Save the lover from whom leased.*

### COUNTESS.

*There's a wife who's proudly prude*
*Though she loves her husband not;*
*There's another, nearly lewd,*
*Swears she loveth none but he;*
*Now the worthiest is she,*
*Never swearing this or that,*
*Who but strives for honesty.*

### COUNT.

*Any woman far from Court*
*Who believes in duty strict*
*In romance falls somewhat short.*
*I prefer the derelict:*
*Like a piece of currency,*
*Stamped with one man's effigy,*
*She can serve the needs of all.*

### SUZANNE.

*If there should a moral lurk*
*In this mad yet cheerful work,*
*For the sake of gaiety,*
*Pray accept it as a whole.*
*Thus does Nature, sensibly,*
*Using pleasures we pursue,*
*Lead us gently to her goal.*

BRIDLEGOOSE.

*Now dear sirs, the c-comic art,*
*Which you shortly mean to j-judge,*
*Apes the life of all of you*
*Sitting there and taking part.*
*When annoyed you bear a g-grudge*
*But although you grumble l-long,*
*All our d-doings end in song.*

# NOTES

GENERAL    There is no comprehensive bibliography of French literature in English translation (comparable to Pane's bibliography of Spanish literature or B. Q. Morgan's *German Literature in English Translation, 1481–1927*.) French plays that have been included in English-language anthologies between 1900 and 1956 are listed in *Index to Plays in Collections* by John H. Ottemiller (New York, Third Edition, 1957). The best introduction to French literature that has been written in English is probably still Lytton Strachey's *Landmarks in French Literature* (London and New York, 1912). Of special relevance to half the authors printed in the present volume is Martin Turnell's *The Classical Moment* (London, 1947, and Norfolk, Conn., 1948).

LE CID (1636)    "With the production in 1636 of Corneille's tragedy *Le Cid*," writes Strachey, "modern French drama came into existence." James Schevill adds:

"Corneille's *Le Cid*, written when Corneille was thirty years old, was influenced by the Spanish play, *Las Mocedades del Cid*, written around 1614 by Guillén de Castro. From the twelfth century on, The Cid was the most prominent figure in Spanish literature, the hero of numerous ballads and particularly of the great epic *Poem of the Cid*, written about 1140. (There are several translations of the latter; the latest is by W. S. Merwin.) In Spain The Cid was identified with the legendary hero, Ruy Díaz de Bivar, who died, supposedly, in 1099. Although several Spanish scholars have denied the existence of Ruy Díaz, the truth is probably closer to what Cervantes says in *Don Quixote:* "There is no doubt there was such a man as The Cid, but much doubt whether he achieved what is attributed to him." For further particulars readers are referred to the work of the great Spanish scholar, Ramón Menéndez Pidal, *The Cid and His Spain*, translated by H. Sutherland, London, 1934.

"The aristocratic idea of *gloire* in *Le Cid* is difficult to understand in the equalitarian society of today. To Corneille, the ideals of honor, integrity, the glory of social standing and reputation, were bound up with the ideal of love. A great love was worthless if it fell short of respect for these binding social concepts. At the same time, in Corneille's age, the new focus of the Renaissance on the heroism and the individuality of man was to result in the flowering of French literature that occurred with the reign of Louis XIV. Much of the dramatic power in *Le Cid,* as in Shakespeare's *Romeo and Juliet,* is derived from the conflict between the changing social forces of the Renaissance and the traditional, aristocratic laws of the feudal past. This conflict is particularly clear in the relationships of Rodrigo and Chimena with their fathers, and of the Infanta with the King.

"Although the action of *Le Cid* is compressed into a crowded twenty-four hours, this should not bother modern audiences, accustomed to the movies and to Shakespeare staged in fluid, Elizabethan style. Corneille himself wrote about the scene of the slap, Act I, Scene 3: 'One may imagine that Don Diego and the Count, leaving the King's palace, keep on walking as they quarrel, and arrive at Don Diego's house, when the latter receives the slap which requires him to enter the house in search of help.'

"All of the French names in this play have been turned back into Spanish names for the sake of unity of style."

LE MISANTHROPE (1666)  Lytton Strachey confirmed the general opinion when he said: "Here, in all probability, Molière's genius reached its height." But there has been no agreement as to what Molière intended to say—or succeeded in saying. Our present translator has defined his own view as follows:

"The idea that comedy is a ritual in which society's laughter corrects individual extravagance is particularly inapplicable to *The Misanthrope.* In this play, society itself is indicted, and though Alceste's criticisms are indiscriminate, they are not un-

justified. It is true that falseness and intrigue are everywhere
on view; the conventions enforce a routine dishonesty, justice
is subverted by influence, love is overwhelmed by calculation,
and these things are accepted, even by the best, as 'natural.'
The cold vanity of Oronte, Acaste, and Clitandre, the malignant hypocrisy of Arsinoé, the insincerity of Célimène, are to
be taken as exemplary of the age, and Philinte's philosophic
tolerance will not quite do in response to such a condition
of things. The honest Éliante is the one we are most to trust,
and this is partly because she sees that Alceste's intransigence
*A quelque chose en soy de noble & d'héroïque.*

"But *The Misanthrope* is not only a critique of society; it
is also a study of impurity of motive in a critic of society. If
Alceste has a rage for the genuine, and he truly has, it is unfortunately compromised and exploited by his vast, unconscious egotism. He is a jealous friend (*Je veux qu'on me di-
stingue*), and it is Philinte's polite effusiveness toward another
which prompts his attack on promiscuous civility. He is a jealous lover, and his 'frankness' about Oronte's sonnet owes something to the fact that Oronte is his rival, and that the sonnet is
addressed to Célimène. Like many humorless and indignant
people, he is hard on everybody but himself, and does not perceive it when he fails his own ideal. In one aspect, Alceste
seems a moral giant misplaced in a trivial society, having (in
George Eliot's phrase) 'a certain spiritual grandeur ill-
matched with the meanness of opportunity'; in another aspect,
he seems an unconscious fraud who magnifies the petty faults
of others in order to dramatize himself in his own eyes.

"He is, of course, both at once: but the two impressions pre-
dominate by turns. A victim, like all around him, of the moral
enervation of the times, he cannot consistently be the Man of
Honor—simple, magnanimous, passionate, decisive, true. It is
his distinction that he is aware of that ideal, and that he can
fitfully embody it; his comic flaw consists in a Quixotic confusion of himself with the ideal, a willingness to distort the
world for his own self-deceptive and histrionic purposes. Para-
doxically, then, the advocate of true feeling and honest intercourse is the one character most artificial, most out-of-touch,
most in danger of that nonentity and solitude which all, in
the chattery, hollow world of this play, are fleeing. He must

play-act continually in order to believe in his own existence, and he welcomes the fact or show of injustice as a dramatic cue. At the close of the play, when Alceste has refused to appeal his lawsuit and has spurned the hand of Célimène, one cannot escape the suspicion that his indignation is in great part instrumental, a desperate means of counterfeiting an identity.

"Martin Turnell (whose book *The Classical Moment* contains a fine analysis of *The Misanthrope*) observes that those speeches of Alceste which ring most false are, as it were, parodies of 'Cornelian *tirade*.' To duplicate this parody-tragic effect in English it was clearly necessary to keep the play in verse, where it would be possible to control the tone more sharply, and to recall our own tragic tradition. There were other reasons, too, for approximating Molière's form. The constant of rhythm and rhyme was needed, in the translation as in the original, for bridging great gaps between high comedy and farce, lofty diction and ordinary talk, deep character and shallow. Again, while prose might preserve the thematic structure of the play, other 'musical' elements would be lost, in particular the frequently intricate arrangements of balancing half-lines, lines, couplets, quatrains, and sestets. There is no question that words, when dancing within such patterns, are not their prosaic selves, but have a wholly different mood and meaning.

"Consider, finally, two peculiarities of the dialogue of the play: redundancy and logic. When Molière has a character repeat essentially the same thing in three successive couplets, it will sometimes have a very clear dramatic point; but it will always have the intention of stabilizing the idea against the movement of the verse, and of giving a specifically rhetorical pleasure. In a prose rendering, these latter effects are lost, and the passage tends to seem merely prolix. As for logic, it is a convention of *The Misanthrope* that its main characters can express themselves logically, and in the most complex grammar; Molière's dramatic verse, which is almost wholly free of metaphor, derives much of its richness from argumentative virtuosity. Here is a bit of logic from Arsinoé:

> *Madame, l'Amitié doit sur tout éclater*
> *Aux choses qui le plus nous peuvent importer:*

*Et comme il n'en est point de plus grande importance*
*Que celles de l'Honneur et de la Bienséance,*
*Je viens par un avis qui touche votre honneur*
*Témoigner l'amitié que pour vous a mon Coeur.*

"In prose it might come out like this: 'Madam, friendship
should most display itself when truly vital matters are in question: and since there are no things more vital than decency
and honor, I have come to prove my heartfelt friendship by
giving you some advice which concerns your reputation.' Even
if that were better rendered, it would still be plain that Molière's logic loses all its baroque exuberance in prose; it sounds
lawyerish; without rhyme and verse to phrase and emphasize
the steps of its progression, the logic becomes obscure like Con-
greve's, not crystalline and followable as it was meant to be.

"For all these reasons, rhymed verse seemed to me obliga-
tory. The choice did not preclude accuracy, and what follows
is, I believe, a line-for-line verse translation quite as faithful as
any which have been done in prose. I hasten to say that I am
boasting only of patience; a translation may, alas, be faithful on
all counts, and still lack quality.

"One word about diction. This is a play in which French
aristocrats of 1666 converse about their special concerns, and
employ the moral and philosophical terms peculiar to their
thought. Not all my words, therefore, are strictly modern; I
had for example to use 'spleen' and 'phlegm'; but I think
that I have avoided the 'zounds' sort of thing, and that at best
the diction mediates between then and now, suggesting no
one period. There are occasional vulgarities, but for these there
is precedent in the original, Molière's people being aristocrats
and therefore not genteel.

"If this English version is played or read aloud, the names
should be pronounced in a fashion *roughly* French, without
nasal and uvular agonies. Damon should be *dah-MOAN,* and
for rhythmic convenience Arsinoé should be *ar-SIN-oh-eh.*"

PHAEDRA (1677)   In the English-speaking world, the name of
Voltaire is a byword, while that of Racine is not. Yet a friend

of Voltaire's relates that, after declaiming a passage from
*Phaedra,* Voltaire "said to me, letting his head fall on his
breast: 'Friend, I'm but a nobody in comparison with that man,'
and it was not the only time he told me that."

From time to time, some English-speaking critic or scholar
has tried to set matters to rights. Lytton Strachey's essay of
1922 was a fine attempt to "sell" Racine to an Anglo-Saxon
public. But could this be done by criticism alone? Was it not
the translators—for there had been a number—who had let Racine down? The translations had sometimes been what is
called accurate but they had never been poetry and they had
never been drama.

In the spring of 1960 it occurred to the editor of *The Classic
Theatre* that there was an American poet who, while he had
not yet written for the theatre, possessed a rare dramatic gift.
It also seemed that he was peculiarly well-equipped to reach
the emotions of Racine's heroine, seize them, and find the English words for them. When Robert Lowell was invited to translate *Phaedra* for this anthology, he answered, less to the surprise than to the delight of the editor, that he had had his eye
on the play for a long time. He has this to say about the task
he then undertook:

"Racine's plays are generally and correctly thought to be un-
translatable. His syllabic alexandrines do not and cannot exist
in English. We cannot reproduce his language, which is refined by the literary artifice of his contemporaries, and given
a subtle realism and grandeur by the spoken idiom of Louis
XIV's court. Behind each line is a, for us, lost knowledge of
actors and actresses, the stage and the moment. Other qualities remain: the great conception, the tireless plotting, and perhaps the genius for rhetoric and versification that alone proves
that the conception and plotting are honest. Matisse says somewhere that a reproduction requires as much talent for color as
the original painting. I have been tormented by the fraudu-
lence of my own heavy touch.

"My meter, with important differences, is based on Dryden
and Pope. In his heroic plays, Dryden uses an end-stopped
couplet, loaded with inversions, heavily alliterated, and varied
by short unrhymed lines. My couplet is run on, avoids inver-

sions and alliteration, and loosens its rhythm with shifted accents and occasional extra syllables. I gain in naturalness and lose in compactness and-epigrammic resonance. I have tried for an idiomatic and·ageless style, but·I inevitably echo the English Restoration, both in ways that are proper and in my sometimes unRacinian humor and bombast.

"My version is *free*, nevertheless I have used every speech in the original, and indeed every line is either translated or paraphrased. Racine is said to have written prose drafts and then versed them. We do not have the prose drafts, but I feel sure that necessities of line rhyme, etc., made for changes of phrasing and even of meaning. In versing Racine, I have taken the same liberty. Here and there, I have put in things that no French classical author would have used. Examples are the Amazon in Theramenes' first speech and the 'muck' and 'jelly' in Phaedra's second speech, Act II, Scene 5. Such interpolations are rare, however.

"No translator has had the gifts or the luck to bring Racine into our culture. It's a pity that Pope and Dryden overlooked Racine's great body of works, close to them, in favor of the inaccessible Homer and Virgil.

"Racine's verse has a diamond-edge. He is perhaps the greatest poet in the French language, but he uses a smaller vocabulary than any English poet—beside him Pope and Bridges have a Shakespearean luxuriance. He has few verbally inspired lines, and in this is unlike Baudelaire and even La Fontaine. His poetry is great because of the justness of its rhythm and logic, and the glory of its hard, electric rage. I have translated as a poet, and tried to give my lines a certain dignity, speed, and flare."

FIGARO'S MARRIAGE (1784)    Begun in 1775, finished three
years later, accepted at the Comédie Française three years
after that, *Figaro's Marriage,* over much opposition, found its
way to the stage after yet another three years, and became
one of the great events of all theatrical history. It was an
immense success with precisely that aristocratic class whose
doom it announced. Louis XVI himself seems to have had more
prescience than his underlings. "At Figaro's monologue, more
particularly at the tirade about state prisons, the king jumped
up excitedly and said: 'It is hateful! It will never be acted!
To render its performance harmless one would have to destroy
the Bastille!'" (Mme. Campan, *Mémoires*).

An English translation was made almost at once by a well-
known man of the theatre of that time, Thomas Holcroft. Holcroft didn't even wait to see a copy of the play but worked
from notes he took at a performance. It is curious that a translation made in this fashion should be the only one to have
been published until the present version of Jacques Barzun.
Lorenzo da Ponte's libretto has, of course, been translated
many times, but is a very different work. (On the relation of
the play to the Mozart-da Ponte opera, see *Mozart's Operas*
by Edward J. Dent, Second Edition, Oxford, 1947.) Beaumarchais' long preface to the play has been translated by Mary
Douglas Dirks and published in *The Tulane Drama Review,*
February 1958. The companion play, *The Barber of Seville,*
has been published in at least two translations: that of Ar-
thur B. Myrick and G. A. England (now available in Brander
Matthews' *Chief European Dramatists*) and that of W. R.
Taylor (now available in Barrett H. Clark's *World Drama*).
Jacques Barzun writes:

"I know of no works more difficult to translate from the
French than the plays of Beaumarchais. The author was a
great jumping wit, and he delighted in making his audience
jump with him for its pleasure. In *Figaro* the 'retortive back-
chat'—to use Shaw's definition of dramatic dialogue—surpasses
in rapidity and allusiveness that in *The Barber of Seville* and
in any other French comedy of the century.

"It follows that even an accurate translation of the words and the meaning may still leave *the point* ill-expressed. When this happens it makes Beaumarchais sound incoherent, as if he were a modern exploring the unconscious and its random associations, instead of a man of the ratiocinative century, in which the mainspring of amusement, intrigue, and conversation was to witness diverse interests intently pursued, though perpetually converging on a common situation.

"I am not at all confident that for every difficult speech in a play that has few of any other kind I have provided a counterpart that matches the original in its two most important facets—that turned toward the previous speaker and that toward the audience. But even when this is achieved there remains the problem of tone. Beaumarchais' idiomatic simplicity rarely drops into crude colloquialism, yet Figaro and Suzanne (and sometimes the Count and his Countess) employ two distinct modes of expression depending on whether they are giving spontaneous answers or 'making a speech.' Indeed, the mixed language of the play is in itself a harbinger of social revolution—which does not prevent the author from indulging his gift of graceful phrasing, rapid but clear, highly organized but sayable. By attempting to provide these things in proportional measure, I have also been breaking new ground, for the versions of *Figaro* that I have chanced to read, in manuscript or print, are, in detail and as wholes, travesties of the play.

"But to do a little better, out of devotion to Beaumarchais and deference to two great languages, has required some compromises. Once or twice I have ventured to change the author's meaning, without (I hope) changing his intention. For example, references to 'the torrent of the Morena' and the Guadalquivir River were rendered as 'mountain torrent' and 'nearest fishpond,' these being the clichés suitable to the occasion. Enough local color is left in the several mentions of Andalusia, the Spanish Empire, Catalonia and the honor of a Castilian nobleman. I have also changed the horse-chestnut trees in Acts IV and V to elms, for obvious reasons that the reader will discover.

"A more important change was that imposed by the need to make plausible and entertaining the great legal quibble in Act III. The French equivocates on the words *ou* and *où*. I had to tamper slightly with two speeches to do something comparable.

"Again, recognizing in Beaumarchais the originator of the modern stage directions, which instruct the actor in his interpretation and costuming, I wanted to include in this translation the character descriptions the author prefixed to the printed play. But among these, several are set down as 'the same as in *The Barber of Seville*.' I have therefore lifted a few lines from the author's edition of *The Barber* and inserted them in the appropriate places.

"The present translation, in short, is for the reader, the actor, and the director. It is scrupulous, but it is not a version for research scholars and even less a trot for schoolboys: the former would be led astray about minutiae and the latter would earn very poor marks. But I entertain the hope that if Beaumarchais has learned more English than 'God damn' since 1784, he will in his present abode bestow an indulgent approval on my effort to reproduce his feelings and fireworks in a tongue other than the one he handled so discouragingly well."

The songs in the text constitute a complete and exact translation of the French. Producers of the play may wish to use the freely adapted lyrics which Eric Bentley wrote for the music that is traditionally sung in *Figaro's Marriage* at the Comédie Française; words and music can be supplied by Samuel French, Inc.

E. B.
1961

Tape recordings of *The Cid* and *Phaedra*, read by Eric Bentley, have been placed in the Lamont Library at Harvard University and the Archive of Recorded Poetry at the Library of Congress.

# APPENDIX

Exploits of the Cid (1618) by Guillén de Castro. Although sources as such have no place in the present anthology the main source of Corneille's *The Cid* is given here because very few students would otherwise have access to it, and, above all, because of its great intrinsic interest. This version of *Exploits of the Cid*, part summary, part quotation, is taken from Lord Holland's *Some Account of the Lives and Writings of Lope Felix de Vega Carpio and Guillén de Castro* (London, 1817).

## ACT I

### Scene 1

#### KING FERNANDO, DIEGO LAÍNEZ

The scene opens with the decrepid DIEGO LAÍNEZ thanking the KING on his knees for the honor he is about to confer upon him by knighting his son, RODRIGO, arming him with his own weapons, and allowing the PRINCE and the QUEEN to be his sponsors at the ceremony.

(To them enter the QUEEN, the PRINCE SANCHO, the INFANTA URRACA, the CID, XIMENA, the COUNT LOZANO, ARIAS GONZALO, and PERANZULES.)

The ceremony of knighting the hero, which is performed at the altar of St. James with a silver bason, a sword, and golden spurs, occasions many expressions of admiration from the persons present at his appearance; many presents and compliments from the KING, and some observations of both the INFANTA and XIMENA on his person, which prepare the audience for the ensuing events of the tragedy, by betraying the leading causes of them in the passion conceived for the CID by both the PRINCESS and XIMENA.

The haughty temper of the PRINCE SANCHO is also preserved in this scene, and affords a contrast to the calm and dignified character of the CID. The latter, however, is not exempt from that propensity to boasting, which seems natural to all the dramatic heroes of Spain. The KING, in presenting him with the sword of a knight, informs him that he had worn it in five pitched battles. The CID replies that he will never sheathe it until it has gained as many in his hands.

The pomp is at length withdrawn, and the KING recalls his four counsellors, DIEGO LAÍNEZ, ARIAS GONZALO, PERANZULES and LOZANO.

KING. Ye four great statesmen, chiefs of mighty name,
Who form my council, give that council fame;
I pray you wait—your monarch bids you stay,
And sit, my lords, for I have much to say.
*The* FOUR COUNSELLORS *sit, two on each side of the* KING.
Of sage advice our kingdom stands in need,
Bermudez, guardian of my son, is dead!
Sad stroke of fate!—the prudent lord expired,
When most the prince his saving care required;
For he, no longer to his books confined,
Betrays, though young, a fierce unbending mind;
Horses and shields, and arms, engross his care,
And all his fiery soul is bent on war:
Where then is he, the stern but prudent sage, ⎫
Who with firm hand shall curb his headlong age, ⎬
And, without breaking, quell so wild a rage? ⎭
Needs must the choice, on which so much depends, ⎫
Lie among those, I call, as you, my friends, ⎬
All four are fit—but yet, since one attends ⎭
My younger sons, since Arias serves the Queen,
Since thou, Lozano, still in mail art seen
To scour the field, and ill the times could spare
Thy active valour from the works of war;
Your monarch's choice would on Diego fall,
But ere he chooses, he consults you all:
All four in this and other counsels share,
Props of my crown, and partners of my care.

ARIAS. And who so fit to fill a trust so great,  
   On which depends a kingdom's future fate,  
   As one in council grey, the pillar of thy state?

PERANZULES. Diego Laínez well deserves the meed  
   From thee, Fernando!

LOZANO.             He deserves indeed!  
   What does he not deserve who lives to see  
   His claims preferred to mine,—preferred, O King, by thee?  
   For I to serve thy royal son desired,  
   And as in hopes I to that post aspired;  
   If I can stoop my sufferings to conceal,  
   If, awed by thee, I stifle what I feel;  
   Still thou must know my wrongs, and well may guess  
   Those thoughts thy presence only can suppress—  
   Diego! in whose tottering frame appears  
   The hand of time, the fatal weight of years;  
   Shall he our Prince instruct in arms, in fight,  
   In all the prowess of a perfect knight?  
   When he the youth should by example teach  
   To scour the plain, or to assail the breach;  
   The way to toil shall old Diego lead,  
   Urge the fleet courser panting in his speed?  
   Or break the lance to shivers in his sight?  
   The daily sports that form my chief delight—

KING. Enough.

DIEGO.       The haughty Count's thy name, they say;  
   And well that title thou hast prov'd to-day;  
   Yes, I am weak, I not deny the crime,  
   Such is the doom of age, and such the power of time!  
   But weak, old, tottering, gasping for my breath,  
   In sleep, in sickness, in the pangs of death,  
   Still could I serve my prince, his youth could turn  
   To high and mighty things, becoming him to learn.  
   Who lives must die—yet dying we may give  
   Of courage proofs, and lessons how to live;  
   And, though these limbs no longer have the force  
   To break the lance, or urge the panting horse,  
   The prince may read, and kindle as he reads,  
   My written actions and recorded deeds.

Achievements past, now crowned with endless fame,
Shall more than present might his soul inflame;
So shall our King, and so the world allow,

LOZANO *steps forward to interrupt* DIEGO.

That none on earth deserves this change—

KING. What now?

LOZANO. I not deserve?

KING. Ah, why this contest seek?
Forbear, my Lords!—your King forbids you speak.

COUNT. Then hands for me, and with a blow, attest . . .

*He strikes* DIEGO.

The angry thoughts my tongue so ill supprest.

PERANZULES. Alas, forbear!

DIEGO. Oh! wretched helpless age!

KING. What ho! a guard!

COUNT. My liege, repress thy rage.
Disturbance then, if thou in patience wait,
Which shakes thy palace, shall not harm thy state;
I own (and let my King his grace accord ⎫
For once in favor of a loyal sword)      ⎬
My hand forgot the presence of its Lord; ⎭
But I, for years the pillar of thy throne,
Thy frontiers guarded and thy battles won,
Thy wrongs redressed; and loth wise kings should be
To lay the hand of power on mighty chiefs like me.
A warlike subject is the Prince's hand,
To act his thought, perform his dread command;
The wing on which his schemes of empire rise,
The heart that warmth, and force, and soul throughout
    supplies.

KING. What ho!

COUNT. Your pardon.—

*Exit.*

KING. Ruffian! villain! stay.

ARIAS. 'Tis yours, oh King, your prudence to display.

DIEGO. Nay, call him, grant him all he asks. 'Tis just
Who most can honour, should enjoy the trust;

And he on whom the smiles of fortune shine,
Proud of his glories, rich in spoils of mine,
In youth, in vigour, insolent and vain,
Flushed with success, may well the charge sustain;
But I,—disgraced, dishonoured as I am,
Depressed with age, but more depressed with shame;—
Fly hence my wrongs in secret to deplore,
Till death my sorrow close, or vengeance fame restore.
I go—

KING.    Nay, tarry. Good Diego, hear—

DIEGO. Pardon, my liege; 'twould ill in thee appear,
To let insulted men approach thy throne;
And, honoured long, alas! I now am one;
Oh, injured blood, of proud Castile the best!
*Exit.*

ARIAS. How fierce he went, how passion tears his breast!

KING. And well it may, for insults great as these—
But what remains? Shall I Lozano seize?

ARIAS. No; to forbear the safer course I hold;
Lozano, Sir, is insolent and bold;
To wealth adds power, and well a cause so great
May shake an empire, and embroil a state;
Nay, other ills to such rash deeds belong,
You seize the culprit, but proclaim the wrong.

KING. 'Tis wisely said—the counsel to pursue,
You to Lozano—to Diego you
Repair, and say, when this sad scene occurred
My door was closed, no mortal saw or heard:
I bid them then the weighty secret keep,
Buried in long oblivion let it sleep;
My high displeasure shall the wretch await,
Who dare reveal this secret of my state—
Away!

ARIAS.    I kin to old Diego claim.

PERANZULES. I boast alliance with Lozano's name.
*Exeunt.*

KING. I'm mocked. Authority shall have its day,
And fear shall teach my vassals to obey.
*Exit.*

## Scene 2

RODRIGO is discovered with his two younger brothers, HER-
NÁN DÍAZ and BERMUDO LAÍN, who converse with him on his
armour.

RODRIGO replies to their compliments, by encouraging them
to expect some honours from the KING, who, he observes, has
enough for everyone. He then renews his vow of gaining five
pitched battles, when his conversation is interrupted by the
appearance of his father.

DIEGO enters with his staff broken. He at first seems inclined
to speak to his sons; and on perceiving that the CID is disarmed, asks him significantly if this is the moment for laying
by his sword. He afterwards dismisses them all with great im-
petuosity, and taking down the sword of Mudarra,[1] finds his
strength unequal to wielding it. He then breaks into a passionate and spirited soliloquy on the helplessness of old age,
and the disgrace of unrevenged affront. After some reflection,
he determines to entrust his sons with the vindication of his
honour, and calls in the youngest, HERNÁN DÍAZ. In conformity
with the tradition preserved in the ballads, he pinches the
young man's hand, and when he complains of the pain, drives
him from his presence with bitter reproaches. The second,
BERMUDO LAÍN, is subjected to the same trial, and in the same
manner disappoints and enrages his father. At length RODRIGO
is summoned. He enters with an expression of surprise, not unmixed with indignation, that his younger brothers should have
preceded him. When, however, his father, taking his hand, ap-
plies it to his mouth and bites it most severely, he can no
longer contain his fury, but exclaims, that if he were not his
father, he would revenge the offense by striking him on the
spot!

"It would not be the first blow I have received," answers
DIEGO. The CID eagerly demands what he means, and he exclaims:

DIEGO. Child of my soul, this anger I approve,
  Such rage I honour, and such fire I love;
  With joy I see thy boiling passions rise,
  And bless thy glowing cheeks and kindling eyes:
  Yes! the warm blood that rushes to thy face
  Descends indeed, from Laín Calvo's race.
  Through Nuño's veins the noble current run,
  Such I received, and such I gave my son!—
  No haughty Count, howe'er he earn the name,
  Shall then attaint it in its course of fame;
  Tho' he, Count Orgaz, would our house disgrace,
  And fixed the daring insult on my face;
  But thou, my son, to raise our house again,
  Washing in hostile blood this latter stain,
  (For what but blood can for such wrongs atone?)
  Shalt cleanse thy father's glories and thy own;
  My hopes on thee and on thy courage rest,
  I called thee last, because I lov'd thee best;
  Because my age, grown fond, had hoped to spare
  My favourite child, my first, my greatest heir:
  I tried thy brethren, but I blushed to find
  In both a coward heart and groveling mind:
  Men without souls, a scandal to our name,
  That but confirmed th' affront, and deeper died my shame;
  'Tis thine then, thine these hoary locks to save,
  And bid me sink with honour to the grave;
  Then summon all thy soul; too well I know,
  I bid thee cope with no ignoble foe;
  Still found his suits to urge, his lance to wield,
  First in the presence, foremost in the field;
  Yet since thy heart can feel, thy arm can fight,
  The dread of shame shall raise thy latent might;
  Think on thy father's wrong, thy own disgrace,
  And wield this weapon to redeem our race.
  Rage chokes my utterance, more I cannot speak, ⎫
  I weep my wrongs,—'tis thine redress to seek, ⎬
  And on that hated head the vengeance due to wreak. ⎭
  *Exit* DIEGO.

RODRIGO remains, and expresses the conflict between his honour and his love in a speech of considerable feeling and poetry. It is, however, too lyrical in metre, thought, and expression. Before he leaves the stage, he reverts to the ordinary verse of *redondilla mayor,* and repeats nearly word for word the greater part of the second ballad or *romance.*[2]

*Exit.*

(Scene discovers XIMENA and DOÑA URRACA at a balcony.)

They converse on the gallant appearance of RODRIGO. The INFANTA, betraying her own admiration of him, banters XIMENA on the warmth of her praises.

(*Enter below* COUNT LOZANO, PERANZULES, *and servants.*)

The ladies observe the agitation of LOZANO, but cannot overhear a conversation between PERANZULES and the COUNT, in which the former endeavors to prevail upon LOZANO to offer some explanation to the KING and to DIEGO for the outrage he had just committed. LOZANO, without justifying his conduct, maintains that honour admits of no explanation but by the sword, says that the plea of drunkenness or madness, which alone could excuse his violence, would disgrace him, and not satisfy DIEGO; and when his companion attempts to intimidate him with the consequences of his haughtiness, insolently dwells upon his own importance and courage, and derides DIEGO for decrepitude, and his sons, or as he calls them, his brats, for their inexperience.

*Exeunt.*

Enter RODRIGO, who perceives the ladies at the window, and with much gallantry to both, marks most respect for the INFANTA, and most love for XIMENA. In the meanwhile his state of mind does not escape the observation of the enamoured XIMENA. He laments his destiny, and even hesitates between his affection to his mistress, and his duty to his father, though he sees LOZANO, who re-enters, conversing with PERANZULES. At length DIEGO appears, and the sight of him decides his wavering resolution. A short and spirited dialogue, which is closely imitated by Corneille, ensues. RODRIGO bids the COUNT step aside, points to his father, tells him that he is his son, and challenges him to meet in some more retired spot. LOZANO

treats his extreme youth with great scorn, and at length with
a very undignified insult, threatens, as he had struck his father, to kick him. This is too much for RODRIGO to bear; they
draw and exeunt fighting, while the exclamations of URRACA
and XIMENA testify their horror at the encounter. The COUNT
cries behind the scenes: "I am slain!" The CID enters, defending himself against the assaults of LOZANO's followers, till
URRACA interferes, and, with the authority of an Infanta, forbids their pursuit of RODRIGO.

*Exeunt.*

# ACT II

## Scene 1

KING FERNANDO enters, enquiring the cause of the disturbance he has heard in the streets, and ARIAS and PERANZULES
arrive to inform him that RODRIGO has killed the COUNT, and
with a sword in his hand escaped, or rather defied the officers
of justice. XIMENA and DIEGO appear at opposite doors, the
former with a bloody handkerchief, and the latter with his
cheek stained with the blood of LOZANO. After an altercation
in short speeches, each pleads his cause at some length, and
XIMENA paints with much passion the impression made on her
mind by her father's wound and death, and observes, in language which Corneille has imitated, that death prevented
him from uttering his injunctions through any mouth but that
of his wound; that they are written on the dust in characters
of blood.

DIEGO says that he arrived as LOZANO expired, and washed
the offense he had received in the presence of the KING on his
cheek with the blood of him who had offered it. While they
are pleading the cause, URRACA and PRINCE SANCHO arrive.
The KING bids XIMENA be comforted, and orders DIEGO to be
arrested. SANCHO, at the suggestion of his sister, intercedes for
his governor DIEGO, and in the course of his intercession, betrays that haughty and ungovernable temper which char-

acterized him through life, by threatening the courtiers, and even his father, with violence, if his suit be rejected. The KING evades the embarrassment in which he is placed, by leaving DIEGO in the friendly custody of PRINCE SANCHO. A messenger summons the INFANTA URRACA to the QUEEN's house in the country; and after the KING has promised XIMENA protection, and she, in several speeches aside, informed the audience that her love is at variance with her duty, all retire.

*Scene 2*

To ELVIRA enter RODRIGO. RODRIGO acknowledges to ELVIRA that he slew LOZANO, and professes to have come to XIMENA to offer to die in her presence. ELVIRA, hearing XIMENA approach with PERANZULES and others, insists on his concealing himself. PERANZULES and attendants retire soon, and XIMENA, thinking herself alone, confesses, in the hearing of RODRIGO, her love for him to ELVIRA. He throws himself at her feet, and offers her his sword to stab him: he relates with simplicity and feeling his cause of quarrel with her father, describes the conflict in his breast between love and honour, and ends by entreating her to revenge her father on him as he had his on LOZANO.

She answers him with great emotion, that he acted with honour in fighting LOZANO, but reproaches him with his want of delicacy in entering her house with the blood of her father yet fresh on his hands. She ascribes his audacity to his confidence in her love, and admits it to be too well founded: her honour she says will induce her to do all she can to bring her father's murderer to justice, but she confesses her hopes that she may not be able to do much. They part in mutual despair.

*Scene 3*

DIEGO, *alone*. Not more the lamb astray in unknown lands,
Bleats for its absent shepherd's fostering hands;

Not more the lion roaring through the wood,
Searches each thicket for his stolen brood,
Than I for thee, Rodrigo!—how my sight
Greets for my son mere shadows of the night!
I gave the signal, marked th' appointed place,
My prudence left no unprovided case;
Has he neglected? can he disobey?
Ah, no! misfortune keeps my son away.
A chilling thought! For were Rodrigo slain,
Hurt, wounded, seized, this heart ne'er beats again.
What horrid fancies glance along my mind—
But hark! I hear some footstep in the wind;
I dare not think it,—'twere delight too near,
Sure my own echoed sighs deceived my ear . . .
Yet,—there again, upon the flinty ground,
Strike the swift hoof—I catch the welcome sound;
'Tis he: I hear him from his horse alight,
It is, it is— Oh, pure, unmixed delight!
My son?

RODRIGO.   My father?

DIEGO.                 Can I trust my joy?
Do I, indeed, embrace my gallant boy?
Bear with me—let me but compose my thought,
And draw my breath, to praise you as I ought:
Oh! you have nobly prospered, nobly shown
A soul in great achievements like my own.
Nobly repaid what from these veins you drew;
Life you received from me, I more than life from you;
Touch then the locks you make with honour gray,
And press the cheek whose stain you cleared away!
My haughty carriage into reverence sinks,
My pride before thy greater glory shrinks,
Preserver of a noble house, from whence
Castile her glory draws, and monarchs their defense.

RODRIGO. Rise, rise, my lord! what strange demeanour's this?
'Tis mine to kneel, thy honoured hand to kiss;
For what poor merit in this arm can be,
Must all my father, be derived from thee.

DIEGO. Say rather I should kneel to reverence thine,
For sure your favours far outbalance mine;
I gave thee being, such as fathers give,
But thou by dint of worth hast made my soul revive.
Enough—
To paint my gratitude, my son commend,
Were an eternal theme, and one I ne'er could end.
Know then, five hundred knights, a chosen band,
Chosen by me, await my son's command;
Each on his jennet, and the meanest there ⎫
Might with the coursers of the sun compare. ⎬
Haste then, my son, occasion offers fair; ⎭
Our King is braved; the haughty Moorish bands
Invade his frontiers, and lay waste his lands.
Last night the scouts arrived, the council sate,
Sad looks proclaimed the subject of debate;
Our lawless foes through hilly Oca sped,
And o'er Naxera's spacious fields they spread;
With fire and sword they waste our fertile plain,
Fortune attends their march, and rapine swells their train.
To hear the captives made, the booty won,
Appalls most hearts, and would provoke my son.
Haste on thy horse, attack the dangerous horde,
And be thy spear successful as thy sword;
So shall the King, the court, the people own,
Thy arm not strong in private broils alone;
Go, serve thy King, thy country's battles fight, ⎫
'Tis in such war that every generous knight ⎬
Redeems lost favour in his sovereign's sight. ⎭

RODRIGO. T'insure this triumph, I thy blessing crave,
The happiest omen that a son can have.

DIEGO. You have it—may it every good impart!
My hand but acts the wishes of my heart.
*Exeunt.*

## Scene 4

Scene discovers the INFANTA URRACA on a balcony in a country house. She breaks out into a soliloquy on the beauties of the country and the pleasures of retirement, in which there are some natural sentiments and some far-fetched conceits. As there is an appearance that Guillén de Castro, in the topics of this speech, meant to produce a contrast to the busy and spirited scenes which preceded it, a few lines as a specimen of his talent for descriptive poetry may not be unacceptable to the reader.

URRACA. How sweet the fields and forests to the eyes
   Of those who know such calmer joys to prize,
   Who let all cares be stolen by delight,
   Their souls surrendering to the sense of sight!
   Oh! sweet variety of hill and vale!
   Here verdant buds, there dusky oaks prevail;
   What, though through woods the roaring lion rove, ⎫
   How many harmless warblers of the grove     ⎬
   Blend with his rage the tender notes of love. ⎭
     Etc., etc.

She continues for some time in a similar strain, till, in contrasting the occupations of a court with a country life, which her mother, the QUEEN, had chosen, her thoughts are led to the quarrel of LOZANO and DIEGO, and the suit of XIMENA against RODRIGO. While expressing her anxiety for his safety, she is interrupted by the appearance of cavalry. RODRIGO, their captain, alights from his horse, and informs her, in a dialogue of great gallantry, that he owes his safety to her interference. He then intreats her blessing for his undertaking against the Moors, but contrives with great respect and address to prevent her from expressing yet tenderer sentiments, which she seems above once upon the point of declaring.
   *Exeunt.*

## Scene 5

The next scene opens with a shepherd flying before the Moors. The MOORISH KING enters, giving directions about the prisoners he has taken, and boasting that he is inferior to no one but Mahomet. In the meanwhile the SHEPHERD has escaped the pursuit of his followers, and from the top of a rock, where they cannot reach him, descries the approach of the Christians, and afterwards the battle and defeat of the Moors, whom he insults with the same epithets that Tom Thumb gives to the gigantic prisoners in the courtyard. ("The monstrous ugly barbarous sons of whores."—Tom Thumb.)

RODRIGO enters. The MOORISH KING surrenders with his followers; but the hero of the piece informs the audience that he must take two more Moorish kings prisoners before the day is over. The SHEPHERD makes a remark on the event, and they all return.

## Scene 6

SANCHO enters with a fencing master, and followed by DIEGO LAÍNEZ, who, perceiving that the PRINCE is seriously incensed, makes the fencing master withdraw. The PRINCE SANCHO acknowledges his wish to fence with his master in earnest, from indignation at his supposed superiority, and from his persuasion that he is to be murdered by a spear and not by a sword; a persuasion founded on a prophecy, and productive, in his mind, of an aversion to his brothers and sisters, for he infers from it that they will be his assassins. While DIEGO is combating his apprehensions and belief in astrology, DOÑA URRACA enters. She is accompanied by a page, and bears a hunting spear stained with the blood of a boar. This circumstance confirms SANCHO's apprehension. Altercations between him and his sister ensue, in which his superstitious character is displayed, and his violence with difficulty restrained.

To them enter KING FERNANDO and the captive MOORISH

KING. The former compliments DIEGO on his son's victory, and the latter relates the wonders of it. When RODRIGO himself appears, the generous prisoner takes his hand and addresses him by the name of *Mió Cide*. SANCHO asks the meaning of the word, and having learnt that it is Arabic for "my lord" or *"mi señor,"* KING FERNANDO confers it as a permanent title on RODRIGO.

XIMENA enters in mourning, with four knights in mourning also. She pleads her cause against RODRIGO in a speech from the ninth *romance*.[3] Some of the original expressions, and even lines, are preserved, though Guillén de Castro has made many judicious alterations and additions.

The KING, after some ambiguous phrases of further intentions, agrees to banish the CID for his murder of LOZANO, but embraces him on taking leave for his prowess against the common enemy. URRACA observes the interchange of affectionate regards between XIMENA and the CID, and on going out expresses her jealousy, as PRINCE SANCHO and the rest do their admiration for RODRIGO.

# ACT III

## Scene 1

URRACA confides to ARIAS GONZALO her distresses arising from the death of her mother, the age of her father, and the aversion of her brother, who is to inherit the kingdom. ARIAS suggests marriage with a foreign prince, which she, from her love of Castile, rejects, but acknowledges that she had entertained thoughts of RODRIGO, till she discovered his affection for XIMENA. In spite of her pretended prosecution of him, she knows his passion to be returned by that lady.

To them enter KING FERNANDO and DIEGO. URRACA, being assured by her father that he has states which he holds by conquest as well as by succession, leaves the stage. The KING declares his intention of deciding his right to Calahorra by single combat, and he chooses the CID for his champion. A servant

announces XIMENA, and the KING says that she has the insolence
and impatience of her father LOZANO, and is always persecut-
ing him with her remonstrances. This remark gives ARIAS an
opportunity of disclosing the information he had derived from
URRACA, viz., that XIMENA is in love with RODRIGO. He suggests
a marriage between them as the best method of silencing her
complaints.

ARIAS and the KING contrive a plan to discover the truth of
this report of her love for the CID, and after directions have
been given in whispers to the attendants, XIMENA appears and
repeats almost verbatim the *romance*[4] in which the circumstance of shooting the doves, and the imprecation against an
unjust KING are preserved. DIEGO combats the truth of the
aspersion against the CID of having killed XIMENA's doves, by
saying, that he is performing a pilgrimage to Santiago. A servant, according to the secret injunctions of ARIAS, announces the
melancholy news that the CID has been slain in the road to the
shrine of Santiago. DIEGO, who is in the secret, affects the
greatest distress; but XIMENA, who does not doubt the truth of
the report, turns pale and faints at the intelligence. The KING
acknowledges the stratagem and the object of it. XIMENA endeavors to deny the inference drawn from her affliction, by
proposing to give both her person and her property to any
nobleman, and half her property to any person of inferior birth
who shall bring her the head of RODRIGO. The KING, from a
persuasion of the invincible qualities of the CID, offers to proclaim the conditions.

### Scene 2

(The CID; two soldiers; the SHEPHERD as a servant; and
a LEPER, who thrusts his arms and body full of sores from
behind the scenes.)

After some idle dialogue and preparations for dinner, in
which the SHEPHERD is the *gracioso*, the CID hears the groans
of the leperous beggar. His servant and soldiers, from fear of
infection, and from disgust at his appearance, refuse to assist
him out of a quagmire into which he has fallen, but the CID

stretches out his arm, kisses his hand, covers him with his gar-
ment, washes his wounds, and sits down to dine with him. He
begins to suspect some mystery, when the LEPER addresses him
by name, and he is rewarded for his charity by the sudden
conversion of the LEPER into St. Lazarus, who foretells his future glories, and announces the approach of the KING. The
KING, DIEGO, PERANZULES appear. A single combat is to decide
the fate of Calahorra, and the Arragonese giant, DON MARTIN
(another Rodomonte, Alcides or Atlas) insolently defies the
Castillian knights, and claims the disputed territory. The CID
steps forth, and notwithstanding the disparity of strength, and
the menaces of his gigantic antagonist, accepts the challenge.

*Exeunt.*

## Scene 3

(XIMENA and her sister, ELVIRA.)

While XIMENA is dreading the event of the single combat, a
letter reaches her, signed DON MARTIN, claiming her person and
property, and announcing his arrival with the head of her father's murderer. She is overwhelmed with grief, and leaves the
stage, acknowledging that she adores the shade of her enemy,
and laments the man she had killed.

## Scene 4

The KING and his three courtiers consult upon the succession
of his states. To them the PRINCE enters, and receives the notice of his father's intention of dividing his kingdom with a
mixture of grief and disdain. The KING threatens him with his
curses.

XIMENA appears in a bridal dress and affects to rejoice in
the supposed death of the CID, but, upon hearing it confirmed,
she acknowledges her love, and entreats the KING to allow her
to surrender her property, but refuse the hand of DON MARTIN.

The words have scarcely passed her lips when the CID appears, recounts his victory, and solicits the hand of XIMENA in marriage. The KING grants his petition; and XIMENA, with affected reluctance, consents, observing, that she obeys the commands of Heaven.

## NOTES TO THE APPENDIX

1. Lord Holland notes: "A native of Cordoba, of Moorish extraction, but afterwards adopted by the Lara family and much celebrated in the national songs for his heroic achievements; he flourished about the year 990."

2. Lord Holland's book contains the text of eight of the ballads and a summary of four more. Here is the second:

> Pensive was the Cid, reflecting
>   That as yet he was but young,
> To engage the Count Lozano,
>   To avenge his father's wrong;
> Well he knew the dreadful party
>   Waiting on that mighty lord,
> Thousands on Asturias' mountains
>   Starting at his lightest word.
> Well he knew how King Fernando
>   Judged the Count Lozano's right;
> His the foremost vote in Cortes,
>   His the foremost post in fight.
> Yet, it all appeared as nothing
>   When his father's wrong he heard,
> First and only wrong that ever
>   Laín Calvo's race incurred.
> Then of heaven he asks but justice,
>   Of the earth a field to fight,
> Of his father leave to combat,
>   Of his honour manly might.
> Thoughts of his unequal boyhood
>   Little terror to him gave,
> From their cradles, noble chieftains,
>   Honour calling, greet the grave.
> Down from out the hanging armour
>   Took he old Mudarra's sword,
> Where, for years, it had been rusting,
>   Dead its great Castilian lord;
> Thinking only such a weapon
>   Such a quarrel can sustain,
> Ere about his waist he girt it,
>   Troubled thus he vents his pain:
> "Reckon, valiant sword, O reckon,
>   "To Mudarra you belong,
> "Grant his strength be mine in battle,
>   "His indeed has been my wrong:

"What, though proud of past achievements,
   "Thou so weak an arm would'st shun,
"Yet I know thee, valiant weapon!
   "Backward never wilt thou run.
"Firm as thy unyielding temper,
   "Shalt thou me in fight behold,
"Thou hast, like a former master,
   "Found a second full as bold;
"Then, if with thy aid I'm vanquished,
   "Frantic with the shame and guilt,
"Will I hide thee in my bosom,
   "To the cross which forms thy hilt.
"Haste, then, to the field of battle,
   "Haste, oh, sword, we loiter long,
"To chastize the Count Lozano's
   "Daring hand and lawless tongue."
Then went forth the Cid determined,
   So determined did he go,
Ere an hour had passed, his weapon
   Had avenged his father's blow.

3. Lord Holland renders the whole ballad thus:

On his subjects' strife deciding,
   Sat the King in chair of state,
Grace and justice, hope and terror,
   On his dread awards await;
Bounteous, yet severe his judgments,
   Evil punish, good reward,
Vice chastised, desert requited,
   Best the subject's welfare guard.
Thirty squires in long procession,
   All in black, and noble all,
Waiting on Ximena Gomez,
   Entered then the Audience Hall:
Those who bore the mace retreated,
   And the court in silence wait,
While Ximena vents her sorrow,
   Prostrate on the cloth of state.
"Sire, six months have now passed by us
   "Since my noble father bled,
"Slain by one, thy partial favor
   "To such lawless actions bred;
"Four times at thy feet I've fallen,
   "Four times do I thus complain;
"Gracious words and promise always,
   "Justice never I obtain.
"Haughty, vain, and young Rodrigo
   "Hath your sacred laws defied,

"Proudly does he still defy them,
 "You protect the stripling's pride:—
"You preserve him, you conceal him,
 "When the favor'd culprit's hid,
"Then, for that they cannot find him,
 "Are your loyal bailiffs chid!
"If good Kings in all their actions
 "Follow God, as need they must,
"Since on earth they bear his semblance,
 "Since from him derive their trust,
"Shall the love, and shall the honour,
 "Shall the name of King belong
"To a man who fails in justice,
 "Nor redresses subjects' wrong?
"Ill advised, misguided monarch!
 "Pardon if I speak not right,
"Wrongs endured, in simple woman,
 "Turn respect to foul despight."
Then replied the King Fernando:
 "Say no more, and cease thy moan,
"Words like thine, sweet maid, would soften
 "Breast of steel and heart of stone:
"If I've saved this youth, I've saved him
 "More for thine than his relief;
"Time shall come, when this Rodrigo,
 "To delight shall turn thy grief."
As he spoke in came a message,
 The Princèss the King requires:
Handing forth Ximena Gomez,
 To Urraca he retires.

4. Specifically, the seventh ballad of Lord Holland's twelve:

  The King had sat him down to dine,
   In Burgos where he dwelt,
  Where fair Ximena hurried in
   To tell the wrongs she felt.
  A mourning dress was all she wore,
   Her cap was crape so black,
  And humbly kneeling on the floor,
   These words of woe she spake:
  "My mother did of sorrow die,
   "I drag a life of pain,
  "Each morn the man offends my eye,
   "By whom my sire was slain:
  "With hawk on wrist he rides, and loves
   "To work me more despight,
  "To fly his falcon at my doves,
   "And kill them in my sight.

"And as my slaughtered fav'rites bleed,
  "My robe with red is died,
"I sent t'arraign the wanton deed,
  "And he with threats replied.
"The King who justice won't enforce
  "His kingdom should not keep,
"No right has he to cross a horse,
  "Or with a Queen to sleep.
"He should not taste of napkined bread,
  "Nor steel about him bind."
The King heard what Ximena said,
  And pondered in his mind:
"Say, I the Cid or take or kill?
  "My Cortes will revolt.
"Say he goes free?—the deed is ill—
  "God will avenge the fault.
"A letter I resolve to send"—
  He spoke—the letter sped—
Scarce off, it reached its journey's end,
  And its contents were read.
The father reads and not the son,
  Which, when the Cid did know,
He cries, "For greeting I use none;
  "What's that you did now shew?
"Bad tidings from the King, I fear?"
  "Nay, nay," his father said,
"It bids you come, but stay you here,
  "And I'll go in your stead."
"Now, Holy Mary, God forbid!
  "And may thy son be curst,
"If where thou go'st," exclaims the Cid,
  "I go not always first."